KEY
SETTLEMENTS
IN
RURAL AREAS

for Viv

KEY SETTLEMENTS IN RURAL AREAS

Paul J. Cloke

Lecturer in Geography
Saint David's University College
Lampeter

METHUEN

First published in 1979 by
Methuen & Co. Ltd
11 New Fetter Lane, London EC4P 4EE

Published in the USA by
Methuen & Co.
an associate company of Methuen Inc.
733 Third Avenue, New York, NY 10017

© *1979 Paul Cloke*

Typeset by Inforum Ltd, Portsmouth
Printed in Great Britain at the
University Press, Cambridge

British Library Cataloguing in Publication Data
Cloke, Paul
    Key settlements in rural areas. —
    (University paperbacks).
    1. Regional planning — England
    I. Title II. Series
    711'.3'0942   HT395.G7

ISBN   0–416–71910–4
ISBN   0–416–71920–1 Pbk

Contents

Preface

In 1957, John Saville admitted that 'the rural planner is groping in a fog of ignorance'. Much of this deficit in rural knowledge has been due to an urban bias in planning, research and problem-solving, necessitated by the speed and scale of urban growth. However, there has been a concomitant period of post-war planning of the rural environment which has developed without the basic research inputs to policy initiation and monitoring. Thus it is that major planned changes have taken place in the countryside in an atmosphere of inexperience on the part of the planners and ignorance on the part of large sections of the general public.

The key settlement policy may be regarded as the principal agent of planned change in post-war rural Britain. Rural settlement policies have usually embodied major elements of the key settlement concept in one guise or another and yet this fundamental part of the rural planning machinery has been very much a part of the fog of ignorance of which Saville spoke. The planners themselves have largely been working in the dark, with little idea of the future ramifications of the policy that they were introducing. Rural people, too, have exhibited a low degree of perception of the planning policy which potentially can cause them direct benefits or disadvantages.

Only recently has the philosophy and practical application of the key settlement policy incurred criticism, but now the floodgates have been opened a stream of disapproval has flowed across the pages of rural planning texts and journals. The total blind faith in the key settlement concept has been replaced by an equally benigh-

ted reliance on any policy or nomenclature which is able to circum-
vent the key centre philosophy. In addition, many respected
commentators have recently expressed the opinion that the key
settlement approach has been short-sighted and that its continued
adoption would be likely to prejudice the long-term health and
stability of rural settlements. As a consequence of these reactions,
the 'concentration versus dispersal in rural planning' debate has
been initiated, the outcome of which will have fundamental implications for the future study and application of geographical planning in rural areas.

Here, then, we have a very relevant section of the 'fog of
ignorance' which demands detailed study. At the outset, several
questions beg for an answer. What is a key settlement policy? This
type of rural planning has been operational now for twenty-five
years or more, and yet there are many who would be stretched to
define exactly what the unique qualities of the concept are. What is
the theoretical background to key settlements if any? It is important to know how and why the policy was first introduced so that
comparisons are available with today's rural circumstances. To
what extent have key settlements been used and how do policies
differ from one to another? Knowledge of key settlement policy
implementation will provide vital spin-off for future rural settlement policies.

All these questions are tackled in the first three chapters of this
book and therefore form separate inputs into the major objective of
this study, namely how well do key settlements work in different
types of rural area? Only by assessing key settlement performance
at county level and below can we adequately decide the future role,
if any, that this policy should play in the future of the countryside.
Chapters 4 and 5 attempt to assess the economic and social ramifications of the key settlement policy through the medium of case
studies of pressured and remoter rural counties. These results are
then fed into Chapters 6 and 7 which link theory and practice into a
statement concerning the value and future potential of key settlement policies in different types of rural area.

The book adopts the basic premise that planners ought to arrest
the trends of depopulation in remoter rural areas and equally that
the concept of conservation in pressured rural areas is one which is
worthy of planning consideration. There are those who would
advocate a strict *laissez-faire* approach to rural planning but the
author remains unconvinced that such a strategy would be a
beneficial one, and he is unrepentant for pointing this study of key

settlements in a positive planning direction.

Neither do I make any apology for treating this subject from a geographical viewpoint. Spatial perspectives may be thought dominant within the book but in many ways the themes of spatial discrimination or spread of opportunities form the nub of key settlement policies, and therefore a geographer's approach is certainly not out of place. The quantitative nature of the case-studies is equally held to be justifiable in that objective policy decisions concerning the future of rural areas will require a considerable amount of evidence to be collected in as scientific a manner as possible. Some imbalances will have been caused by the narrowing of the book's focus to the situation in England and Wales. Growth centre policies akin to key settlements have been used in many countries on the continents of Europe and America and it is to be hoped that some of the conclusions reached in the British context will find application elsewhere.

Finally I should acknowledge a few of the numerous debts incurred in the presentation of this study. I am most grateful to the following individuals and organizations for permission to reproduce copyright material: the editor and publisher of *Regional Studies* for figures 1.1 and 1.2, previously published in Cloke (1977a), on which article my section on 'An index of rurality' in Chapter 1 draws heavily; Leicestershire County Council for figure 7.1 taken from *Rutland Structure Plan: The Main Choices*; the editor and publisher of the Geographical Papers series from the Department of Geography, University of Reading for figure 7.2 taken from Bather *et al*. (1976). I am also indebted to the editor and publisher of *The Village* for permission to include material published by them (Cloke, 1977b).

My initial interest in rural geography and planning was stimulated by Brian Woodruffe at Southampton University and developed under the guidance of Robin Best and Gerald Wibberley at Wye College. Much of the research on key settlement policies was carried out under the sponsorship of the Social Science Research Council and some of the final touches were made possible by the Pantyfedwen Research Fund. Invaluable assistance was also received from the various planning departments and community councils of Warwickshire and Devon. To the personalities and organizations named here, and to others too numerous to mention I express my sincere thanks.

Thanks are especially due to Sadie, whose canine antics have provided hours of amusement during the writing of this book.

However, most of all I am grateful to my wife, Viv, who has offered patience and encouragement throughout the span of this research and whose practical assistance in the typing of the manuscript has been priceless. Her contribution has been far beyond the descriptive power of mere words.

1
Rurality and Rural Change

The administrative system of rural planning has failed to respond to changing social and economic needs of villages and rural industry and is leading rapidly to an imbalanced growth pattern throughout Britain ....

Graham Moss's (1978, 131) indictment of post-war rural settlement planning typifies a current sense of dissatisfaction with the theory and practices which have been enlisted to deal with the pressing problems caused by anachronistic settlement patterns in a dynamic countryside. This general discontent has led geographers and planning practitioners alike to embark upon a critical review of rural planning which is both long overdue and essential for the forward planning of the rural areas.

One product of the generally recognized need for rural re-examination has been an extreme reaction against current planning systems. Indeed, the warnings sounded by many authors, including Cherry (1976), Davidson and Wibberley (1977), Gilg (1978) and Woodruffe (1976), have provided some justification for those critics who postulate sweeping changes in rural planning methods. On the other hand, there has been a realization that rural areas have invariably been the poor relation in the worldwide study and practice of town and country planning. Naturally, the speed and scale of urban growth have necessitated an urban bias in post-war planning, research and problem-solving. It is, however, unfortunate that this concentration on urban problems and their solutions has been detrimental to countryside planning in that the understanding of rural planning systems has been hampered by the use of diluted urban and regional planning techniques which are ill-suited to the rural scale. Consequently there would appear to be some support for the viewpoint that this hard-earned experience should not be discarded lightly. While most workers in the rural field would fall somewhere between these reactionary and ameliorative stances, few would deny the urgent need for a fuller understanding of rural systems and processes, especially in view of the opportunities for implementing new or improved types of policy under the Structure Plan framework.

Perhaps the single most important facet of post-war rural settlement planning has been the key settlement policy. This planning device has often been regarded as a panacea for the rural ills existing both in areas of remoteness and in areas subjected to intense urban pressures, and has therefore formed the basis of most rural settlement policies in one guise or another. The widespread implementation and continuing importance of the key settlement policy has made it a prime contender for critical attention under the more general review of rural planning and its methods. Indeed, it is no longer feasible for planners to accept this form of rural planning without first considering the efficacy with which the policy has been implemented in the past and the denouement resulting from the policy's impact on present and future rural activities.

Much of the recent discussion concerning key settlement policies (e.g. McLaughlin, 1976; Ash, 1976) has been of a theoretical and moralistic nature revolving around the relative merits of 'concentration' and 'dispersal' in rural planning. However, several stages of investigation into the whole key settlement issue are required prior to such discussion if future policy decisions are to be based on hard evidence rather than conjecture, and on understanding of systems and processes rather than reactions to sets of circumstances. One of the central themes around which criticism has been levelled against the key settlement policy concerns the seemingly blind adoption of this form of planning, regardless of both the type of rural area involved and of the particular problems encountered in the particular region to be planned. Therefore at the outset of any examination of the key settlement policy it is necessary to define what is meant by 'different types of rural area', and having done that, to summarize the changes taking place within these areas which have generated the environment in which the key settlement policy was put into operation.

1.1   An Index of Rurality

Most people will have an intrinsic awareness that rural areas are 'different' from urban areas and that there are internal differences within rural areas themselves. However, the task of translating these perceived differences into meaningful spatial distributions is a difficult yet important one, for by studying different categories of rural area the various planning mechanisms operating within them may be better understood. To achieve an effective spatial categorization of rural areas, the concept of rurality itself must be defined.

Definition of rurality

Until recently, planners have leaned heavily on sociological theories of rural and urban relationships. Two basic models have been invoked in this context. The original idea of 'rural' and 'urban' as two poles of a dichotomy was soon found to be unrepresentative of the real world situation (Stewart, 1958). As Sorokin and Zimmerman (1929, 16) pointed out, 'in reality the transition from a purely rural community to an urban one ... is not abrupt but gradual'. Realization that the extremes of the dichotomy were easily recognized but that the threshold between their respective influences was not readily identifiable, led to the conceptualization of the rural- (or folk-)urban continuum pioneered by Redfield (1941). Support for this concept came from investigators such as Queen and Carpenter (1953, 38) who noted a 'continuous graduation in the United States from rural to urban rather than a simple rural-urban dichotomy'.

However, the continuum model has also been seen to be unrepresentative in that it is both oversimplified and misleading (Mitchell, 1973). By way of compensation increasing complexity has been introduced into the theory of rural-urban relations. Pahl (1966a, 327) argues that the continuum concept might be replaced by 'a whole series of meshes of different textures superimposed on each other, together forming a process which is creating a much more complex pattern'. A natural progression from this idea is outlined by Bailey (1975, 117-18), who argues that 'the crux for the sociologists is that the defining parameters of social problems are the same for rural as for urban areas'. Thus the treatment of the rural-urban distinction in sociology has changed from the study of two extremes to the recognition of common social variables in these extremes, which allow a unified field of study, and preclude the separation of 'rural' from 'urban'.

When faced with a fluid conceptual framework such as this, it seems likely that an inductive approach might yield more positive and useful results when attempting a definition of rurality for use in the planning of rural areas. This approach inherently accepts some form of continuum model, and rightly so, for geographers and planners are not yet ready to follow sociologists into a non-spatial view of rural and urban as a unitary area, simply because of the vast differences in scale, resources and environment between the two extremes.

An inductive approach suggests that certain selected variables may be measured to ascertain whether an area inclines towards the rural or urban pole. The definition of rurality is therefore inherent in the choice of these variables, and so it is necessary to include some test of significance to ensure that the selected variables are indicative of rural or urban (and therefore non-rural) inclination. Schnore (1966, 135) warns that all such definitions incorporate a degree of arbitrariness. 'In this case, the major difficulties stem from the fact that the characteristics which have been singled out for attention ... are literally variables, i.e. they exhibit differences in degree from place to place and time to time.' However, these difficulties would appear to be advantageous in the construction of an index. Areal variation is necessary to gain a widespread pattern of the distribution of rurality, and variation over time is likely to offer an interesting insight into the changing nature of rurality.

In 1971, the Department of the Environment (1971a, 1972) reported on an investigation into the nature of rural areas and small towns in England and Wales. Incorporated in this study was the measurement of three variables to define rurality, and the calculation of an index by which degrees of rurality could be measured. This study pioneered the inductive approach in this field but an updated index has since been developed which makes use of multivariate statistical techniques (Cloke, 1977a). The need to replace subjective and nebulous expressions of rurality with a more objective statistically-based view is paramount as a foundation to the study of rural areas and their settlements. It is therefore important to produce a definitive statement of the different types of rural area which exist, with particular reference to those areas using the key settlement planning system.

The indexing technique

The use of multivariate techniques to create an index of rurality was based on the measurement of sixteen variables for each rural district in England and Wales for 1961 (table 1.1). These data were subjected to a principal component analysis in which selection of the input variables suggested that the principal component itself would indicate the overall concept of rurality. The resultant loading scores showed that a subset of nine variables were the most efficient contributors to the principal component and so this subset was reintroduced into the analysis (table 1.2). Finally, the revised loading scores were used as weightings in a standardized indexation procedure, which produced index values between -12 and +15 (see Cloke, 1977a). A highly negative index value denotes an extremely rural area, because that value is produced by high scores in those variables directly correlated with rurality (table 1.2) and

Table 1.1   Indexing variable list

Variable name	*Census data*
1 Population density	Population/acre
2 Population change	% change 1951-61, 1961-71
3 Population over age 65	% total population
4 Population men age 15-45	% total population
5 Population women age 15-45	% total population
6 Occupancy rate	% population at 1½ per room
7 Occupancy rate	Household/dwelling
8 Household amenities	% Households with exclusive use of: (a) hot water; (b) fixed bath; (c) inside W.C. (1971)
9 Occupational structure	% in socio-economic groups: (13) farmers – employers and managers; (14) farmers – own account; (15) agricultural workers
10 Commuting-out pattern	% residents in employment working outside the rural district
11 In-migration	% population resident for less than 5 years
12 Out-migration	% population moved out in last year
13 In/out migration balance	% in/out migrants
14 Distance from nearest urban centre of 50,000 population	–
15 Distance from nearest urban centre of 100,000 population	–
16 Distance from nearest urban centre of 200,000 population	–

lower scores in those variables which are inversely correlated with rurality. Alternatively, a highly positive index value has been brought about by a bias towards those variables which are inversely correlated with rurality, and so extreme non-rural tendencies are indicated.

The same procedure as above was used to calculate a comparable index using data from the 1971 census. Loading scores for the sixteen variables and for the revised subset are shown in table 1.3. Many operational difficulties had to be overcome in order to achieve comparability between the 1961 and 1971 indices. However, the resulting analysis of change between the two dates does provide an interesting insight into the long-term patterns of rural change (see Cloke, 1978). Of more direct relevance to this discussion of variations in types of rural area are the spatial manifestations produced by the indices.

Spatial patterns of rurality

Figure 1.1 illustrates the spatial distribution of the rurality index

Table 1.2   Variable loading scores for 1961 index

Variable	Loading score	Revised loading score
Population change 1951-61	0.73984	0.77151
Household amenities	0.73780	0.73826
Population women 15-45	0.72098	0.76131
Commuting-out pattern	0.68591	0.73575
In-migration (5 years)	0.64610	0.58545
Population density	0.59345	0.66164
In/out migration balance	0.49956	–
Population men 15-45	0.39421	–
Occupancy rate (household/dwelling)	0.30663	–
Occupancy rate (Persons/room)	0.08919	–
Out-migration (1960-1)	0.05655	–
Distance from 200,000 urban node	-0.59700	–
Population over 65	-0.61408	-0.60623
Distance from 100,000 urban node	-0.67039	–
Distance from 50,000 urban node	-0.71716	-0.67525
Occupational structure	-0.78833	-0.81771
Percentage of current variance explained	35.8%	50.8%

Table 1.3 Variable loading scores for 1971 index

Variable	Loading score	Revised loading score
Population women 15-45	0.81910	0.83468
Population change 1961-71	0.75264	0.78473
Occupancy rate (household/dwelling)	0.70324	–
Commuting-out pattern	0.69741	0.72182
Household amenities	0.63919	0.65360
In-migration (5 years)	0.60671	0.61294
Population density	0.59169	0.62476
Population men 15-45	0.53790	–
In/out migration balance	0.32784	–
Out-migration (1970-1)	0.12379	–
Occupancy rate (persons/room)	-0.19560	–
Distance from 200,000 urban node	-0.56135	–
Distance from 100,000 urban node	-0.68744	–
Population over 65	-0.70138	-0.69705
Distance from 50,000 urban node	-0.76455	-0.71370
Occupational structure	-0.79594	-0.82194
Percentage of current variance explained	39.3%	52.4%

for 1961. A simple quartile classification has been used to separate the rural districts of England and Wales into four categories ranging from extreme rural, through intermediate rural and intermediate non-rural, to extreme non-rural. The term 'non-rural' is preferred to 'urban' because the index is specifically designed to investigate rural indicators. Consequently, variables which are inversely correlated with the rural extreme are not strictly urban pointers, although the two meanings often coincide.

Four major belts of extreme rural (Category 1) areas are clearly visible from the index distribution. These are:

(1) The south-west peninsula, including all of Cornwall, the more remote parts of Devon, and the south-western extremities of Somerset, Dorset and Wiltshire.
(2) Wales and its borderlands, excluding the southern industrial belt and the extreme north-east.
(3) Most of Norfolk, north Suffolk, and the Wash areas of Lincolnshire.
(4) A discontinuous Pennine belt, stretching from north-east Yorkshire and Westmorland to western Northumberland.

Table 1.4 shows the index-derived extremes of rurality and non-rurality. From this it can be seen that mid-Wales is the most rural of the four Category 1 belts outlined above. The general indication given by the 1961 index is that rurality is greatest in areas of remoteness (cf. Ministry of Housing and Local Government,

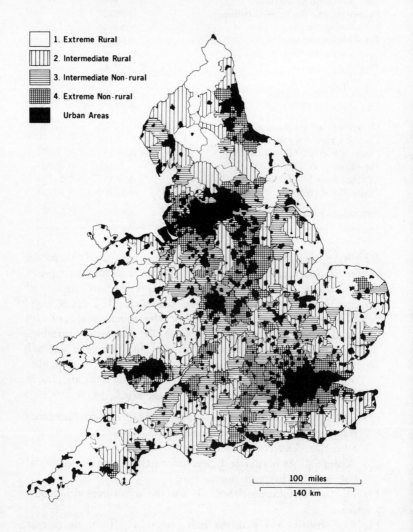

Fig. 1.1   Rurality in 1961

1967), and in particular the upland remote areas.

The distribution of intermediate rural areas (Category 2) falls into two distinct zones. These areas are much in evidence adjacent to the upland Category 1 belts, for example in south and central Devon, south and north-east Wales, and bordering much of the Pennine belt. Category 2 is also indicative of lowland agricultural areas such as those surrounding the Norfolk Category 1 belt, and those in localized patches, examples of which are to be found in the Kent-East Sussex and Worcestershire-Gloucestershire border areas.

Category 3 districts are classified as intermediate non-rural. Many districts in this category are to be found on the periphery of urbanized lowland England, demonstrating in some cases the outermost spread of urban pressure exerted on the rural environs both by the London conurbation, and by the Central Urban Region

Table 1.4   Extreme rural and non-rural districts

Extreme rural			
1961		*1971*	
Knighton	-11.1467	Newcastle Emlyn	-11.7423
Tregaron	-10.5027	New Radnor	-11.6030
Machynlleth	- 9.7260	Painscastle	-11.1780
Lleyn	- 9.5482	Reeth	-11.1006
Reeth	- 8.7134	Machynlleth	-11.0400
Aberaeron	- 8.5928	Knighton	-11.0331
Hiraethog	- 8.4933	Lleyn	-10.9616
New Radnor	- 8.4781	Llanfyllin	-10.4203
Twrcelyn	- 8.3026	Penllyn	-10.0365
Stratton	- 8.0768	Kington	- 9.8148
Extreme non-rural			
1961		*1971*	
Pontypool	14.4459	Whiston	14.8817
Elstree	14.2878	Meriden	14.7064
Watford	13.8896	Warrington	11.7249
Warmley	13.4983	Workingham	10.5329
Billesdon	13.3226	Highworth	10.2997
Easthampsted	11.7899	Hartley Wintney	10.1267
Eton	11.7495	Easthampsted	9.9822
Luton	11.6273	Grimsby	9.8194
Whiston	10.8848	Wigan	9.7234
Darlington	10.8569	Blaby	9.7165

(as defined by Osborne, 1964) with its outliers in south Wales and Durham. Elsewhere, districts of this category denote the influence of smaller-scale urban centres such as Hull, Cambridge and Exeter.

Rural districts showing extreme non-rural tendencies are found in Category 4. As expected, these areas (with the exception of the Peak District) form well-defined rings around the conurbations of the Central Urban Region, except for the north-west conurbation where the ring is only partially formed. Table 1.4 highlights the fact that the areas around London are well-represented among the most extreme non-rural districts. Indeed, only London has exerted sufficient pressure to extend this ring beyond those rural districts immediately adjacent to the urban administrative area. Here, a definite growth axis of Category 4 districts has spread into Oxfordshire and Berkshire. Extreme non-rural districts are also found away from the main conurbations. These districts illustrate the urban influence of more peripheral urban nodes such as Plymouth, Bristol, Norwich and Grimsby.

The overall picture of rurality in the rural districts of England and Wales in 1961 is one of a rather fragmented gradation from non-rural to rural. Generally, remoteness would appear to be highly correlated with rurality, but the rural districts in central England form a more diverse pattern of overlapping spheres of influence. There are very few examples, the best perhaps being to the south of Bristol, where a perfect continuum of rurality can be viewed in the form of a well-ordered concentric gradation of the four categories of rurality. The unevenness of the gradient from extreme non-rural to extreme rural is emphasized by the contrast between the gradual westward slope of increasing rurality from London, and the abrupt change from Category 4 districts in the West Midlands (particularly in the Seisdon area) to the Category 1 extreme rural areas of Shropshire. It is apparent from this change that distance is not the only factor which explains the spread of urban pressure, and a study must be made in particular of agricultural land use and the effects of planning restrictions in order to understand the complexities which complicate any continuum that might exist.

A similar basic pattern of rurality is displayed in the 1971 distribution (figure 1.2). The four principal belts of Category 1 extreme rural areas remain, but of these only the south-west peninsula retains a virtually unchanged position. Those districts bordering the South Wales conurbation appear to have assumed an

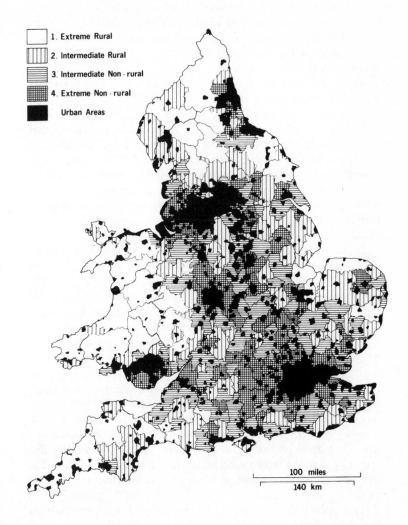

1. Extreme Rural
2. Intermediate Rural
3. Intermediate Non - rural
4. Extreme Non - rural
Urban Areas

100 miles
140 km

Fig. 1.2   Rurality in 1971

increasingly rural nature, while elsewhere in Wales, the peripheral urban centres of Milford Haven, Cardigan, Holyhead and Bangor appear to have exerted greater urban influence on their surrounding areas than was the case in 1961. This has resulted in a decrease in rurality in these districts. The number of extreme rural districts comprising the Pennine Category 1 block has increased, whereas a decrease in rurality may be noted in north Norfolk.

These observations comply with the general hypothesis that lowland areas are increasingly being subjected to urban pressures, causing a decrease in rurality, whereas in upland areas rurality appears to be self-sustaining. Once again table 1.4 shows that mid-Wales is the most extreme Category 1 area. Intermediate rural areas have a similar distribution to that of 1961 except that in several areas this category has been eroded by intermediate non-rural districts, as the pressure from urban centres has increased, or where green belt policies have caused certain urban pressures to leapfrog to more peripheral rural districts. This erosion can be clearly seen in the northern parts of Kent.

At the other end of the scale, the intermediate and extreme non-rural classifications both appear to have spread outwards from the major urban nodes, especially in south-east England. The western axis of urban pressure from London, visible in 1961, has been consolidated and extended almost to Bristol, while a similar axis has developed north-westwards from London. In central England generally, the model of an urban hour-glass (Smailes, 1961) or dumb-bell (Best, 1965) linking the London and Central Urban regions is mirrored very clearly in the pattern of surrounding rural districts which are indexed as intermediate or extreme non-rural. It is interesting to note that although Champion (1974, 69) in his work on the changing extent of urban land, recognizes a 'clear separation of the two regions by the only weakly urbanized belt extending from Wiltshire to the Wash', the 1971 rurality distribution demonstrates a substantial erosion of this separation. The indications are that these patterns of urbanization are possibly evolving more towards Hall's (1973, 302) projection of 'Megalopolis England', although there are evidently pitfalls in the use of this terminology.

Also noticeable from the 1971 distribution is a spatial devolution of urban pressure away from the conurbations, and London in particular, towards the more provincial urban nodes such as Peterborough, Lincoln and Grimsby. Table 1.4 demonstrates that the London area is less well-represented in the list of the most extreme non-rural districts than in 1961, and this gives further proof of increased urbanization elsewhere in England and Wales. An exception to this trend is evidenced by the observation that the south-west cities of Plymouth and Exeter have suffered a relative decrease in their influence over their rural hinterlands.

Generally, the relationship between rurality and urbanization in 1971 follows the broad pattern outlined by Best and Champion (1970) in their study of the conversion of agricultural land to urban use. However, two significant departures from their findings are apparent from figure 1.2. The first is that the 'rural gap' (see p. 22 of their article) between the London and Central Urban regions is shown to be rapidly closing. Secondly, and perhaps more important, the 1971 distribution of rurality shows a significant spread of urbanization from the London conurbation, both westwards towards Wiltshire and north-eastwards towards East Anglia. Neither of these trends are highlighted in the calculations of conversion of agricultural land, but nevertheless could be important pointers to future growth areas.

1.2 *Changes Affecting Rural Settlement Patterns*

The construction of an index of rurality for England and Wales is an attempt to formulate previously subjective ideas into one concise statement of rural-urban differentials. Statistical indexation techniques have been used in order to introduce as much objectivity as possible into the classification of different types of rural district. As such, neither the index nor its resulting distributions encompass innovative thinking, but are rather a rephrasing of current theoretical developments into a more compact and workable framework. A numerical interpretation of rurality, and consequent differentiation between varying districts, provides a fundamental and necessary starting point for research involving contrast or comparison between rural areas.

The spatial manifestations or rurality (as expressed by the index) are complex and dynamic, and so the two broad categories of 'pressured' and 'remote' have been distilled from the foregoing analysis to act as a framework for the summary of some of the problems linked with changes in rural areas (figure 1.3). It will be seen that pressured and remote areas are each characterized by particular types of rural problem and that key settlements, where used in different rural situations, are required to carry out very different planning functions and to react to various troubles in the

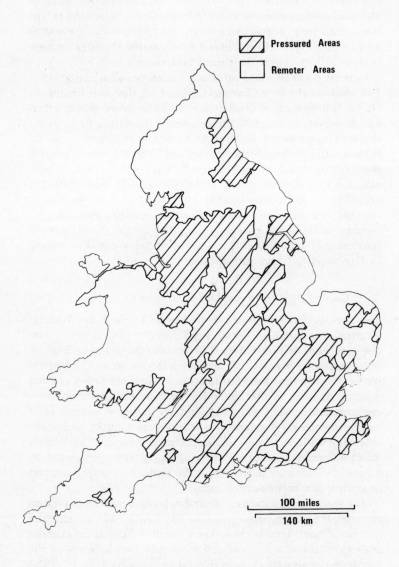

Pressured Areas

Remoter Areas

100 miles

140 km

Fig. 1.3 Pressured and remoter areas in England and Wales

countryside. The classification of 'advantaged', 'disadvantaged' and 'deprived' rural settlements (Moss, 1978) is deferred at this stage since these categories represent end-states reached by various causal factors and therefore do not help in the understanding of rural processes themselves.

Problems of pressured rural areas

In his discussion of the urbanization of the British countryside, Clout (1972, 46) suggests that 'in less than a quarter of a century since Britain entered the motorway age the country will have experienced possibly the greatest social upheaval since the Industrial Revolution'. This social upheaval will have been brought about by the rapid spread of urban influences into the countryside, contributory factors to which are:

> the extending system of motorways, greater use of private cars, rising level of real income and leisure, and the improved servicing of villages with water, electricity and other basic services, bringing these amenities up to the standards hitherto found only in towns. (Ministry of Housing and Local Government, 1967, 3)

The most marked result of this process is the level of population increase both in Rural and County Districts (table 1.5) and in the small towns and market centres which were an integral part of the previous rural settlement pattern (table 1.6). Such growth is not a new phenomenon (see Ashby, 1939). Indeed the search for residential space by the affluent and the lure of cheap housing for the less

Table 1.5   Population in Rural and County Districts (000s)

	1951	1961	Change 1951-61 (%)	1971	Change 1961-71 (%)
England	7,428	8.176	+ 10.1	9.739	+ 19.0
Wales	766	778	+ 1.6	838	+ 7.7
Scotland	1,475	1.472	- 0.2	1,527	+ 3.8
Total	9,669	10,426	+ 7.8	12,095	+ 16.0

Source: Woodruffe's (1976) interpretation of 1971 Census data

Table 1.6   Population in small towns (000s)

	1951	1961	Change 1951-61 (%)	1971	Change 1961-71 (%)
England	1,493	1,664	+ 11.5	2,079	+ 24.9
Wales	297	304	+ 2.6	334	+ 9.8
Scotland	533	546	+ 2.4	596	+ 9.2
Total	2,323	2,514	+ 8.2	3,009	+ 19.7

Source: Woodruffe's (1976) interpretation of 1971 Census data

affluent have been two essential components in the outward spread of urban areas over the years. However, the scale of urban diffusion has increased with heightened personal mobility to the extent that rapid urbanization of previously rural areas has brought about many urgent problems for the planners.

The arrangement of these pressured rural areas is more complex than might at first be imagined. Generally the intensity of commuting appears to fall with increasing distance from the urban centre in question, but as Masser and Stroud (1965) have highlighted, specific local factors are able to modify small-scale commuting patterns. Planning policies play a major role in the determination of these patterns. Restrictive policies such as the imposition of a green belt can curtail residential growth in certain areas whilst other policies (for example the Warwickshire Interim Settlement Policy, 1966) have been more sympathetic towards estate development within commuter zones. Personal residential selection procedures will also mould the local distribution of pressured rural areas. It is inevitable that some villages will be perceived as more fashionable than others and so will attract a greater demand for housing (Humphreys, 1974). Kendall (1963) has shown that the attitudes of landowners can restrict growth in rural settlements, and the reverse can also be true if substantial amounts of land are made available at one time. Other factors such as varying lines of communication, the internal workings of residential information systems and policies for the decentralization of employment will also modify the degree of pressure exerted on any particular rural area.

A number of surveys (e.g. by Hampshire County Council and

Mass Observation Ltd, 1966) have investigated the reasons why people move into rural settlements. These studies suggest that urban pressure on the countryside originates not only from commuting newcomers, but also from people with retirement in mind and from the requirement of some workers for proximity to the various types of employment which have a rural location. However, urban pressure also arises from changes within the village community (Emerson and Compton, 1968). With the decline in agricultural jobs much of the manual employment now takes place in towns and this has led to a trend of commuting from this section of the village community. This movement has meant that rural communities were themselves in a fluid state even before the integration of newcomers became a serious problem. Together, these changes have upturned several rural sub-systems.

In the housing sub-system, for example, increased demand from 'outsiders' has had to be accommodated both by the building of new dwellings and, to a lesser extent, by the conversion of agricultural workers' dwellings. At the same time demand from local people has often led to the building of new council estates, and so a social split has been created between new and improved private housing on the one hand, and the council housing occupied by 'local' people on the other (Scott-Miller, 1976). In a wider context, the decision has also had to be made whether to allow growth in all pressured settlements or whether some are more suitable than others to accommodate the influx of 'urbanites'. Strong arguments have been advanced (e.g. by Fairbrother, 1970) for the conservation of high-quality rural settlements, but should such reasoning result in policies of no growth in certain settlements, then those settlements would immediately become residentially desirable, property prices would increase, and eventually the settlement would be liable to 'gentrification' by the affluent (see Wibberley, 1972). Furthermore, smaller properties which might have been suitable for younger, less prosperous families have tended to be bought up and used as second homes (Saville, 1966; Bielckus *et al.*, 1972).

The balance of the rural social sub-system has also been upset. Pahl (1965a, 49) in his classic study of commuter settlements in Hertfordshire concluded that 'the traditional world of a small, established middle-class with a large working-class population has been invaded by a new middle-class commuting element so that now the middle-class is numerically the greater'. The middle-class newcomers have tended to maintain all their contacts outside the settlement and so integration into the existing community has been slow, and in some cases has not been attempted at all. Thorns (1968) contrasts this pattern of social linkage with that of farm-workers in periurban areas who are very closely orientated around their own village. Social activities within the village reflect this social conflict in microcosm, with the traditional organizations and events which revolve around church and pub in rural communities being shunned by many newcomers in favour of more middle-class pastimes such as the badminton club or the drama group (Frankenberg, 1966).

Social segregation in pressured rural settlements is often given geographical expression through the tendency both by developers and by local authorities to group houses of equal value or rent together. In this way, clusters of socio-economic groupings are formed which serve to further impede social integration in these settlements. Segregation is also manifested in other directions. For instance, Clout (1972) recognizes that the influx of middle-class commuters often brings about a change in the status and leadership structure of the village. Very often such institutions as the Parish Council or Meeting become the domain of the vociferous newcomers who having furnished themselves with their own dwelling in a rural environment take it upon themselves to ensure that this environment is not spoilt by an influx of additional new housing into the settlement.

The in-depth investigation into the unbalancing of the rural social sub-system, conducted by Pahl (1965b, 1966b), concludes that 'the introduction of a certain type of middle-class commuter, seeking a meaningful community, by its presence helps to destroy whatever community was there' (1966b, 998). A situation such as this presents the planner with several planning issues, not least of which is the question of whether a settlement should be planned to attain a particular social balance. If so, the optimum balance for a particular settlement would have to be defined, and this is a task that has so far evaded planning methodology. However, Thorburn (1971, 129) makes the point that 'any idea of balance pre-supposes that the total number of people in each class who live or want to live in villages accords with the balanced position sought, and there is some evidence that this is not the case'. In this instance, the only foolproof method of maintaining social balance in rural settlements is to assume control of house occupancy, and as yet planners have not seen the problem of social imbalance in villages as meriting such a radical solution.

Changing demographic structure has also upset the equilibrium in pressured villages since the turn of the century. The numbers of middle-aged and elderly people in rural settlements have tended to increase in locations where estate development of low-cost housing has not occurred. Where such estates have been built, large num- bers of younger families have arrived with the consequent pros- pects of a first-generation boom in the birth rate.

These changes in themselves are not seen as pressing rural problems, but in recent years the rate of change in pressured rural settlements has accelerated, often without the benefit of positive planning action to cushion the effects of increased pressure. The provision of services and infrastructure, for example, is at best a steady rather than immediate process, and the sudden influx of new population into the pressured areas has created severe prob- lems for educational and sewage-disposal building programmes. Thus the pressured rural areas have suffered problems which indi- vidually would not have been too problematical but which collec- tively have caused an accelerating imbalance in the physical and social milieu of the rural settlements involved. It is this speed of change which has forced planners to discard the 'adhoccery' which is so deplored by Pahl (1966b) in favour of more positive planning policies in general, and the key settlement type of policy in particular.

Problems of remote rural areas
Although the national trend has been one of growth in rural areas, Woodruffe (1976) provides evidence that almost a third of all rural districts are continuing to lose population. Generally, these are the areas situated at some distance from centres of urban population and which are therefore unaffected by most of the pressures of urbanization described above. Consequently the pro- cess of decline both in agricultural employment and in the rural social structure have not been superceded by in-migration of urbanites, and so the planning problems posed in such areas are largely distinct from those occurring in pressured rural areas. The major urban influence in the remote areas is that of second-home ownership and of the gentrification of villages of high environmen- tal quality. However, this very selective form of in-migration does little to solve the basic socio-economic problems caused by remoteness.

The actual extent of these remote rural areas has been the subject of some debate (see, e.g. H.M. Treasury, 1976) but it is evident from figure 1.3 that major tracts of rural land in Britain may be described as remote rural areas, and certain characteristics may be detected which are common to all or most of these areas. Principal among these characteristics is the occurrence of rural depopulation, which may be viewed as both the initiator and the end-product of the social and economic ills of rural areas. Rural depopulation itself has been studied in great detail (notably by Saville, 1957; Mitchell, 1950), and several general statements can be made about the factors influencing this phenomenon and the problems resulting from it. A case-study in Devon (Economic Committee of the Community Council of Devon, 1969) has highlighted the complex urban-rural relationships which contribute to rural out-migration.

> Two of the major contributory factors have been the 'push' from employment in rural areas and the 'pull' of employment in urban areas. The 'push' was started by the availability of cheap imported food and animal fodder which followed improved methods of communications. Farmers tried to cut costs and increase output by substituting machinery for labour. The demand 'pull' has been the higher wages offered by manufacturing industries in urban areas in order to attract workers from rural areas because of the shortage of labour. (p. 7)

A second factor to be considered in this context is the nature of the settlement pattern itself. With the decline in traditional rural manufacturing industries and the corresponding awareness of the economics of industrial centralization, a scattered distribution of villages and hamlets designed for self-sufficiency has become a liability in terms of the provision of transportation services to urban employment. Thus those settlements beyond commuting range of the nearest employment centre have lost their residential attraction to many groups of working people. It is not only transport which has become uneconomic in this way. Other services, notably in the areas of education and retailing have followed the trend towards centralization while rural areas still lag behind their urban counterparts in terms of the basic infrastructure of piped water, electricity and main-drainage facilities. These factors have some importance in the explanation of rural depopulation, but they should not be overemphasized. Both Bracey (1958) and Mitchell (1950) have produced case-studies which question any strong connection between lack of services and depopulation.

A third contributory factor in the process of depopulation is the apparent belief that the standard of living in urban areas is far higher than in the rural settlements. Bracey (1970) lists several urban attractions which have some bearing on rural out-migration, these being: better shopping facilities, a greater range of social amenities, better housing, improved welfare, better transport, better education facilities and a wider range of social and intellectual contacts. Similar 'pull' factors were emphasized by House (1965) in a case study of rural north-east England. However, Green (1966), while noting the propensity of young people to move out from remote rural areas, makes the point that the remaining rural population are in no way to be written off as demoralized or living in the past. Indeed they demand much the same level of living standards and services as the urban dweller although there is a disgruntled acceptance that some rural services may be less conveniently situated than their urban counterparts.

Rural depopulation often produces an imbalance in the age and class structure of a remote rural area. In a situation where employment is lacking it is generally the younger age groups who will move away to seek jobs elsewhere. Thus a residual rural community is formed which is over-represented by very young and ageing members. Similarly the balance of class structure will be tipped towards those people who can meet the financial requirements connected with second-home ownership or long-distance commuting, and also towards those people who do not have the required affluence or personal mobility (or indeed the inclination) to move out of the remote rural areas once they are established there.

Wallace and Drudy (1975) see the combined forces of rural depopulation as a 'vicious circle'. Following a theory originally proposed by Myrdal (1957), they note that 'As a result of the decrease in population fewer services are demanded and these in turn contract. For this reason the economic attractiveness of the area in question is reduced further and the vicious circle is complete' (p. 17). The social aspects of this circle are emphasized by Winter (1971) who considers that a threshold point is reached in a declining population where service facilities can no longer be supported, thus leading to a decline in living standards and further incentives towards out-migration.

Until the late 1960s rural depopulation was recognized as being an ever-present feature of remote rural areas (see Lowenthal and Comitas, 1962). Gillette's (1923) prognosis that rural villages and towns would decline and eventually disappear was always seen as a distinct possibility. More recently, however, the future scale of this phenomenon has been questioned, particularly in the context of models of the future urban and rural form which tend to emphasize rural growth at the expense of conventional cities (see Sarre, 1972; Cloke, 1978). The Government Inderdepartmental Group report on rural depopulation (H.M. Treasury, 1976, 2) concurs that 'there are some reasons for thinking that things may be changing and that the problems of these [remote] areas, or at least some of them, will be less serious in the future'. This optimism is based on the fact that out-migration was slowed in some remote rural areas during the 1960s. However, this loss of momentum may have been caused at least in part by high levels of unemployment on the national scale and so this evidence cannot be fully accepted. In any case, it is clear that rural depopulation, along with its cause-and-effect relationships with social and economic rural sub-systems, continues to be the major planning concern in many, if not all, of the remote rural areas in question, and planners will continue to be faced with the problem of finding workable policies for these areas.

1.3   *The Key Settlement Solution*

It is clear that within the countryside there are many different shades of rurality, each representing a particular combination of social and economic problems. At one extreme, planners are faced with the problems of providing housing, services and employment within the framework of a scattered depopulating settlement pattern. At the other extreme, planners are called upon to accommodate the physical and social vestiges of urbanization whilst at the same time preserving settlements of high environmental quality. All the more surprising, therefore, is the realization that the key settlement type of policy has been introduced in all types of rural area, forming a kind of universal elixir for multiple rural ailments. This policy revolves around the fundamental concept of concentrating rural resources into certain selected centres. However, other policies also include some forms of concentration and so it is essential at this stage for the term 'key settlement' or 'key village' to be strictly defined.

In the past these terms have been coined to cover a multitude of different rural policies, and two examples from recent research serve to demonstrate that discrepancies in terminology continue to exist within the study of rural planning. Parsons (1976), in a case-study of village planning in Norfolk and Nottinghamshire, defines key village policies as those 'which propose the concentration of rural facilities into selected centres but do not extend concentration to the location of development' (p. 19). Alternatively, Rawson and Rogers (1976, 16) see a key settlement policy as one 'where certain villages will gain new housing'. However, if these definitions are taken at their face value then they could be applied to any rural planning policy operational in Britain as there will invariably be some element of housing and service concentration in planned rural areas.

What separates a key settlement policy from other forms of rural planning is not only that a comprehensive function in terms of housing, services and employment is attributed to the growth centre itself but also the fact that a key settlement policy incorporates an overview of the settlement pattern as a whole and lays special emphasis on the relationships between the key settlement and the other settlements served by it. It will be seen in Chapter 3 that key settlement policies in the planning context evolved from an emphasis on service provision, through housing development priorities, to a broader consideration of the functional status and potential of settlements, the economic environment and the operation of the settlement structure in general. This being the case, the key settlement approach forms a distinctive planning method as shown by its use in counties such as Cambridgeshire, Devon, Durham and Warwickshire at various intervals over the last twenty-five years.

Origins of the concept
It is important to the overall study of key settlements to gain an initial understanding of the circumstances and environment in which this type of policy was conceived. In fact the conception of the key settlement form of planning can be traced back to two dominant personalities of the inter-war and immediate post-war period, and it was from the ideas and initiatives of these two men that a formalized key settlement policy was adopted, first by Cambridgeshire and then by other counties. The first of these innovating personalities was Harold Peake, who came to the forefront of rural planning affairs at the end of the First World War. His major concern was to plan for the future of English rural settlements at a time when it was not generally realized that villages needed to be planned at all. Peake was perhaps one of the first to accept that 'we cannot bring to life an organism which has

died a natural death' and that 'it is scarcely worth while to re-create it on its own model' (1922, 220). Consequently, he turned his thoughts towards an ideal village form, which would be of sufficient size to overcome basic service thresholds.

> All the everyday requirements of health, education and recreation, needed by most of the inhabitants would be found within the village itself, while the population would be sufficient to command reasonable transport facilities to the neighbouring town, where they could satisfy their rarer needs. (p. 232)

Peake's contribution is greater than just providing the academic germ of the key settlement concept. He prophesied the changes that were about to take place in rural areas, and demanded planned action at an early stage so that rural imbalances could be accommodated on a gradual day-to-day basis rather than in retrospect. This planning need was recognized to be broader than a series of simple village plans. Peake emphasizes that 'if the remodelling is to be a success it must be the result of regional not merely village planning, or scraps will be left over which cannot readily be united with others' (1916-18, 249).

Little has been written of Peake and his far-sighted endowments to the field of rural geography and planning. Accordingly, it is fitting to quote from the final paragraph from his book *The English Village* (1922, 236) which presents a situation which bears an almost frightening resemblance to the conceptual problems tackled by researchers up to the present day.

> Now is the time, while all our country cottages are being replaced to re-plan our villages upon some well-considered model. Let us not 'muddle through' this as we have done through so many important crises of our past history, lest we stereotype a system which has outworn its usefulness, and fail to seize the opportunity which is now offered to us to construct villages capable of sustaining a community life in keeping with modern conditions.

While Peake may be viewed as an academic whose ideas have far-reaching conceptual relevance to modern-day rural planning concepts, Henry Morris went one stage further and was able to put his ideas into practice in the contemporary rural planning context (Ree, 1969). During his period of office as Chief Education Officer of Cambridgeshire (1922-54) Morris, through the medium of having to provide educational services to a dispersed rural settlement pattern, came to a fundamental understanding as to the direction in which the overall planning of rural areas should go. He soon realized that 'the village has ceased to be an independent social unit' (Morris, 1942, 18) and that 'the only alternative to the complete subordination of the countryside to the town is the adoption of the rural region as a cultural and social unit, parallel to that of the town' (p. 19).

Ree (1973) expands the two basic ingredients of Morris's solution to the problems of the rural areas. Firstly he said of Morris that 'he insisted that the vision of planners should extend to a far wider horizon than was usual. They should be concerned not merely with economic efficiency, not merely with sewers and roads and housing, but with the total scene' (p. 19). The second half of the Morris philosophy was that 'we ought to see our way to the organic provision of education for the whole adult community' (p. 20). A combination of these two beliefs led Morris to propose and instigate his plans for 'the village college' (Morris, 1925) which was to be the centralized secondary school for a number of contributory villages by day, and a centre for adult education and for social functions outside normal school hours. The idea of a centralized focal point for a rural area was one which paved the way for a broadened key settlement concept. Moreover, twenty village colleges were actually built, more than half of these being situated in Cambridgeshire.

Henry Morris the man has been the subject of some criticism in recent times. Poster (1969) suggests that his ideas were indebted largely to the experience of the Danish folk high-school movement and to the writings of an American educational philosopher called John Dewey. However, Henry Morris the figurehead and administrator is to be esteemed in that he was the first agent of successful concentration in rural planning and as such prepared the path for the ensuing key settlement type policies.

Key settlement objectives
Out of the creative vision of individuals such as Peake and Morris emerged the concept of selective concentration in rural planning, which was further expanded and augmented both by the theorizing of academic planners and geographers (see Chapter 2) and by the monitored use of the policy in the practical planning field (Chapter 3).

In pressured rural areas the key settlement type of policy has been used as an efficient method of controlling rural growth. Two basic objectives are expected from the policy in this context. Firstly, the concentration of residential development into certain selected centres enables a similar polarization of infrastructure and services, and this tends to be the optimum economic pattern for the provision of such facilities. The second justification for the policy's use concerns the ability of a settlement to accept residential growth. A key settlement policy (in theory) allows the conservation of settlements whose environmental quality is such that further large-scale growth would be inappropriate. Moreover, it should be possible to ensure that those settlements selected as growth centres are environmentally and socially capable of receiving the designated expansion. Key settlement policies in pressured rural areas are therefore an exercise in channelling growth and, as such, are in theory more easily workable than in areas where growth has to be attracted.

Key settlement policies in remote rural areas have been used in situations where little current growth exists and so the policy provides the framework for an exercise in the promotion of growth. Contiguous with this objective is the stemming or even reversal of rural depopulation. The designation of key settlements where employment is either on hand or within easy travelling distance creates a location for intervening opportunities within the depopulating settlement hierarchy. In this way it is hoped that migration will be limited to internal rural movements from the remotest settlements to the holding points provided by the key settlements. Two further reasons have been called upon to justify the use of key settlement policies in remote rural areas. Firstly, this type of policy is seen as the most efficient and economic means of servicing a scattered settlement pattern. In addition, the policy is a discriminating vehicle through which available resources can be concentrated on those growth centres which are situated in areas of greatest need. All in all, the remote rural areas present more difficulties for the successful operation of a key settlement policy, and success will very often depend on concomitant policies for the attraction of additional employment and facilities within the area concerned.

2
Conceptual Evolution of Key Settlements

The original ideas of Peake and Morris have been widely adapted and augmented by other theoretical considerations in the rural planning field, and the key settlement policy has been moulded from a configuration of these various concepts. The influence of these various theoretical and conceptual developments on the initiation and continued use of key settlement policies has been considerable for two main reasons. Firstly, the period of time during which the key settlement idea was being adopted by rural planners coincided with a phase of high levels of integration between the academic discipline of geography and the planning profession. Thus it was that subjects of theoretical interest to geographers were *ipso facto* of direct relevance to planning thought and, as a consequence, a definite requirement can be discerned at this time for planning policies to be founded on proven theoretical considerations.

The second link between key settlement policies and conceptual matters concerns the way in which planners felt the need to justify the policies which they enacted. In order to explain and defend the use of key settlement policies in rural areas, planners tended to isolate points of spatial and economic theory which suggested that policies of concentration would be most relevant to the solution of rural problems. A basic paradox is apparent here, in that the very concepts from which the key settlement notion was originally developed, have also been used to provide a retrospective and independent justification for key settlement policies already in use. Therefore a vital analytical input to any overall assessment of this particular planning strategy is to examine the application of each individual theory, or group of concepts, to key settlement policies in rural areas, with the aim of discovering whether key settlement planning was founded on, or retrospectively justified by, the various concepts in question. To this end, the application of relevant theoretical notions such as growth centre theory, central place theory and threshold analysis to the key settlement idea is now discussed in some detail.

2.1 Growth Centre Theory

At first glance, the theory of growth poles and growth centres offers an ideal solution to the planning problems encountered in remote and pressured rural areas. This is particularly true of the popularized growth pole model which illustrates two opposing forces governing the movement of economic prosperity. The first of these forces is that of 'backwash' (Myrdal, 1957) or 'polarisation' (Hirschmann, 1958) which concerns the tendency for central nodes to attract factors of production, be they entrepreneurial skill, labour, raw materials or savings, from their surrounding areas. Backwash appears to lend itself as a neat model for the planning situation where economic and population overspill into a rural district needs to be controlled and channelled into the reception centre (or centres) most suited to accept such growth.

The second force associated with the growth pole model is that of 'spread' or 'trickle down', where economic development and prosperity are transmitted from a centre to its periphery, for example by the transfer of income earned in the centre to the service sector of surrounding settlements. Similarly, this spread effect is a convenient analogue model on which to base the planning of remote rural areas, with their problems of lack of employment opportunities, difficulties in infrastructure and service provision, and resultant depopulation.

Superficially, then, growth pole theory appears to give ample justification for the concentration of development into key growth centres in pressured rural areas and the rationalization of growth into key centres in remote rural areas, thus taking advantage of backwash and spread effects respectively. However, the growth pole model has evolved through investigation at the regional and national levels, and the model's operational ability in microcosm is very much dependent on the diluting effects of scale.

Small-scale growth centres

The term 'rural settlement' is often taken to define those settlements which are regarded as rural by the planners and thus are subject to distinct rural policies, such as the key settlement policy, under the Development and Structure Plans. However, in any theoretical discussion of small growth centres, the scale inherent in the key rural settlement idea must be further defined so that the size of a key settlement may be equated with the minimum size of a centre which would be able effectively to carry out the different roles of a growth centre.

Richardson (1973, 5) notes that 'the arbitrariness of all attempts to delimit cities casts some doubt on the value of the concept of city size'. This is equally true of the quest to give numerical expression to the difference between an urban and a rural settlement. For example, Smailes (1944), Bracey (1952) and Smith (1968, 1970) have all embarked on classifications of the settlement hierarchy but have not given theoretical population ranges to their different classes. Correspondingly, Berry (1967) has studied discontinuities in the settlement hierarchy and has grouped settlements according to how many functions they perform. Thus a town performs between 28 and 50 functions, whereas a village ranges between 10 and 25. However, it is again noticeable that no population figures are placed on these groups.

There are, of course, multitudinous problems in delineating a threshold between 'rural' and 'urban' settlements, especially when it is considered that settlements in reality form a continuum between the two extremes. Also, regional and functional differences will distort any numerical expression of such a threshold. However, it is useful to summarize the attempts that have been made in this direction. Table 2.1 shows the maximum settlement population that is defined as rural by certain researchers.

For example, the figure of 15,000 is seen by Green (1971) as the maximum population of a country town, whereas Best and Rogers (1973) suggest that a small settlement will begin to take on the type of service functions which are characteristically associated with larger settlements, at about 5000-7000 population. A group of planners led by Thorburn in 1966 suggested that 8000 was the optimum size for a village, and inherent in this statement is the idea that a village of this size is still a village. At the other end of the scale, Everson and Fitzgerald (1966) see the maximum population of a country town as 2500. No attempt will be made here to

Table 2.1   Suggested maximum sizes for a rural settlement

1,000	Everson and Fitzgerald (1969 – *Village*
1,500	Stirling (In Green, 1971)
2,500	Everson and Fitzgerald (1969) – *Country town*
	U.S. Bureau of Census (1966)
5,000	Green (1971) – *Village*
5,000–	Best and Rogers (1973)
7,000	
8,000	Thorburn (1966)
10,000	Town Map Threshold
15,000	Green (1971) – *Country town*

select one threshold population figure to divide rural and urban settlements. Rather, the body of opinion sampled above will be held as a standard against which the various facets of growth centre theory may be measured.

It must be remembered that Perroux's (1950) original conceptualization was of a growth pole in *economic space* and that if this initial growth pole theory is to be of any use to the planner (except as an analogue model) then it must be translated into *geographic space* whereby development is polarized around 'growth centres' (Darwent, 1969). Therefore, the growth centre concept can be seen to have detached itself, at least in part, from the theory which gave it birth, and this has led to growth centres themselves being variously defined with each definition placing more or less emphasis on the question of scale. One widely used definition describes an urban core (and its surrounding area) which is capable either of spontaneous population and economic growth, or of potential growth which could if required be stimulated by government intervention (EFTA, 1968). This definition would seem to offer some scope for growth centres at the rural scale. Other researchers are less liberal in their definitions. For example, Hermansen (1972) argues that geographical growth centres must incorporate growth pole firms. Definitions in this vein are, however, so strict as to preclude all but the biggest urban nodes from the requirements of a growth centre.

Given the EFTA definition, growth centres appear to offer themselves as tools for planning policy which are suitable in size, form and composition as well as in the goals and objectives that are required. At the same time it is important to note that experience in this field has shown that, although the normative value of the growth centre concept, especially to planners, is considerable, the explanatory value is limited and should not be overemphasized. Even the normative value is more heuristic than specific. Darwent (1969, 21) points out that such ideas as 'it is better to concentrate investment in centres than to scatter it around' and 'bigger centres will be better than smaller ones in the amount of growth produced from a given level of investment' abound in the literature, without any concrete theory to justify them.

Despite this conceptual uncertainty, growth centre policies are practised at both national and regional scales in a variety of forms for a variety of reasons. Moseley (1974) summarizes the four principal growth centre mechanisms as economics of infrastructure and service provision, economics of agglomeration, the spread of development to peripheral areas and the introduction of intervening opportunities in areas of depopulation. Whether these mechanisms may be adapted to serve the needs of rural areas is again determined by questions of scale. Can small towns and large villages fulfil the polarizing role which has so far been identified only in the larger urban centres, and if so what forms of public and private investment are needed to secure the success of this role? So far, few detailed answers to these questions have been offered, and to do so requires a systematic investigation of each of the growth centre components, in relation to the minimum size at which they might continue to operate efficiently.

Economies of infrastructure and service provision
The notion of rationalizing the provision of infrastructure and services so as to take advantage of economies of scale is an integral part of the growth centre concept. Thus the building of one big school or high-capacity sewerage scheme is economically more acceptable than building several smaller schools or sewerage systems. The same applies to the provision of services by the private sector. Several small retail outlets with scattered clientele are less viable than one or two larger shops with all their customers within easy reach. These conclusions are supported by the North Walsham Area Study (Norfolk County Council, 1976), which undertook to test the hypothesis that the concentration of new housing development in or around existing centres provides the greatest overall benefit at the least net cost to the community. The general results of this study indicated that the savings generated by policies of concentration amounted to £5m-£40m so far as capital

costs were concerned (depending on various sewage-disposal options) while the revenue costs of dispersal would be one-third higher than those of concentration.

It would seem that a small scale of operations does not create any difficulty in this case, for in any given situation a concentration of service provision will give greater economic viability than a dispersal. Unfortunately there are several distorting factors involved here. The above statement would be true if a new settlement pattern was being created from scratch; but as it is, present settlements represent large investments, the value of which may only be realized by their continued use. Settlement viability thus becomes a matter of 'the relative cost of providing residential and other settlement services from the existing pattern or producing these services from some other pattern' (Whitby *et al.*, 1974, 165). This relative costing is perhaps best achieved using a cost-benefit analysis approach as was used in the South Atcham Study (Warford, 1969).

Economic thresholds in service provision are reasonably straightforward but when social thresholds are considered the optimum settlement pattern becomes a question of policy rather than of the economic range of a good. For example, in remote rural areas population levels are often below many of the economic thresholds and thus services such as public transport and food-distribution facilities cannot be viably maintained. Therefore, there seems little doubt that economies can be achieved by concentrating the provision of infrastructure and of economic services. However, this does not take into account the hardship that would be inflicted upon the non-mobile elements of the rural population should concentration of services into growth centres also apply to social services such as those dealing with public transport, education and health needs. In pressured rural areas the service threshold is usually more easily attained and there is a strong case to be made for concentrating additional services and infrastructure into key growth centres in order to take advantage of economies of scale. Social policy would also point in this direction so as to avoid the externalities incurred by additional development in settlements where further growth would be environmentally damaging.

In theory the growth centre concept of centralization of service provision is equally applicable to rural areas as it is to larger regions. However, by the same token, rural planning policies would have to be attuned to the needs of local people in order to prevent the idea of concentration being applied throughout the settlement hierarchy, resulting in larger and more urban settlements replacing rural growth centres of smaller scale.

Economies of agglomeration

Growth pole theory places great emphasis on the pole firm or industry being able to stimulate the growth of linked firms through the generation of external economies. Such agglomeration will also produce internal economies of scale accruing from expansion of output within the new site, and transfer economies due to linkage with and proximity to buyers and suppliers. It has been argued, for example by Thomas (1972), that these three types of economy are all needed to maintain the self-sustaining growth that is vital if the growth centre is to promote the desired spread or backwash effects. Apparently, then, the best method of achieving these economies is to concentrate all growth investment into a key centre or centres.

Pressured rural areas by definition offer the advantages of location near to urban centres and labour sources, and a higher quality of transport and site infrastructure than their remoter counterparts. Indeed such pressured areas may wish to control the spread of industry rather than attract it. The effects of scale are more far-reaching in the remoter rural areas. Experience in mid-Wales, where relatively few jobs have been created but very high unit costs have been incurred, suggests many difficulties for industry at the rural scale in assuming the role of the regional growth pole. It seems unlikely that the type of industry attracted into rural areas can set up linkages so as to take advantage of external, internal and transfer economies. Much rural industry is either very small, or consists of branch factories which link to higher-order urban centres, or has pre-existing linkage to the agricultural output of the area. Self-sustained growth as defined by the presence of industrial linkages accompanied by an upward curve of investment or production cannot take place in the rural environment because the sheer mass and number of production units involved will only agglomerate successfully when surrounded by urban population and infrastructure. Berry (1970) and Shackleford (1970) put the threshold for self-sustaining growth at roughly 250,000 population.

If self-sustaining growth is defined in less rigid terms, then the concept might again be applicable to the rural scale. For example, Moseley (1973b) has shown that firms in individual small towns in East Anglia derive some advantage from industrial growth in nearby expanding towns. At even smaller scale, it is feasible that self-sustaining growth can be achieved by all-purpose cooperatives run by small communities such as Llanaelhaearn in North Wales which has a population of 250. Here, a cooperative has funded a small pottery industry and cottage knitting activities and has plans for additional employment growth. In some respects, self-sustaining growth of sufficient scale for the community involved might be attained in a situation such as this.

However, in the terms laid down by growth centre theory, rural areas are at the bottom end of the growth hierarchy and a clear correlation exists between size and probability of further growth. The only slight indication to the contrary has been found by Moseley in Thetford and Haverhill, which have populations of around 13,000. Links between industries in these towns and local suppliers in the periphery and in the centres have been established to some extent here, and this may serve as an example to other rural areas with similar problems. At present, rural industrial growth is very often government-sustained (rather than self-sustained) through a continuing system of grants, loans, tax relief and other government pressures. Despite criticisms of this policy it may well be the only way in which this aspect of growth centre theory can be fulfilled even in a small way in rural areas, and again public policy must balance social benefit with the economic cost needed to achieve the necessary growth.

Spread of development to the periphery

Whereas a growth centre's ability to attract factors of production from its hinterland has not been seriously questioned, the ability of the centre to spread development and prosperity centrifugally is not so definite. This aspect of growth centre theory is crucial to the solution of planning problems in remote rural areas for two reasons. Firstly, the opinion is often expressed, as by Nichols (1969), that unless such a spread effect capability is discernible in a given area, the area in question cannot be included in growth centre theory. Secondly, it is implicit in many public planning policies that growth centres do spread development to their peripheries, and the political acceptability of these policies relies on this concept of spatial impact.

It is obvious that the balance between the backwash and spread mechanisms is of great importance. In theory, the labour force attracted by the employment of the growth centre will, in part, be drawn from the periphery as commuters, in which case these workers will return some of their increased prosperity to the location where they live. It is also possible that decentralization of capital will occur in the form of branch plant establishment, this theoretically being a result of either economic or government forces. Finally Richardson (1969) outlines a socio-economic spread from growth centres whereby a demonstration of new values in the centre erodes the conservatism of the periphery and thus acts as a stimulus to economic growth.

The work of Lucey and Kaldor (1969) in Ireland, and Moseley (1973b) in East Anglia, indicates that the spread of development to the periphery is only applicable to the rural scale in very limited circumstances. Spread by industrial linkage will not occur unless frequent contact with suppliers is required by growth centre firms. It is more likely that any industry in rural key growth centres of large-village or small-town scale will be the supplier for, or even branch factory of, larger growth centre firms, and so linkage will take place up the settlement hierarchy rather than down into the periphery. Nevertheless, spread will be indirectly brought about by the change in the economic and perceptive position of the commuter and his influence on the area in which he lives. For example, local service provision may then be enhanced over and above the strict threshold of the settlement concerned.

The strength of these changes is difficult to assimilate. Berry and Neils (1969) and Moseley (1973a) delineate a spatial surface of development around their studied growth centres. Both agree that a growth centre needs a minimum population of 25,000 to have any appreciable impact on this surface. There is some doubt as to whether this figure should be taken as definitive, there being no theoretical justification for such a threshold, and more proof is needed than can be supplied by two case-studies. Indeed, Moseley in East Anglia and Bertrand (1970) in Brittany have produced results which indicate that small growth centres with populations of between 5000 and 15,000 have a clear impact on the development surface through their employment opportunities. Also, little research has been carried out into the impact of the dispersal of ideas and attitudes which would not be portrayed by the development surface technique.

There is no theoretical reason, therefore, why small-scale growth centres cannot spread small-scale benefits to their peripheries, especially if they are of sufficient size to attract firms which are willing to use local suppliers and local labour. However, in practice several doubts are cast on the ability of small centres to exert centrifugal forces. Certainly, even if employment is provided for 50 to 100 people, then the benefits are spread at least indirectly to the periphery; but in terms of the generation of linked economic activity, which is the dictum of growth centre theory, the backwash effect is more in evidence than the spread effect.

Growth centres and depopulation

The ability to stem depopulation is, in effect, a measure of the success of the growth centre concept as applied to remote rural areas. If private and public sector services and infrastructure are improved, and if employment opportunities are provided which in turn spread prosperity into the hinterland, then a situation is brought about whereby an area previously undergoing depopulation will have more to offer the population living there. As a result, the population of the area will begin to stabilize, if not in the periphery settlements, then certainly in the growth centre itself.

In pressured rural areas it is hoped that the spread and backwash effects will be so balanced as to attract any population growth to the key centres, this being achieved by severe restrictions on housing development elsewhere. Thus growth needs to be controlled and channelled rather than initiated, and it is clear that planners have had more experience and success in the controlling of growth than in starting it. Therefore, it is the remote areas which look to the growth centre concept to help in problems of depopulation. It is now generally recognized that there are several push and pull factors affecting the migration of rural dwellers to urban centres, and so growth centres would have to cater for the widespread employment, transport, housing service, infrastructure and social needs of the rural population if out-migration is to be prevented.

Both House (1965) and Hannan (1969) emphasize that a lack of employment opportunities is the most important reason for migration. In answer to observations such as these, the planners have turned to the introduction of small-scale industries in the hope that these will be a sufficiently powerful attraction to stem the depopulation process. The example of mid-Wales shows that the capability of remote rural areas to attract the right type of industry is limited. Garbett-Edwards (1972) concludes that the dispersed settlement pattern of the mid-Wales area does not allow sufficient attraction of industry for the stemming of depopulation. He does, however, allow that the provision of employment opportunities is the answer to depopulation problems and that the general development of mid-Wales is inextricably linked to industrial growth. This opinion is borne out by the fact that the integrated management of the Highlands and Islands is beginning to counter the regional outward drift of population, although much of this stabilization seems to have been brought about by the magnetism of Inverness, a town of 35,000 population, as a stopping-off point for migrants.

In fact, the ability of growth centres to stem depopulation is rather an unknown quantity. In terms of employment provision, the small rural growth centres are at a great disadvantage as they lack the sheer size needed to attract growth pole type firms. Nevertheless, the remainder of the pull and push factors causing migration can be dealt with to a certain extent by the increased provision of a range of services and an adequate physical infrastructure which can be provided in the growth centres because of scale economies. These improvements of opportunity may well have some impact on the depopulation process provided that suitable employment is present within commuting range. Outside this journey-to-work threshold, depopulation is likely to be exacerbated by additional out-migration to the growth centres themselves.

Limitations of rural growth centres

It is an interesting summary of the question of scale in growth centres to compare the maximum size approximations for rural settlements (given in table 2.1) with the estimates for the minimum population size at which growth poles are said by different sources to function either in part or as a whole (table 2.2). This comparison shows that, even accounting for the difficulties involved in placing a numerical value on a vague concept such as a village or a town, a key rural settlement cannot perform theoretical functions of the growth pole and centre.

For example, empirical investigation suggests that agglomeration economies promoting sustained industrial growth are not attained without a threshold population of at least 25,000 and that a fully functional growth centre needs a population of 250,000 before achieving self-sustained growth. The only dissenting note from this evidence is instanced by the study *A New Town For Mid-Wales* (Economic Associates Ltd, 1966) which suggested that a centre of 70,000 population would be sufficient to promote self-sustaining growth and to spread development and prosperity.

Table 2.2   Suggested minimum sizes for growth centre attributes

250,000	Berry (1970)	*Self-sustaining growth*
	Shackleford (1970)	
	Fox (1966)	
200,000	Moseley (1974)	*Migration interception*
70,000	Economic Associates Ltd (1966)	*Self-sustaining growth*
50,000	Misra (1972)	*Investment spread*
30,000	Allen and Hermansen (1968)	*Employment linkage*
	Moseley (1974)	*Infrastructure provision*
25,000	Lewis and Prescott (1972)	*Development spread*
	Berry and Neils (1969)	
	Moseley (1974)	
15,000	Carol (1966)	*Infrastructure provision*
13,000	Moseley (1974)	*Employment linkage*
5,000	Green and Ayton (1967)	*Service provision*
3,000	Moseley (1974)	*Service provision*

This suggestion was finally shelved in favour of a number of smaller growth points, but there is a case for arguing that some of the more successful English and Scottish new towns do function as fully-fledged growth centres, and these have populations of well under the quoted 250,000 threshold. Indeed, their present population is often no more than 50,000.

Few case-studies have been carried out concerning the role of small towns and large villages as growth centres. Moseley's (1973b) is often referred to simply because it is one of the very few such studies in the British context. Another relevant example is the *Small Towns Study* carried out in East Anglia (East Anglia Consultative Committee, 1972). This report sees growth centre theory as having only a tenuous relationship with the problems facing the planners in East Anglian small towns. In particular, the scale of investment in employment and infrastructure implicit in the growth centre concept is perceived to be far greater than that planned for the small towns even in the long term.

In view of both theoretical and empirical evidence, we can draw the general conclusion that key rural settlements are not of sufficient scale to provide a full range of growth centre attributes. However, it is important to question whether this full range of regional-scale attributes are needed in a centre in order to cope with rural-scale problems. It is apparent that small-scale growth centres cannot bring about industrial agglomeration economies and linkages; but are these necessary at the rural scale?

It is possible to recognize two tiers of rural growth centres which are a workable part of the growth centre concept. The higher in the settlement hierarchy is the substantial rural town with a population of up to, say, 15,000. A population base of this size would allow a good deal of employment growth, especially if government help was enlisted. Some spread effects would then be exerted by the centre at least to those parts of the periphery within commuting range. This larger centre would have the capacity for high-order provision of services (both economic, social and cultural) and physical and social infrastructure, and these facilities along with the increased employment opportunities go some way towards removing the causes of rural depopulation (as seen around the East Anglian towns).

A second-tier rural growth centre would have a population between 3,000 and 5,000 and this settlement would function principally as a centre for service and infrastructure provision, although some small-scale employment could also be provided. Such a centre would service the mobile peripheral population as well as those employed in agricultural and related industries. This centre would also have the capability of acting as a stopping-off point for out-migrants. The introduction of some industry is important. Saville (1957) notes that without key rural settlements offering some employment, the process of out-migration will continue to create communities with disproportionately old population structures. Encouragement in this respect comes from growth centre policies in northern Sweden (Bylund, 1972) and Newfoundland (Courtney, 1972) where depopulation is beginning to be stemmed by the intervention of small-scale growth centres of less than 3,000 population.

In pressured rural areas there should be little difficulty in setting up either tier of rural growth centres as outlined above. Backwash effects are promoted by planning restrictions on growth outside the centres and incentives for growth within the centres. Problems of scale are not so acute in this context, and the location near to larger urban centres often means that the rural areas are themselves within the commuting periphery of higher-order urban growth centres and so receive spread benefits from this source.

There are more problems involved in setting up growth centres in remoter rural areas. For one thing, it is difficult in such a situation to deny growth to any settlement merely on the grounds that it is not a planned growth centre. In this case, development potential must be recognized as well as present suitability for growth. However, the numbers of growth centres selected must be balanced against the need for sufficient size or potential to ensure that the desired objectives are met. Too many centres will spread growth too thinly while too few will exclude peripheral rural areas from any prosperity emanating from the growth centre spread mechanism.

The lack of theoretical justification for small-scale growth centres does not necessarily mean that growth centre themes should not be implemented in rural areas. Lemon (1973) notes that the Development Board appear to have been preoccupied with the growth point concept in their dealings with mid-Wales and the Highlands and Islands, where the concept seems out of scale with the problems to be solved. If this is so, then other countries are equally guilty in this respect. Growth centres in rural areas are widely used, for instance in the Appalachia region of the United States (Ryan, 1970) and in Ireland (O'Riagain, 1971). Despite this criticism, there certainly is a case for applying the growth centre concept to the small rural scale, providing that the expectation of results from the policy does not exceed the small-scale answers that small-scale growth centres are able to produce. It is difficult to conceive of any other settlement policy that offers the problem-solving capabilities that are given by the growth centre concept, and if a system of growth centres is adopted, then individual rural problems can be specifically treated within this sympathetic planning framework.

2.2   *Central Place Theory*

If the growth centre concept is able to give some tentative theoretical justification for the promotion of rural key settlements, then central place theory has an equally important contribution to make in terms of an understanding of the relatively unplanned settlement hierarchy that has developed over the centuries in rural areas. Christaller's (1966) original postulation of a hexagonal service area surrounding each settlement paved the way for a recognition of a nested hierarchy of settlements, with the ranking of an individual settlement in this hierarchy being dependent on the size of the settlement and its level of service provision (see Losch, 1938-9).

The theoretical recognition of a universal settlement hierarchy proved to be a significant progression in geographical and planning conceptualization. Christaller produced evidence of a sequence of marketing centres of differing levels in Bavaria and there followed a series of attempts to measure and define the settlement hierarchy in developed countries such as Britain and the United States. In fact the first of this series, by Dickinson (1932) in East Anglia, was independent of and concurrent with the work of Christaller. Dickinson highlighted the existence of a hierarchy of settlements by introducing the concept of a nucleated settlement which acted as a focus for the servicing of a surrounding tributary area. This recognition of a service centre-hinterland relationship had a direct bearing on the planned promotion of service centres within the countryside. Dickinson's (1942) work in East Anglia was followed by Smailes' (1944) attempt to delimit urban fields in England and Wales, and much of this work formed the basis for policies contained within the early Development Plans.

Measurement of centrality
The early research of Dickinson and Smailes highlighted the importance of centrality measurement to the planner. It was realized that it is easier to build upon a 'natural' settlement hierarchy than to substitute a more artificial order of service provision. Therefore the accurate measurement and classification of the centrality of various settlements was seen as a high research priority, particularly in the rural setting where minimum service thresholds were deemed as critical in the retention of rural populations.

Two basic methods of centrality measurement have emerged, and the development of each has continuing importance to rural planners as part of the process for identifying and selecting key centres in the countryside. The first method is the use of service indicators, as pioneered by Dickinson and Smailes, and quantified by O'Farrell (1968) in County Tipperary. Service indicators have been important in the key settlement selection process (particularly following the 'hot cross bun' legislation), but are subject to criticism (see Carter, 1972) on the grounds that selected indicating criteria are often arbitrary and that the resultant settlement categorization can be erroneous.

The second method of centrality measurement concerns the delineation of hinterland areas and is typified by the work of Green (1950), Carruthers (1957) and Johnston (1966) using bus service data. Once again this work was included in the policy-formation process for rural Development Plans and their reviews. Although

bus services are now an outmoded measure of functional associations, flow research has continued, notably using telephonic communication data (Davies and Lewis, 1970), although this line of
research has tended to stop short of the rural scale.

Central place theory and the rural scale
The relevance of central place theory to key settlement policies in
rural areas stretches beyond the use of centrality measurement
techniques in the early Development Plans. An appropriate vehicle
for the examination of this relevance is provided by Bracey's (1962)
investigation of the English central village, a phenomenon which
he defined as 'the village with more shops and services than one
would expect for its size which is operating services for neighbour-
ing villages and hamlets' (p. 170). Three orders of central village
were listed from an analysis of the distribution of retail and service
outlets in Somerset. Settlements were designated first-order central villages if they had 20 shops or more, second-order central
villages if 10-19 shops were present and third-order central villages if 5-9 shops were available. Furthermore, the spheres of
influence of these various central villages were measured in terms
of the range and extent of mobile services emanating from the
centre and serving smaller settlements in the rural hinterland.

Bracey's findings are demonstrative of several areas in which
central place theory can be applied to rural key settlements.
Firstly, the initial realization that 'natural' centres did exist within
hierarchies of settlements was an important influence on the early
Development Plans. The original central place research of the
1940s and 50s corresponded with a formative period in planning
history and it is certainly the case that at least one county,
Wiltshire, made direct use of Bracey's research in its Development
Plan (Wiltshire County Council, 1953). It is also likely that the
stipulated procedures for Development Plans concerning the map-
ping of services and facilities in the various rural centres (see
Chapter 3) reflected the general atmosphere of the current central
place research findings. However, the relevance of central place
theory even transcends the mere recognition and cataloguing of
rural centres. At the time of the Development Plans, planners
perceived a logical progression from the identification of existing
rural centres to the continuing support of these centres as the focus
for investment in rural areas. In effect, many planners were
attempting to build up certain key rural settlements into the ideal
central village model whereby additional service provision on one

central location would benefit a wide rural hinterland. The early Development Plans' emphasis on existing central places thus not only set the pattern for trend planning in rural areas, but also had some considerable bearing on the introduction of key settlement policies which stress the importance of a centre's ability to service its surrounding area.

This link between rural planning and central place notions has continued, especially after early doubts as to the accuracy of the hierarchy concept had been dispelled by Berry and Garrison (1958). As Chapter 3 reveals, planned support has tended to be given only to the highest one or two grades of central place in the rural settlement hierarchy, rather than to the three or four categories proposed by Bracey. Newman (1967), in a study of the Irish rural settlement pattern, affirms the view that regional planning necessarily involves the promotion of a hierarchy of central places, and it is apparent that central place theorization has provided a framework and data base from which key settlement type policies have evolved in rural areas.

A second important feature of the central place concept concerns the changing nature of the settlement hierarchy over time. Clawson (1968, 287) foresaw that

A great many of the small rural towns will wither greatly, and some will die and disappear by 2000. Some have already died and disappeared in farming areas. The process within and between such towns will be cumulative, in a downward spiral. As their business volume declines they will be less able to offer services that will attract farmers, who will gradually go to larger towns at farther distances.

The understanding of change in the settlement hierarchy and of the subsequent planned solutions to the problems arising from this mutation, has been considerably enhanced by the study and conceptualization of the variations in central place hierarchies. One particular planning problem – depopulation – was studied by Johnston (1965) who concluded that the settlement pattern as a whole, and village size in particular, has influenced the degree to which an area has retarded depopulation. In a more general context, Hodge (1966) highlights the characteristics of declining small settlements in North America. He found that it was the smaller settlements that were suffering a deterioration of status because they were not able to offer a wide range of goods and services. This was particularly the case when these settlements were located within the range of larger towns. Furthermore, two levels of successful central place were detected. Many small-scale centres were present serving purely local needs while a few larger-scale centres with higher-order facilities remained to service wider areas of the rural hinterland. Trends such as these are of particular significance to the planning of rural areas. As Clout (1972, 140-1) explains

> Country planners in many parts of the world have attempted to pay due attention to these 'automatic' trends as they formulate policies for future service provision in the countryside. Such policies in a given rural area involve selecting a limited number of settlements where population numbers may be increased and the range of service provision extended, and designating the remainder for future stability or even contraction.

Once again, it is noticeable that the influence of central place theory in rural areas has given impetus to the key settlement concept.

A further example of how the changing central place hierarchy is of relevance to selective rural planning is afforded by the experience of creating primary settlement patterns on Dutch polderland recently reclaimed from the sea. For instance, the East Flevoland polder was originally designed to be served by twelve rural growth centres, but experience from previously settled polders (notably the North East) has shown that a more concentrated pattern is required (Thijsse, 1968). Consequently, only four growth centres, each with increased population targets, are now proposed. The rural planner's ability to keep pace with increasing personal mobility and its consequent outworkings in the rural settlement pattern, will depend to a considerable degree on a constant monitoring of the central place hierarchy. The general trend, however, is clearly one of higher levels of settlement concentration and so, at least from this point of view, the concept of key settlements is becoming increasingly relevant.

Finally, central place concepts have been extensively used in the selection of rural key settlements. Bracey (1962) noted that the distance separating one central village from the next was usually in the region of five or six miles. This distribution bears a remarkable resemblance to the pattern of selected key settlements in Devon (see Chapter 5) and is equally similar to the planned growth centre distribution in many other rural counties. What is more, it will be suggested in Chapter 4 that central place functions or even sheer population size have been the dominant factors in the selection of individual key settlements. If this is to be the case in the future, then O'Farrell's (1968, 32) assertion that 'a conceptually sound methodology and an objective technique for quantifying the centrality of functions and centres is the only valid basis upon which to make meaningful comparisons', assumes a greater relevance in the comparison of two settlements in order to choose one for key status.

Thus far the theorization of central places has been seen to offer a major contribution to the planning of the remote rural areas, but little has been said of the pressured areas where settlement hierarchies have more complex linkages with urban centres. To redress this balance it should be pointed out that the conceptualization of thresholds and the range of a good has some implications for pressured rural areas, although planning ramifications of thresholds and ranges are again predominant in the remoter rural areas where threshold minima rather than maxima are encountered. These concepts are sufficiently discrete to warrant separate consideration, but they should be viewed as one limb of central place theory, the whole body of which has been seen to be making a particular contribution to the use of key settlement policies in rural areas.

2.3 Thresholds and the Range of a Good

The theorization as to market centres and the hinterlands which they serve gave rise to two concepts which have assumed considerable significance in the planning of rural areas. A threshold has been defined as the minimum population that is required to bring about the offering of a certain good for sale or to sustain any service, and the range of a good as the maximum distance over which people will travel to purchase a good or derive a service offered at a central place (Carter, 1972). The relationship between these two notions formed the basis of Christaller's theoretical central place system. However, thresholds and the range of a good, particularly the former, have been widely adopted *per se* in the decision-making process for service provision in rural areas.

Green (1971), a practising planner, highlights the conflict between the service aspirations of rural dwellers and the trend of concentrating services into larger units of distribution, and many early Development Plans took note of this conflict by measuring the rural thresholds for various services. For instance, Cambridge-

Table 2.3   Rural settlement categorization according to services

	Population range	Facilities available
Grade 1	170- 600	Public house, post office general store, village hall
Grade 2	600-1100	As above, plus primary school, playing field, garage
Grade 3	1100-1800	As above, plus police house/station, butcher, ladies' hairdresser, resident doctor
Grade 4	1800-3000	As above, plus electrical goods shop, licensed club, hardware shop, gents' hairdresser, bank
Grade 5	3000 +	As above, plus secondary school, chemist's shop

Source: Cambridgeshire and Ely County Council (1968, 88)

shire County Council (1968) was able to identify five broad groups of rural settlement according to the services and facilities present (table 2.3).

A considerable amount of research was also carried out by Norfolk County Council in order to ascertain the viability of certain services and facilities in the rural areas of that county (Green, 1966; Green and Ayton, 1967). Table 2.4 shows the threshold approximations for a list of such services and it follows from these observations that

> If it is accepted that methods of retailing are changing in favour of larger catchment populations, that some degree of competition is desirable, and that a chemist is a necessity, the minimum population to support an acceptable range of retail shopping may be 8,000 or even more. (Green and Ayton, 1967, 4)

There has been much debate as to the minimum size for a viable rural service centre. Covering the entire rural planning spectrum, Green and Ayton consider that the minimum population needed to support a reasonable range of local facilities is 5,000, whereas West Suffolk County Council (1968) suggest that 1,500 is the maximum figure beyond which a rural settlement becomes socially unmanageable. Views on this subject have changed over time. In the early 1950s there was general agreement that 500-600 population represented a viable rural settlement (see, e.g., Bonham-

Carter, 1951; Mitchell, 1951), and the First Review of the Devon Development Plan (Devon County Council, 1964) continued this strand of thought when it concluded that a village with a population of 500 represents a fairly well-balanced community and is able to act as a local centre. However, the increasing use of service thresholds as indicators of settlement viability has led to the acceptance of the need for higher levels of population to create viable rural settlements and this in turn suggests the requirement for the expansion of a few selected villages and the quiescence or decline of the remainder. Thus it is apparent that the study of rural service thresholds has directly influenced the concentration of rural settlement patterns and the use of key settlement policies.

Thresholds and the range of a good have been put to specific use in two stages of the rural planning process as well as at the general level of policy formation discussed above. Firstly, the range of a good has been incorporated into the determination of threshold levels for the provision of various goods and services. By adding an element of physical distance, the threshold population required for economic viability may be made up of either the growth of a single centre or the demand from a centre and its hinterland, or indeed from a series of linked centres and their hinterlands. The concept of the range of a good is contributory to the size and distribution of

Table 2.4　Typical service thresholds in Norfolk

Population	Service
300	Grocery shop
2000	Butcher
2000-2500	Single doctor
2500	Draper
2500	Household goods
3000	Baker
4000	Chemist
5000	Home nurse
5000	Primary school
6000	Three-doctor practice
8000	Health visitor
10,000	Secondary school

Source: Green and Ayton (1967, 4)

the various key settlements which form the basis of a settlement concentration policy.

A second specific application of these notions has resulted from the conceptualization of threshold theory, which was pioneered by Malisz (1969) and brought into the regional planning context by Jackson and Nolan (1971, 1973). A 'threshold' in this context describes a certain stage in the development of a settlement where further progress is hindered by the need for a particular service or infrastructural facility which represents a considerable investment. One of the difficulties in the implementation of key settlement policies is the programming of growth, particularly in the pressured rural areas. Very often, the development of a key settlement is concerned with indivisible units of investment such as a sewage treatment plant or a new school. Jackson and Nolan (1971, 288) point out that

> The population of a settlement can grow satisfactorily only up to the time when it meets its next threshold limitation. In this respect, the optimum growth of a settlement is to be seen not as a continuous process but as a succession of steps caused by the indivisibility of certain basic investments essential for growth.

In the context of programming development at the rural settlement scale, the authors cite the example of Lytchett Matravers in Dorset, which had a population of 1,500 in 1965 but which has been designated for expansion to 5,500 by 1981 (Dorset County Council, 1965). The application of threshold analysis (Dorset County Council, 1972), especially with regard to the need for a new school, new road surfaces and new drainage systems, is reported to have optimized the investment programming system and minimized the disruptive periods of basic infrastructure and services. These are the very difficulties currently being experienced in several pressured rural areas, for example the expansion of Southam in Warwickshire, and consequently it would appear that threshold analysis could be of particular value in the programming of key settlement development. On the other hand, several dangers are inherent in the singular use of the threshold concept. It has been noted that this approach encourages the planner to plan for the least number of threshold violations so that the returns from large-scale fixed investments may be optimized. Accordingly, the concentration of services and facilities has been advocated on these grounds. However, the economic analysis of thresholds is merely one part of a planning process in rural areas which also involves social and other non-economic considerations that have to be accounted for. Consequently, thresholds alone should not be allowed to dictate rural planning policy.

It must also be remembered that thresholds are not universally applicable. Any threshold is specific to one service or facility in one area with one settlement pattern at one point in time, and although certain thresholds are fixed by the public sector (for example, school catchment areas), it would be unwise to treat thresholds as immutable phenomena. Nevertheless, if these difficulties are heeded, the study of thresholds and the range of a good will continue to play an important role in the planned concentration of rural settlement patterns and in the phasing of key settlement development.

2.4   *Other Related Concepts*

In any discussion of the conceptual background to key settlement policies, mention should be made of three concepts and techniques which bear an important relationship to the notion of concentration in rural planning. The first of these is directly linked to the use of threshold analysis as described above. One of the major disadvantages of thresholds is that they do not take account of social and other non-economic factors, and consequently the use of cost-benefit techniques has been advocated to replace, or at least to complement, the study of thresholds. As Clawson (1966, 280) insists,

> The essence of an enquiry into optimum settlement patterns is the consideration and the synthesizing of all relevant factors, yet one has to start somewhere, taking up each factor in turn and inter-relating the others to it, and summarizing the whole into some form of balance sheet, monetary and otherwise.

Thus, it would seem that the cost-benefit approach does afford a mechanism which is able to account for non-economic variables as well as quantifiable costs and benefits in the decision between various planning alternatives.

Perhaps the best-known use of cost-benefit analysis in the rural context was contained within the South Atcham Study (Warford, 1969), which attempted to cost the various factors involved in alternative water supply proposals. However, other important contributions have been made in this respect. Gruer's (1971) research is particularly interesting because her results from a cost-benefit analysis appear to oppose service concentration, which is traditionally supported by the concept of economies of scale. In this case, the alternative policies for the provision of outpatient clinics were compared and it was found that if the cost of loss of labour and the cost of travel are included in the analysis, then the cost of consultants travelling to peripheral clinics was usually less than the social costs of patients travelling to centralized services.

Unfortunately, the harsh realities of rural planning have tended to supercede the idea that what is good for the consumer of a service will also benefit the supplier of that service. Shaw (1976) outlines four possible future policies for Norfolk's rural settlements as being:

(1) To concentrate growth in the largest settlements.
(2) Dispersal by allowing a standard rate of growth in all villages.
(3) Dispersal by making use of any spare service capacity, taking account of physical constraints.
(4) Development of dispersed villages of 500-800 population.

A cost-benefit analysis on these alternatives would presumably aid the selection of an optimum policy direction for Norfolk from the point of view both of the supplier and the consumer of services. Clearly, the recognizable physical costs of supplying services have in the past weighed more heavily in the policy-making process than have any intangible social costs and benefits. However, the Norfolk County Council (1976) case study of the North Walsham area has attempted to rectify this situation by assessing social and non-monetary costs as well as economic costs. The conclusion is reached that both the capital and revenue costs of servicing the dispersed settlement patterns advocated by policies 2 to 4 are extremely high compared with the costs involved in a policy of concentration. Furthermore the non-monetary costings are found to favour the strategy of concentration apart from the two specific problems of school closure and the stimulation of community activities. Shaw argues that these two factors, coupled with the additional freedom of a greater choice of residential location in rural areas, are sufficient to warrant the acceptance of the higher service costs inherent in policies of dispersal.

It may well be that social costs and benefits have not been noted sufficiently in the planning of rural areas, and if this is so, the application of the cost-benefit technique (itself by no means infallible) may sponsor a wider perspective in rural policy formation. However, in these times of economic stringency, restraint on public expenditure will invariably nullify the practical application of cost-benefit analysis in rural areas so long as established planning attitudes predominate. This being the case, cost-benefit analysis may be more usefully employed in the understanding of certain specific parts of the rural system, for example the mechanics of depopulation (see Speare, 1971).

Hudson's (1969) analogue model comparing the location of rural settlements with the process of 'competition' in plant ecology also offers an interesting vista on the development of key settlements. He describes three stages of change in rural settlement distributions: colonization, where the occupied territory of a population expands; spread, where density increases and small-scale dispersal of settlement occurs; and competition, where the smaller settlements are weeded out in favour of larger service centres which are able to serve more extensive hinterlands because of increases in personal mobility. If it is accepted that 'unless geographical explanations (or predictions) have a theoretical justification, the recognition of spatial regularities is of little value' (Hudson, 1969, 366), then this model goes some way towards explaining the 'natural' evolution of planned key settlements.

Finally, the importance of settlement morphology must be noted. In the past, the existing internal pattern of development has often regimented the way in which a settlement has been planned, and has supported the practice of trend planning in rural areas. Morphology has thus hindered the overview of the entire settlement pattern which key settlement policies have sought to engender. It has, however, aided the cause of conservation for those settlements not suitable for designation as growth centres, and, at a broader level, it is claimed to be able to aid policy-option exploration and heterogeneous global settlement (Christakis, 1975). The science of ekistics has made many such claims, but thus far the practical application of morphology has been at a very basic and local level.

All of the above concepts have, to a greater or lesser degree, played some part in the inception and development of the key settlement policy. However, it would be prudent at this stage to remember that of at least equal importance in this process was the planners' need for a definitive and seemingly innovative policy from which it was evident that the problems of the rural areas were being tackled. The key settlement type of policy was presented as a convenient blueprint at the right point in time, and even had it no acceptable conceptual background, then it is likely that one would have been manufactured in order to give this popular policy some credence. Whether or not this has, in fact, happened is difficult to assess. Some of the above-mentioned conceptual links are tentative, while others appear to be firm. What is clear is that this policy has been shrouded in economic rather than social theory and this may account for many of the difficulties which have been enountered in counties where the policy has been used.

3
Evolution of Key Settlements in the Planning Framework

3.1 Early Legislation and Plans

Prior to 1932, planning legislation had concerned itself with the problems of housing and public health in built-up areas, but the Town and County Planning Act of that year gave first recognition to the need for planning in rural areas. This rather perfunctory and inadequate Act made provision for rural areas which were being developed, or which were under threat of development, to produce a planning scheme with the object of

> controlling the development of land comprised in the area to which the scheme applies, of securing proper sanitary conditions, amenity and convenience, and of preserving existing buildings or other objects of architectural, historic or artistic interest and places of natural interest or beauty, and generally of protecting existing amenities. (Section 1)

Any scheme required the cooperation of at least seventy-five per cent of landowners involved, and this clause alone was instrumental in the bypassing of many of the above objectives so that some form of planning scheme might eventually be produced. However, the very production of such schemes caused local authorities to take note of some of the problems occurring in rural areas. For example, the Warwickshire Joint Planning Committee (1935) recognized the practice of large-scale residential building in the countryside regardless of service availability. They also noted that this scattering of development had resulted in financial and constructional problems in the provision of essential public services.

The scheme prepared for the Durham region (Durham County Council, 1932) outlined the loss of employment due to pit closures and suggested that some contraction of villages might be necessary as a result of their decline. However, the plan took no action to put this suggestion into operation.

It is evident that some regional planning schemes of the 1930s recognized the difficulties of servicing an outmoded settlement structure, and pointed to the need for settlement rationalization in general and the designation of key settlements in particular. Indeed, one county took practical steps towards the concentration of rural services and facilities. The Cambridgeshire Joint Town Planning Committee (1934) planned for the grouping of villages around a key settlement which was to provide educational and social facilities for the cluster, and these plans were carried out incorporating Henry Morris's idea of village colleges in the key settlements.

Fifteen years passed before the next major planning legislation, but the interim period contained several ancillary Acts which had a significant bearing on the settlement policies to follow. For example, the various Housing (Rural Workers) Acts between 1926 and 1938 led to the building of new dwellings for agricultural workers by local authorities; the Rural Water Suppliers and Sewerage Act, 1944, enabled local authorities to make a basic provision of these services to rural areas; and the Education Act of 1944 required local authorities to produce a plan for the building, expansion or closure of schools in its area. The locational decision-making process associated with education contraction or expansion, the siting of new agricultural dwellings and sewage-disposal and water-provision schemes, forced local authorities to consider the whole question of concentrating service provision (and to some extent residential development also), so that investment arising from this legislation might be optimally utilized.

Perhaps the official cradle of the key settlement concept can be found in the evidence to the Second Report of the Minister of Health's Rural Housing Sub-Committee in 1937, which recommended that new rural housing development should only take place in villages, so as to economize on service provision, preserve the countryside and maintain the social advantage of community life. The key settlement concept was also hinted at in the Scott Report on Land Utilisation in Rural Areas (1942) which was to have a profound influence on post-war planning in the countryside. Within an overall framework of preservation and planning for rural areas, the report directed that all new development should be restricted, wherever possible, to larger villages and smaller towns, thus favouring the concentration of services and facilities. The Fourth Rural Housing Report (1944) also made mention of the key settlement idea.

A crop of key settlement policies appeared under the auspices of the Town and Country Planning Act of 1947, which was the basis for post-war rural planning procedure. The Act dictated that 'every local authority shall carry out a survey of their area and submit to the Minister a report of the survey together with a development plan' (Section 1). What is more, plans produced in this manner were backed up by the ruling that planning permission had to be obtained before any material land-use alteration could be carried out.

Rural settlement policies contained within the Development Plans often enacted ideas which had previously been expressed in the regional planning schemes, but the form in which these ideas were presented was regimented by certain ministerial circulars. Ministry of Town and Country Planning Circular 40 (1948), for example, advised that surveying in rural areas should be concentrated on the social and economic functions of the larger settlements. Therefore, the major surveying effort associated with the Development Plans in rural areas was restricted to a cataloguing of educational, health, medical and other social and retail service provision, while a settlement's capacity for residential development, for example, was understandably given little attention as this was perceived as an urban problem at this time.

Circular 59 (1948), from the same ministry, required the planning authorities to map the location of centres for social, educational and health services as a series of circles, divided into quadrants ('hot cross bun'), each quadrant indicating where a certain service existed or was planned for that centre. East Sussex (1953), for example, identified centres where educational and public health facilities were to be maintained or established. In fact, the Development Plans contained considerable variation in hot-cross-bun coverage. Some counties, including Nottinghamshire (1959), Shropshire (1960) and Staffordshire (1960), illustrated the majority of settlements with this notation. Other counties (e.g. Huntingdonshire, 1954) used it solely to identify key settlements. In many ways the hot-cross-bun maps were the first physical manifestation of the ensuing key settlement policies and as such sparked off a good deal of controversy both from villages whose inhabitants felt that village vitality would be impaired by not being selected as a growth point, and from the selected villages where inordinate growth and consequent loss of community life were feared. Such reactions have been an inevitable and consistent consideration in the enforcement of key settlement policies over the years, and have become increasingly important with the advent of greater public participation in planning.

Government advice continued to give support to policies of settlement rationalization even though such policies were of a controversial nature. For instance, *Advice Notes on the Siting of New Houses in Country Districts* (Ministry of Town and Country Planning, 1950) suggested that the economic provision of services in rural areas could only be brought about by the selection of certain villages for expansion. It was also conceded that in certain extreme economic conditions, the only course open to planners was to 'demolish and clear the village and resettle the inhabitants in new centres where employment, houses and services can be provided'.

3.2   *The Development Plan Policies*

With this background of legislation and advice it is not surprising that the rural settlement policies contained within the Development Plans varied only as to the number of settlements selected rather than whether selection should take place at all. Because of the apparently similar nature of selective settlement policies, it is necessary at this point to distinguish between two main categories of policy:

(1) A policy which dictates that new development will be channelled into larger villages. For example, Kent County Council (1958) classified settlements simply into villages suggested for moderate expansion and villages which were not suggested for any expansion. This type of policy tends to take an inward-looking view of the planning of each settlement and the hallmark of this group is that formal government advice appears to have been accepted without too much local innovation.

(2) A key settlement or 'king village' or 'rural centre' policy which is ideally far broader in scope than (1) in that it takes account of the functional status and potential, the economic environment and the operation of the settlement structure in general. Thus,

the key settlement policy may be distinguished by an outward-looking view of how the key settlement will serve the rest of the settlement pattern. It is this type of policy which is the principal concern of this discussion.

Generally, key settlement policies were favoured more by counties with problems associated with a high level of rurality than by periurban counties whose policies were simply geared towards development control. However, the key settlement policies themselves varied considerably from county to county, particularly in terms of the detail in which the policy is presented, the scale of the policy, the chosen role of the key settlements and the planning of settlements not selected as growth centres.

Detail of policy presentation
The key settlement policies included in the original Development Plans exhibit a good deal of variation in detail, although there is a uniform choice of the county areas as the areal policy basis. The Hampshire (1955) policy merely isolated certain settlements where development would be favoured and indicated that applications for development elsewhere would be considered on the merits of the individual case. The Cambridgeshire written statement (1954) was similarly vague. On the other hand, Somerset (1958) produced a more detailed fourfold classification of settlements.

(a) Towns and main villages which act as local centres.
(b) Settlements showing evidence of developing, and which from their position and circumstances might become main villages.
(c) Settlements, which although not showing evidence of developing, could serve as local centres for areas not now enjoying good facilities.
(d) Other settlements.

Perhaps the most detailed of policies accruing from the Development Plans is that of Durham (1954) which detailed the amount of development that would be permitted in each individual settlement, and so left little room for manoeuvre in the face of public outcry against the policy (Blowers, 1972).

This variation in policy detail should not be confused with the strength of a policy, nor with a policy's ability to fulfil its chosen objectives. There are some situations where a detailed policy might prove detrimental to the selected planning goals, and others where a more vague policy is at least an efficient as a detailed one. For example, Lindsey, Lincolnshire (1955) selected a large number of rural service centres with the intention of engendering development, but Jones (1975) in a study of rural settlement policies, indicates that the detailed policy provided too many options for too little growth in the remoter areas of the county. Moreover, the same policy, applied to villages adjacent to the major towns in Lindsey, was inadequate to deal with the increase in demand for commuter accommodation, and failed to 'contain' the pressure. Again, where there has been little expansion of housing in some remoter rural areas, a vague policy statement can prove as adequate as a more detailed statement in that neither could do more than the other to increase the prevailing levels of growth.

It is clear that when studying the impact of a key settlement policy in a particular area, the written presentation of the policy is not as important as the manner in which the policy is perceived and operated by the planners concerned.

Scale of the policy

Less variation is apparent in the numbers of key settlements selected by different counties than was found in the detail of their policy presentation. It has already been noted that key settlement policies were principally drawn up by the more rural counties such as Cumberland (1955) and Northumberland (1956), and the settlement pattern prevailing in these counties was one of numerous small villages. Plans for settlement rationalization tended to reflect this settlement pattern by selecting large numbers of key settlements.

There are several reasons behind the choice of so many growth centres in each county. Firstly, the concept of rural growth centres (or at least rural service centres) was pioneered by these Development Plan policies, and so with little previous experience of such policies to draw on, planners were not able to predict with any accuracy the effectiveness and dynamism of rural centres of various size categories. Selection of key settlements according to threshold populations for various services led to an emphasis on the minimum size for a growth centre almost without regard to the numbers of settlements attaining that minimum size. Associated with this factor of inexperience was the inherent novelty of the key settlement concept. Jones (1975) notes that the prevailing attitude of the time would appear to be one whereby the selection of a village as a key settlement was like the touching of a talisman, after which the planners could sit back and wait for the flood of applications.

When these considerations are coupled with the political pressure exerted by each settlement to gain 'key' status, and the planners' wish for an even geographical spread of key settlements, then it is not surprising that the early key settlement policies opted for maximum coverage of these key centres. Thus Cheshire (1959) proposed forty-one village centres as well as twelve rural centres, and Durham envisaged the investment of considerable capital in seventy centres.

Role of the key settlement

The classic role of the key settlement in the Development Plan policies is summed up by the policy for parts of east and south-east Somerset:

> There is need for a long-term programme to increase rural facilities in this belt and in this connection it is suggested that little would be achieved by dissipating public money on services widely elsewhere, instead it would be better to select a few villages which from their size, position and communications, appear to have some likelihood of developing as main villages to act as small centres for their surrounding rural areas. (Somerset County Council, 1958, 55-6).

The major emphasis on concentration of service provision can be explained on three counts. Firstly, the legislation and government advice on which the Development Plans were based was almost entirely concerned with the cataloguing of existing services and planning for the fulfilment of future service requirements. Secondly, little consideration to the planning of residential development in rural settlements was thought to be necessary, as 'the demand for private housing in rural areas was not very strong in the early fifties and essential housing needs were satisfied by the building of local authority houses' (Woodruffe, 1973, 116). Finally, one of the major causes of concern in the remoter rural areas was that of continuing depopulation. The rural counties believed that the provision of well-serviced key settlements would act as a stopping-off point and therefore would help to stem the tide of depopulation (House, 1965).

The planning of residential development was restricted in most counties to recognizing the lack of modern utilities and proposing to remedy the situation in most villages as and when finance and labour were available. In fact the rural areas nearest to major urban centres, which were most likely to incur demand for residential development, received little attention at this time. The key settlement policy adopted by Nottinghamshire (1959) was the exception to a situation where few counties went as far as to formulate rural settlement policies on the basis of the rural community structure surveys contained in the Development Plans.

One interesting deviation from the stereotyped service provision role of key settlements is afforded by the Cheshire policy. In this case 'urbanized villages' were recognized, these being rural settlements of considerable population size situated adjacent to towns or settlements which have become extensions of the built-up area. Increases of population in these settlements were deemed undesirable although services or urban standards were to be provided.

Cheshire also provided an early example of the bifurcation of key settlement functions. Twelve settlements of above average population and yet situated away from any urban node were selected as 'rural centres'. Service provision in these settlements was to be brought up to the standard of that in a small town so that the rural centre could service a considerable rural hinterland. Significantly, the policy also sought to attract industry and employment into these centres, a task also undertaken by Northumberland for their key settlements. In addition to the rural centres, forty-one second-tier villages were selected to act as localized service centres. This division of the key settlement role into two tiers was one which found favour with later key settlement policies.

One further variation in the role of key settlements is apparent from the reports of survey presented by East Sussex and Nottinghamshire. Both reports suggested that service provision and facilities could be shared amongst a close-knit group of villages (or village cluster). However, in neither case was this suggestion taken up in the written policy statement, although the village cluster concept has been resurrected several times since (e.g. by McLaughlin, 1976a).

Role of non-key settlements

It would be easy to concentrate solely on the role of the key settlement itself when tracing the development of key settlement policies in the planning of rural areas. Indeed, the charisma of a key settlement policy revolves around the ability of the selected settlement to fulfil certain specified aims and objectives. Yet much of the emotion and political outcry engendered by this type of policy concerns the plight of those settlements which are not selected for specific service investment and therefore were often not viewed as viable centres for further growth. Such settlements were paid little attention in many of the initial Development Plans. Cambridge-shire, for example, merely indicated that every application to develop in non-key villages required individual determination in the light of local circumstances. This vague type of policy was also adopted by Hampshire. On the other hand, several counties were more ready to apply the rationalization process to both poles of the rural settlement continuum. It is clear that a policy designed to rationalize an outmoded settlement pattern in rural areas experiencing little or no growth will selectively channel initial prosperity into the key settlements at the expense of other, less privileged, communities. Indeed, population flows from small village to key settlement were encouraged as an answer to rural out-migration. Only in the long term could non-key villages expect to receive a backwash of investment and perhaps prosperity.

Durham was the county which gave fullest commitment to a policy of total settlement rationalization. A fourfold classification of settlements was augmented by detailed accounts of the invest-ment projected for each category. It is worth recording these four categories in detail, if only because of the huge public outcry which resulted from that part of the policy concerned with the 'killing-off' of the Category D villages, which were usually mining villages associated with pits that had closed down (Barr, 1969). The four settlement categories were:

(a) Those settlements in which the investment of considerable further amounts of capital is envisaged because of an expected future regrouping of population, or because it is anticipated that the future natural increase in population will be retained.

(b) Those settlements in which it is believed that the population will remain at approximately the present level for many years to come. Sufficient capital should be invested in these com-munities to cater for approximately the present population.

(c) Those settlements from which it is believed that there may be an outward movement of population. Sufficient capital should be invested to cater for the needs of a reduced popula-tion.

(d) Those settlements from which a considerable loss of popula-tion may be expected. No further investment of capital on any considerable scale should take place. This generally means that when the existing houses become uninhabitable they should be replaced elsewhere, and that any expenditure on facilities and services in these communities which would involve public money should be limited to conform to what appears to be the possible future life of existing property in the community.

In fact Cumberland also designated 'D-villages' where 'development is unlikely to occur', but less opposition was raised to this policy.

The range of attitudes towards non-key settlements, from allowing suitable development to taking positive steps to relocate the settlement's population in a more rational location, appears to be associated with the nature of the county involved. The more remote rural counties, generally with a larger number of key settlements, tend towards a restrictive attitude where non-key settlements are concerned, even though this usually takes the less controversial form of preserving the *status quo* rather than an embargo on further investment. By contrast, the counties adjacent to centres of urban population have more growth and development to allocate and so are able to adopt a less strict viewpoint on the question of suitable development in non-key settlements. Even this attitude is questioned in later policies.

3.3   *Development Plan Review Policies*

Only very limited government advice in rural settlement planning was given to local authorities between the appearance of the initial Development Plans and the submission of the early reviews. However, two new items were introduced to the rural settlement planning agenda during this period. In 1955, local authorities were encouraged to establish green belts, with the consequence that villages within this new designation were to be prevented from further development other than by infilling or rounding off. The second new influence in the rural settlement planning context was the Town and Country Planning Act of 1962 which merely consolidated the 1947 Act and had little effect on the form of development planning (Ratcliffe, 1974). Development Plan regulations were amended in 1965 so as to discontinue the use of 'hot cross bun' symbols on county maps, but information still had to be submitted about service centres in the rural settlement pattern.

However, when the Development Plans were first reviewed,

many counties found it necessary to make extensive revisions to their previous rural settlement policies. In this instance, the revisions were not dependent on detailed government advice but rather were a reflection of the fluctuating conditions and problems in rural areas. Alterations in policy were forced upon some authorities because of a rise in demand for rural housing, principally from urban workers. Moreover, the pressure for rural residential development raised fundamental questions about the future size and structure of rural settlements. Indeed, a system of informal non-statutory plans evolved in many counties in order that development control and revisions in county policy could keep pace with the rapidly changing situation.

Several general observations may be made concerning the key settlement policies contained within the Development Plan reviews. Certain counties made no changes to their initial Development Plan policies (e.g. Huntingdonshire, 1959). Others made extensive policy alterations due in part to unstable external factors and in part to being given the opportunity to rethink or at least spend more time on the Development Plan policies. These changes can usefully be summarized under the headings used in the discussion of initial Development Plan policies. In this way, inter-county variation may be monitored while a concurrent analysis may be made of the major differences between the policies of the initial Development Plans and the Development Plan reviews.

Detail of policy presentation

A much greater degree of detail was incorporated into the key settlement policies of the reviews than had previously been the case. Frequently the previous division between key settlements and others was replaced by a three- or fourfold classification of settlements. On the other hand, Somerset (1964) in fact produced a policy using fewer settlement classifications than before, but it is interesting to compare the three detailed village schedules with the less detailed initial Development Plan policy quoted above. The schedules were as follows:

(1) Villages intended as centres for social, education or health services. Favourable consideration to be given to satisfactory proposals for the development of these villages. Amounts of development will depend on the character of the village, local physical features, accessibility and the need for economy in the use and provision of public services.

(2) Centres considered suitable for more limited development in the form of infilling consistent with the established character of the village and with such essential public services as exist or can reasonably be anticipated.
(3) Small villages and hamlets. Development is not precluded in these settlements. The local planning authority will give sympathetic consideration to development needed for the livelihood of any established rural community.

Very often the overall policy was supported by a series of informal village plans and maps (e.g. Cornwall, 1969) which were prepared in order to complement previous survey work, and to facilitate the planning of individual key settlements. The use of plans such as these became an increasingly frequent second stage in key settlement policy planning. With this trend towards local planning within the county policy system, the later reviews were able to include estimates of the amount of population growth to be permitted in the various settlement classifications. Huntingdonshire (1972) for example, budgeted for an increase of at least 1000 persons in its major growth villages. It must be stressed, however, that many other counties deliberately omitted the inclusion of population increase estimates so that developers could not point to written planning policy as a justification for development which might be deemed unsuitable in planning terms.

Generally, the key settlement plans of this era give more detailed explanation to the background of their policies than previously. This is particularly evident in the consideration of residential development as well as service provision. In some cases, the review stage is the first in which counties have considered it necessary to give a formal statement of a key village policy. Such was the case with Lancashire (1962), which was preoccupied with urban matters in the initial development plan, but residential pressure in rural areas compelled a consideration of rural matters in the review, and the formulation of a key settlement policy resulted. This policy was justified at length:

> In order that the rural economy may be sustained, the amenities of the countryside preserved and the social and other facilities improved, it is considered that development in rural areas should be carefully controlled while provision will be made where appropriate for the consolidation of the existing settlement pattern by the influx of new population. (p. 79)

Two general evolutionary trends are highlighted by the Lancashire policy. In the first place it attempts to portray a comprehensive picture of rural settlements and their needs rather than looking at the problem from one particular aspect. Secondly, the concept of settlement 'consolidation' in pressured rural areas (as opposed to settlement rationalization in remote areas) is introduced, whereby major emphasis is placed on the individual settlement's ability, on physical, social and aesthetic grounds, to cater for new residential development.

Devon (1964) was obliged to produce a definitive rural settlement policy for entirely different reasons. The high level of rural depopulation taking place in the county was not forecast in the initial Development Plan, and the review proposed a strict key settlement policy, orientated mainly around service provision, to counteract these out-migration trends.

Scale of the policy
Very few counties altered the number of key settlements provided for by their original plan. Indeed, the policy introduced by Devon at the review stage designated more than sixty key settlements, and so it would appear that the preference for a large number of rural growth centres was maintained in the reviews. Even Huntingdonshire, despite its being such a small county, was able to name eight major expansion settlements and nineteen minor expansion settlements. The only exception to this rule appeared in the Northumberland (1966) review where the Education Authority's decision to halve its programme of primary school provision led to a drastic amendment of the key settlements policy so that only those villages with primary education facilities were fostered as rural growth centres.

Apart from such specific alterations in the pattern of essential service provision, there would seem to be very little reason for any change in the scale of key settlement policies at this time. The 1961 Census followed immediately after the formulation of the initial development plans, and the mid-term ten-per-cent Census was not able to supply detailed information on the progress of the rural areas. Therefore, it was the 1971 Census which in many cases provided the first opportunity for a detailed review of all aspects of key settlement performance. Even those counties which produced further detailed surveys on their own account found that the early reviews came too soon after the often delayed instigation of the initial rural settlement policy to enable a positive judgement as to the optimum number of growth centres in the county.

Role of the key settlement

The function of key settlements designated under the Development Plan reviews was appreciably wider than in earlier policies. Perhaps typical of the policies applied by the remoter rural counties was that of Devon, which designated key settlements in order to:

- provide the best environment for the countryman.
- encourage the setting up of new activities and sources of employment in the country.
- secure the most economic distribution of public utilities ... and social services.
- make an adequate system of public transport services in rural areas a practical objective.
- preserve the rural landscape.
- maintain a convenient distribution of readily accessible village centres, particularly in areas of rural depopulation.

The introduction of new employment into the countryside and the concern about transport linkage between settlements were objectives which were introduced or reemphasized by most of the key settlement policies in remoter rural areas.

In addition to these widening criteria for concern in the reviewed policies, the guidance and control of residential development assumed major importance in the role of key settlements. Amounts of development to be permitted depended on the character of the village, local physical features, accessibility and the need for economy in the use and provision of public services. The requirement for greater detail in the consideration of individual settlements partly arose from and partly gave rise to an emphasis on the development of informal local plans. In fact, local planning was given formal impetus with the circulation of Planning Bulletin 8 (Ministry of Housing and Local Government, 1967), which suggested a staged process of policy formulation and settlement plan preparation in the light of information currently available. Stage three of this process, following initial appraisal and county policy formation, was the preparation of plans for small towns and villages.

For those rural counties experiencing urban pressure, the introduction of green belt legislation led to the imposition of severe restrictions on settlements within the green belt areas. Few key settlement policies came under the influence of green belts at this time, although it is possible that the severe green belt restrictions imposed within counties such as Warwickshire may have led to the adoption of key settlement policies in order to channel any development forced to leapfrog the green belt into settlements capable of accepting such growth. The few key settlement policies operative in periurban counties were little altered at the review stage, although Hampshire (1969, 2) revealed a possible separation of service and residential development roles in stating that 'certain villages will be selected to serve as local service centres for the rural area around them, although this will not necessarily imply further growth'.

The Development Plan reviews thus gave important impetus to the requirement for a more comprehensive role for key settlements. An increased demand for residential development in the countryside often necessitated the detailing of how much residential growth was acceptable in each key settlement, and factors such as conservation, public transport and employment opportunity provision became increasingly apparent as part of the key settlement function.

Role of the non-key settlements
The trend towards rural policies in the form of a three- or fourfold settlement classification enabled counties to attribute a more specific function to those villages not selected as key settlements. A case in point is Cornwall, whose classification of non-key settlements consisted of:

B. Centres which are suitable for a smaller amount of development depending on the extent and capacity of existing or proposed services.
C. Centres which are suitable only for the location of a very limited number of additional dwellings.

As in the initial Development Plans, different counties adopted differing tolerance levels towards development in smaller settlements. Somerset (1964, 3), for example, takes a sympathetic viewpoint:

The policy set out above does not mean that development in small communities will not be permitted; the Local Planning Authority will be prepared to give sympathetic consideration to development needed for the livelihood of any established rural community.

This leniency towards smaller settlements was certainly not a standard attitude amongst counties as a whole, as many, including

West Suffolk (1963), found it necessary to include at least one category of village where growth would be inappropriate because of the situation and structure of the existing settlement.

In general, though, there was a softening of the strict attitude adopted in some of the initial Development Plans towards the non-key settlements. In some cases, settlements were upgraded in the light of changing social trends. Increased growth in coastal districts resulted in the upgrading of several Cumberland (1964) mining villages which had been previously scheduled for abandonment. Elsewhere, a softening of written policy on non-key settlements came as a result of adverse public reaction to the previous plan. The Durham policy, which attracted much public antagonism, was extensively revised (1964). The former Category D was discarded in favour of a less harsh categorization of settlements in which new capital investment was to be limited to the social and other facilities needed for the life of the existing property. Again some upgrading of settlements took place so that an increased number of small villages were able to receive small amounts of public investment. It is necessary to add a note of caution at this point. There is often a suggestion of window-dressing in this flexible attitude towards the smaller settlements in that there are cases where little difference can be detected between the operation of the rigid development plan policies and the seemingly more flexible review policies.

One exception to the trend of increasing flexibility was the new policy presented by Devon (1964), which indicated that in villages other than key settlements, 'residential developments should be restricted, and only permitted after regard to ... availability of public utilities and social services, the adequacy of approach needs and public transport together with their location in relation to key settlements and urban centres' (p. 166).

It is important to reiterate that the detail in which a policy is presented does not always reflect the strength of that policy when in operation. Much depends on the planner's interpretation of a particular part of the policy at any one time. If, for instance, a rural key settlement is flourishing in terms of population, service and perhaps even employment growth, then the planner may feel able to allow some growth in surrounding smaller settlements. If, however, the key settlement is not attracting growth, or if matters of village conservation are paramount at that time, then a less favourable attitude will be taken towards peripheral development. In this way an apparently flexible policy may be subject to strict interpretation and vice versa.

Having said this, it is clear that the key settlement policies outlined in the reviews had progressed from the earlier policies. Progress is particularly evident in the more comprehensive roles afforded to the key settlement and in the policy changes effected in the light of ten years' experience of key settlements, particularly the steps taken towards local planning and public participation.

3.4   *Structure Plan Policies*

The Town and Country Planning Act of 1968 was an attempt to remedy the deficiences of previous legislation. Under its auspices, the Development Planning procedure was replaced by a two-tier framework for planning involving the formulation of structure plans and local plans, both of which were able to overlap local authority boundaries if necessary. The statement of large-scale policies and proposals contained in the Structure Plan was to provide the backcloth for the detailed working out of these policies in the smaller-scale local plans. These considerable changes to planning methodology were put into operation by the Town and Country Planning Act, 1971 (Amended 1972). However, it is important to note in the rural planning context that, although the new plans were required to relate to such topics as population, employment and housing, there was no obligation to include the planning of rural settlements *per se*.

The time-lapse between the approval of the first Development Plan reviews and the forumulation of the structure plans has in many cases been so long that the reviewed rural settlement policies have themselves become outdated and in need of further review prior to the submission of the Structure Plan. Several interim settlement policies (notably Norfolk, 1974; Leicestershire, 1971; Nottinghamshire, 1966-9) have been produced together with many more informal reviews of policy. The importance of these interim statements is such that policies outlined in them have not been revised to any great extent in the ensuing Structure Plans.

Some Structure Plans have yet to be produced, particularly for counties where the problems of the rural area are a major concern. Inevitably these are the very counties whose limited resources do not allow rapid progress of the involved Structure Plan procedure. However, sufficient rural settlement policies incorporating the key settlement concept have appeared to permit some tentative discussion as to the nature of this new breed of key settlement policies. Noticeable differences have emerged between policies produced for pressured counties and those for remoter counties. Consequently these two areal types merit separate discussion.

Pressured rural areas

Perhaps the most striking feature of this latest series of policies is the increasing number of urbanized counties which have adopted the key settlement concept. This trend was foretold by a series of interim settlement plans detailing the problems of rural areas experiencing urban pressure. Nottinghamshire produced a series of such reports, each dealing with the particular problems of individual rural regions, but each offering a similar settlement policy solution to these problems. For example, in the plan for East Retford R.D. (1966) it is considered preferable to expand a limited number of selected communities rather than to allow an even spread of development in a large number of villages. The plan argues that this concentration of growth will permit the economic provision of public services and ensure that the selected communities are conveniently situated with regard to employment. In this way, the key settlement acts as a centre for service provision, residential development, conservation of other settlements, and also serves as an important node in the journey-to-work network. Similar key settlement roles were adopted by the Leicestershire (1966) interim policy, although this involves a more complex fivefold classification of settlements.

It is not surprising then, that urbanized counties such as Staffordshire (1973) and Northamptonshire (1977) have included key settlement policies akin to the one quoted above in their Structure Plan documentation. Staffordshire's policy attempts both the channelling of growth in periurban areas and the stimulation of growth in rural areas which are more remote from the urban centres. The plan names the selected key settlements and outlines the amount of population growth planned for each. Further innovation has been introduced in the form of the planning of a new village to act as one of the growth centres.

No uniform level of detail is displayed in this group of policies. The Warwickshire policy, which is discussed in detail in Chapter 4, again names its selected key settlements, but gives less detail as to the permitted levels of growth in each centre. The strength and the weakness of the Warwickshire policy is the complex indexation process entered into in order to select the growth centres. Development potential, land constraints and existing commitments are all given detailed analysis for each settlement but there is a suspicion that parts of the index are misleading and others are superfluous.

The Northamptonshire policy names six rural service centres and three limited growth villages. Settlements in the former category will act as service nodes where additional employment and population will be accommodated while those in the latter are merely seen as locations for housing growth. This policy is indicative of a noticeable trend in Structure Plans to supplement the multiple-role key settlements with a number of villages specifically selected for growth in the housing sector alone.

The policy for Leicestershire is different again. Following a survey of existing commitments, population distribution and the service role of villages, it was decided to simplify the interim policy, which consisted of five rural settlement categories, and to classify settlements into one of three groupings: (1) potential expansion; (2) restraint; and (3) local needs. The first grouping is a fairly standard classification which incorporates those villages and small towns from which the key growth settlements will be selected. It is stressed that the village plans for these settlements will be the final arbitors of the growth levels which are acceptable in a particular instance.

Of more interest is the restraint village category which groups together the remaining villages, apart from those where growth will be restricted to the needs of the local community. The scale of growth in these restraint settlements will be strictly dependent on existing commitments and local environmental conditions and services. Included in this category are some villages which were designated as key settlements in previous policies but which have reached a stage of expansion where it is considered that environmental conditions dictate the restriction of further growth. This demotion in the settlement hierarchy raises a very important question in the use of key settlement policies in periurban counties; namely, the long-term decision as to whether key settlements are to be permitted to grow *ad infinitum* and so become settlements of urban size and character, or whether after a certain period of growth, the key settlements are to be allowed a period of consolidation during which the onus of residential growth is shifted to other settlements. If the latter solution is accepted, as it has been by Leicestershire, then there is a risk of a gradual urbanization of the countryside as each settlement is allowed to accommodate its growth potential. Preferably, some compromise can be reached between these two extreme situations, but the dangers of neglecting the long-term ramifications of a rationalization policy in rural growth areas should not be ignored.

Remoter rural areas

Remoter rural counties have been slow in submitting their Structure Plans but there is evidence of interesting policy variation both from submitted plans and from the many preliminary publications which form part of the public participation process. What is clear is that many rural counties are continuing to adhere to the key settlement formula, even though the term 'key settlement' has in many cases been discarded in favour of less provocative nomenclature. The basic key settlement concept varies from county to county. Worcestershire's policy (Hereford and Worcester County Council, 1973) merely states that substantial growth over and above existing growth commitments in rural areas will be generally confined to a limited number of selected villages. The plan for Herefordshire (Hereford and Worcester County Council, 1976), however, favours the restriction of growth to the larger market towns, with village development being confined to settlements where the necessary services and facilities exist or can be economically provided.

An important stage in the development of key settlement policies is marked by the publication of the Norfolk Structure Plan (1977). The problems facing Norfolk are perhaps typical of those affecting a number of rural counties, and so the proposed solutions to these problems in the Norfolk context may give some indication of the format of many future key settlement policies.

The criteria dictating policy selection in Norfolk were those determining:

(1) The appropriate balance in the attraction of development and the allocation of resources between the major urban areas and the rural areas.
(2) Whether, within the rural area, the small towns or the villages should receive the greater emphasis.
(3) Whether, within the rural area, general assistance should be offered to all areas, or whether resources should be specially allocated to selected areas with the greatest need or potential.

As with most counties, the choice of policy in Norfolk is severely compromised from the beginning by the high level of outstanding investment commitments, particularly in urban areas, and so the encouragement of investment in rural areas, especially in employment provision, can only be viewed as a long-term venture. Apart from the factor of existing commitments, the policy response to the aims and opportunities outlined above was heralded by the Interim Settlement Policy (1974) whose advice had been largely carried over into the settlement policy outlined in the Structure Plan. Several departures from the conventional form of key settlement planning are to be found in the Norfolk scheme. Perhaps the most marked innovation concerns the apparent division of key settlement roles so as to form a nested hierarchy of rural centres, each differing in scale and functional priority. Previously, functional bifurcation in key settlement policies had amounted to a basic twofold division between major and minor growth centres. The Norfolk policy retains the major/minor distinction but applies it to three differing types of centre:

(a)   *Growth centres* (major) and *town centres* (minor) with priority on investment for employment opportunities;
(b)   *Village service centres* and *minor village service centres* attracting investment in public services and community facilities;
(c)   Villages for various scales of residential development.

There is a high incidence of overlapping between each settlement category, as might be expected from a policy which aims to provide economies of scale in service provision and residential development. Thus, all but one of the thirteen villages scheduled for residential development are also named as village service centres. Alternatively, sixteen of the twenty-five village service centres are earmarked for residential development at one scale or another. The pattern which emerges from this confusion of details is summarized in figure 3.1. Apart from the all-embracing growth centres, each category gravitates towards a certain functional point or an axis between two such points.

Besides the extreme detail of presentation and an apparent splitting of the key settlement roles, at least in policy formulation if not so much on the ground, the Norfolk policy exhibits other interesting variations of the key village theme. For example, great emphasis is placed on the existing stock of planning permissions, and the inevitability of their restricting the range of policy choice available to the planner. Trend planning has become an integral part of all rural settlement plans, but in this case (as in the Leicestershire plan) some attempt has been made to recognize past mistakes. Expiring planning permissions in unsuitable settlements will not be renewed, and in extreme cases the costly process of the revocation of planning permissions is being considered. Another example of this trend planning is the planned acceptance of residential development in commuter villages which possess only a minimum of services and facilities.

The Norfolk policy, in naming the settlements selected for residential or service development, by the same act isolates the 300 or so villages which can expect no improvement in the level of services or infrastructure. In these cases, there will be a presumption against further housing development permissions, except some minor infilling and individual houses which enhance the form and character of the village. It is interesting to note that counties using a key settlement policy for the first time do tend to adopt a strict no-growth attitude towards the non-key settlements. Counties such as Devon and Northumberland appear to have gradually relaxed this strict attitude as their experience of key settlements has lengthened.

The example of the Devon policy is an interesting one because it demonstrates the planners' response to a lengthy experience of key settlement planning. Sub-regional centres and key inland towns (renamed area centres) from the Development Plan policy retain their basic functions. However the key settlement category has been replaced by *local centres*, 'where it is the intention to maintain existing community services or improve services where major resources are not required to achieve this', and by *selected local centres*, 'where major resources may be made available to improve services' (Devon County Council, 1978, 58). This policy has broadened the scope of village planning in Devon in several ways. Firstly, the two local centre categories encompass 100 rural settlements compared with sixty-eight key settlements in the previous policy. However, the major emphasis will be centred on the forty selected local centres, thereby responding to the criticism that investment had been spread too thinly under the key settlement system. Secondly, Devon's attitude towards non-key settlements has been relaxed from a supposition of no growth to a firm recognition of the need for the continuing viability of small rural settlements.

These changes demonstrate an awareness that an inflexible policy of concentration in rural areas may be profitably superceded by an acknowledgement of the planning needs of all levels of rural settlement whilst continuing to strive for the economies offered by the centralization of resources. In other words, the key settlement policy is being given a more human face.

Conclusions

The evolution of key settlement policies within the planning framework has to a large extent been governed by two cause-and-effect criteria. A causal factor in this process has been the changing circumstances occurring in rural areas whereby problems caused by urbanization pressure particularly on the rural housing system have been added to the more traditional concern with providing services for a depleted rural population. The effect of these changing conditions in the countryside has been to evoke a response from

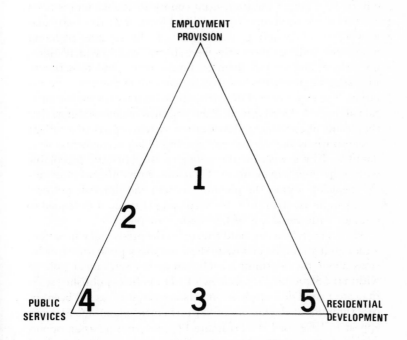

1. Growth centres
2. Town centres
3. Village service centres selected for residential growth
4. Other service centres
5. Centres selected for residential development without service upgrading

Fig. 3.1   Functional differentiation between Norfolk rural centres

central government in terms of legislation and advice which has been geared towards policies of centralization for both services and housing. The fact that the enactment of these policies on the ground has come some time after the changing circumstances were actually recognized does not detract from the generalization that the different priorities inherent within key settlement policies over the post-war period were a direct government guided response to particular planning problems in the countryside.

Although the general format and policy direction of key settlement planning can be explained in terms of these cause-and-effect criteria, the policy variation from county to county represents a reaction to localized conditions and problems, and to the particular viewpoints of planning staff involved. Given the planning guidelines, individual counties were able to produce widely differing policies and yet call them by similar names and subscribe to similar strategic themes based on the concept of resource concentration. The experience of planners who were active in the formulation of the early Development Plans and their reviews suggests that the details of settlement classification systems, particular village categorizations and the size and spacing of key settlements, were dominated by a wish for the policy to be politically acceptable within the county in question. Therefore, with different individuals operating within the planning system and different political factors to be satisfied, it is not surprising that counties tended to produce wide variations of key settlement policy.

These generalizations hold true up to the present-day situation, although it would be unwise to draw too many premature conclusions about the continuing evolution of key settlement policies within the Structure Plan framework. The policies published so far indicate a good deal of variation between counties, as has been the case throughout the history of key settlement planning. Planners appear to have used the Structure Plan preparation as an opportunity of promoting individual preferences of presentation, flexibility and to some extent policy, despite the fact that freedom of policy choice is severely compromised by commitments carried over from previous policies.

However, there is already a marked increase in the use of key settlement policies in pressured areas. This is directly associated with a rapidly increasing demand for housing in rural areas, along with a concern for the conservation of certain settlements whose environments are not suitable for the acceptance of further growth. So long as these two factors remain of importance to pressured rural areas, then it is probable that key settlement policies of one form or another will continue to be adopted as part of the settlement consolidation process.

The current economic situation adds to the likelihood that the remoter rural counties will also turn to policies that will enforce some form of concentration and rationalization of the rural settlement structure. Again, the conservation of growth for economic reasons is linked with the wish to conserve the most attractive parts of the rural environment.

It would, therefore, appear that the key settlement type of policy will continue to play a major role in the planning of rural settlements at least until the end of the current structure plan period and probably beyond that time, especially if the present emphasis on trend planning continues. Although considerable variation has occurred in the presentation and detail of the various policies, there is also considerable variation in how rigidly and how successfully the key settlement plans are implemented in different areas. It is to this aspect of key settlement policies that further analysis is now devoted.

4
Key Settlements in a Pressured Rural Area: a Case-study of Warwickshire

The key settlement policy has been used to tackle the problems experienced in both the pressured and the remote rural situation. Two case-studies follow in which the performance of this type of policy in a pressured and a remoter rural county is evaluated. In this way any shortcomings of key settlements can be seen in the light of varying social and economic conditions.

It is appropriate at this point to recognize what is perhaps the greatest pitfall in case-studies of this type. In pure science, experimentation without accompanying controls is often worthless, and yet in the social sciences where control is more difficult, changing circumstances are often attributed to one factor alone without any reference to the possibility that such change might have occurred for some other reason and that the influence of the factor under observation could in fact be negligible. Similarly, it would be easy to perceive changes in rural areas and to ascribe these variations solely to the key settlement policy which was in use at the time. However, it is possible that some, if not all, of these changes would have taken place whatever planning policy was operational.

The selection of a pressured rural study area was governed by the relatively small number of periurban counties which operate a specialized key settlement type policy. After consideration of the problems of rurality demonstrated in Chapter 1, Warwickshire was selected as the county for investigation.

4.1 *The Rural Settlement Policy*

Warwickshire (figure 4.1) forms part of a national growth region in which people and jobs have increased four times as fast as in England and Wales as a whole since 1931. A major proportion of this growth has been accommodated in the urban areas, but as these have become increasingly congested, a strong demand has developed for growth in the substantial rural areas adjacent to the major conurbations of Birmingham and Coventry.

Rural areas were virtually ignored in the Development Plan (1956), but the build-up of demand for housing in the rural areas was such that an 'Interim Policy Statement' was produced in 1966 which brought Warwickshire's villages under much stricter control. Taking the county as a whole, thirty-three rural settlements were considered suitable to receive limited growth, while a further sixty-three were adjudged as being capable of residential infilling of one scale or another. Little development was expected to take place elsewhere in the rural areas. Having adopted this type of policy (which itself cannot be termed a key settlement policy because it deals only with residential development), it was a logical progression for Warwickshire's planners to opt for further concentration of resources when next the problems of the rural settlements were reviewed. This review took shape under the Coventry-Solihull-Warwickshire Sub-Regional Planning Study (Coventry City Council *et al.*, 1971) which recommended that: 'urban growth in the next twenty years should be less fragmented than in the recent past and rural building should be further restricted by the County Council's policy of selective restraint on village expansion' (p. 4). A policy of settlement selection was seen to provide the most economic means of service provision, while localized centralization of growth would protect those settlements considered unsuitable for further development. For these reasons the population increase proposed by the study for the rural areas was to be no more than 40,000.

The suggestions contained within the sub-regional study were largely accepted in the basic tenor of the Structure Plan although growth in rural areas was to be further restricted under this strategy to 25,000-30,000 additional population. This level of growth was seen as 'sufficient ... for the needs of the rural community ... although this would not be substantially greater than the expected natural increase of the rural population' (p. 13). The use of 'natural increase' as a standard for the desirable level of increase of the rural population has met with some criticism both formally and informally. The Structure Plan states that 'What is most important is that those who are brought up in a village and

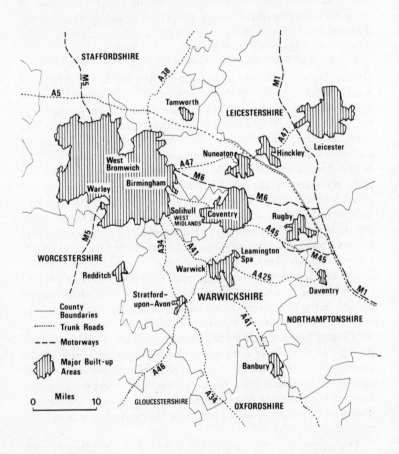

Fig. 4.1 The case study area (pressured). (As a result of local government boundary reorganization, that part of Warwickshire between Coventry and Birmingham was incorporated into the new West Midlands Metropolitan County. For the purposes of temporal comparisons over the period 1965–75, this area is included in many of the ensuing analyses.)

wish to continue living there, or those who find employment in a village and wish to live nearby should be able to do so' (p. 13). Yet it is admitted that new development on the scale proposed 'will not always go to local people' and again that 'often at present the new houses being built are of types too expensive for the young local families to purchase' (p. 13). Little indication is given as to the planning measures to be used in meeting this demand from local people for local housing. Problems of this nature are encountered wherever restrictive settlement policies are administered, and the vague offer of plentiful available housing in the nearest key settlement is not always sufficient to relieve this important localized problem.

On the other hand, a rural settlement policy of this scale is not likely to swamp the countryside with new development, thereby compromising any future plans for preservation and conservation. Sixty-one Conservation Areas are at present designated in the rural areas, and this emphasis on conservation of settlement structures goes a long way towards explaining the reticence to allow little more than natural-increase population rates, which the Rural Settlements Supplementary Report to the Structure Plan (Warwickshire County Council, 1973b, 7) considered 'the minimum needed to satisfy local needs'.

Warwickshire's key settlements
Given the selected rates of population increase it is clear that

> not every settlement is capable of accommodating growth even when it is restricted to the level of natural increase. Neither is it always desirable for growth to occur in a settlement even though it is physically capable of absorbing it. (Warwickshire County Council, 1975, 13)

Therefore, the Structure Plan fell back upon its previous policy of channelling growth into suitable settlements. This policy decision was partially enforced by the level of commitments in previously selected growth centres. However, the planners also saw the opportunity to create a more comprehensive and all-embracing settlements policy whereby all facets of planned rural systems could be coordinated around the growth settlements. Two tiers of key settlements were designated. Eleven first-tier settlements were named as being suitable and having growth potential for 'moderate expansion' of more than 1000 population by 1986. In addition, eight second-tier key settlements were selected as being suitable for 'modest expansion' of a total of 100-500 persons by 1986 (table 4.1).

These key settlements were given the role of absorbing the growth pressures of their hinterlands, thereby relieving pressures on other minor settlements. It is important to note that the Structure Plan also intended that key settlements should act as service centres for their hinterlands and it was the stated policy to encourage as wide a range of facilities as possible within each settlement. Manufacturing and service industries were not generally encouraged in rural areas, these again being principally zoned for urban areas. However, where appropriate industrial developments were proposed, these were also to be located in the key settlements. The Supplementary Report on Rural Settlements took the almost unprecedented step of defining the hinterland of each key settlement, and this gives emphasis to the fact that the

Table 4.1   Warwickshire's key settlements

1	*Moderate expansion (1000 + population)*
	Alcester
	Arley
	Atherstone
	Balsall Common
	Bidford-on-Avon
	Kingsbury
	Polesworth
	Shipston-on-Stour
	Southam
	Studley
	Wellesbourne
2	*Modest expansion (100-500 population)*
	Bishops Itchington
	Coleshill
	Curdworth
	Dordon
	Hockley Heath
	Kineton
	Stretton-on-Dunsmore
	Wolvey

Warwickshire key settlement policy with its coverage of the residential, service, employment and conservation needs of the rural area goes a long way towards a comprehensive consideration of the rural settlement hierarchy as a single system.

Of course, with any policy of settlement selection there are those settlements where growth will be severely restricted in favour of the selected key settlements. The Structure Plan policy was clearly stated in this respect: 'In general, new developments will not therefore be encouraged outside the key settlements, but there may be exceptional circumstances where individual dwellings or very small groups of dwellings could be justified' (Warwickshire County Council, 1973a, 14). In fact there were a number of objections to this part of the rural settlement policy at the public participation stage. It was felt by many that an inflexible application of the policy could lead to the stagnation of the smaller non-key settlements. In response to these fears, the Secretary of State, in paragraph 27 of his letter of approval, modified the draft policy so as 'to provide for reasonable flexibility in the operation of the rural settlements policy'. In the draft structure plan, part of paragraph 4.3(i) concerning non-key settlements allowed that 'in certain circumstances, where the nucleus of social and public utility services exist, development on a limited scale – i.e. single houses or very small groups of houses – may be permitted on the merits of the case (p. 37). This was modified by the Secretary of State to read:

> ... i.e. single houses or very small groups of houses and where it is required to meet the needs associated with the agricultural economy to support the viability of a village or in other circumstances when there are particular local requirements – may be permitted on the merits of the case. (pp. 41-2)

Although the modification was designed to create greater flexibility, it may well have had the opposite effect. Whereas previously any development in non-key settlements could theoretically take place where service levels were of the required standard, the modified policy dictates that development can take place only when needed in order to provide a specific local need – either social or economic – and then only in a settlement where services are sufficient. Therefore, it would appear to be more difficult for the planners to accept development in small settlements than before the modification.

The key settlement selection process

The success of any key settlement policy will depend in part upon the selected growth settlements and whether these settlements are best able to serve the needs of their hinterlands. The method used by Warwickshire to select the specific key settlements on which the overall policy is based has been the subject of much critical discussion, notably by Jones (1974) and Woodruffe (1976). This selection procedure is worthy of further discussion for two reasons. Firstly, the key settlement system is the king-pin of the entire Structure Plan policy for the planning of rural Warwickshire. Therefore, if key status is apportioned inappropriately, the policy for the settlement structure as a whole will suffer. Secondly, the selection procedure was hailed as an innovative process of selecting the constituent key settlements in what might become a standard rural settlements policy in 'pressured' rural areas.

The selection process required all rural settlements with a population of 200 or above, and a few with less population but possessing good facilities, to be analysed to see which were most suitable for growth. In all, 154 settlements were considered during three stages of analysis. The first stage concerned *Development Potential*, where fourteen variables (table 4.2), representing various attributes of services and infrastructure, were measured in each settlement. No explanation is given as to why fourteen variables were chosen or whether further variables were tested and then discarded as being unsatisfactory. In this case, variables such as the presence of a village hall or a children's playground have a considerable bearing on the life of a settlement and thus might have been included as part of the measurement of growth suitability. However, the fourteen variables selected would give a fairly comprehensive picture of a settlement's potential if it were not for the unsatisfactory nature of the measurements adopted to represent

Table 4.2   Development potential variables

1 Landscape	8 Job Accessibility
2 Townscape	9 Shops
3 Residential visual environment	10 Farmland
4 Pollution	11 Sewerage
5 Health services	12 Road access
6 Primary schools	13 Bus access
7 Secondary schools	14 Rail access

some of them. For example, sewerage and sewage-disposal facilities were measured by spare capacity whereas educational facilities were measured by distance from schools of certain sizes, and no mention was made of whether these schools were under capacity. Invariably, no development would be permitted unless there was spare capacity in accessible educational establishments. Other variables, notably those concerning accessibility, were measured, using unproven and seemingly unrepresentative formulae. It may be considered that the points raised here are minor ones, but when considered *in toto* it does seem that the involved nature of this measuring procedure might prove to be misleading.

According to the selection process, scores for the fourteen variables were standardized to a range of 0-5. These scores were then weighted according to four strategies: the first giving the highest weightings to the conservation of good farmland and the availability of sewerage; the second to good townscape and landscape; the third to residential environment and general accessibility; and the fourth to conservation and residential environment. Again, no reason for each particular weighting is given in the report. The 40 highest-ranking settlements for each strategy were listed (58 in all) and then those appearing in the 40 highest in either three or four of the strategies were short-listed producing a total of 33 settlements. This short-list was then carried over to the next stage of the analysis.

The second analytical stage involved *Land Constraints* and sought to assess the scale of development which could be absorbed by each settlement both by spreading outwards in the four cardinal directions and by infill. Scores of 0-10 were recorded according to the presence or absence of physical barriers which might hamper development. However, the report admits that 'the subjective nature of this study meant that it had to be applied with caution' (p. 21) and that 'a thorough survey of each settlement would have been necessary to do this [assessment] adequately and available resources did not permit this' (p. 20). It would seem, then, that as this stage was only used to further refine the short-list produced by the development potential stage, it might have proved more productive to have carried out thorough surveys of the short-listed settlements rather than concentrate on the less detailed analysis for all 154 settlements.

Finally, the procedure took account of *Existing Commitments*. In 1972, existing planning permission or local plan development area commitments amounted to some 7,500 dwellings in rural Warwickshire, or 22,500 persons assuming an occupancy rate of three persons per dwelling. The report stressed that it was necessary to establish whether these commitments were in appropriate settlements and whether their distribution around the county was satisfactory.

The final selection of key settlements depended on a combination of the above three analyses. An additional factor was also considered: 'since key settlements are intended to absorb the natural increase of their hinterland population, it was important to geographically dispense them throughout the County and not to concentrate them into certain areas' (p. 23). In fact, the eleven settlements selected as first-tier key settlements were the eleven settlements with the highest existing commitments. All of these

Table 4.3   Settlements short-listed for key status

	Interim policy status	Parish population 1971	Existing commitments (persons)[1]	Mean development potential	Land constraint scores	Structure plan status
ALCESTER R.D.						
Studley	1	5950	1092	130	4	K1
Alcester	1	4657	1752	135	3	K1
Bidford-on-Avon	1	2822	1137	118	5	K1
ATHERSTONE R.D.						
Atherstone	–	7708	4500	127	3	K1
Polesworth	1	7395	654	123	2	K1
Kingsbury	1	6011	1572	114	3	K1
Dordon	1	3337	240	131	1	K2
Mancetter	–	2510	–	114	1	–
(Ansley)	–	2314	231	110	4	–
Baddesley Ensor	2	2165	–	118	2	–
Baxterley	–	342	–	110	4	–
MERIDEN R.D.						
Coleshill	–	6297	240	147	2	K2
Balsall Common	1	4058	1740	135	8	K1
Water Orton	–	3505	–	141	4	–
Ardley	2	2933	1200	122	5	K1
Meriden	1	2433	–	134	4	–
Middleton	–	691	–	110	8	–
Curdworth	–	653	231	117	4	K2

Table 4.3 Continued

	Interim Policy status	Parish population 1971	Existing commitments (persons)[1]	Mean development potential	Land constraint scores	Structure plan status
RUGBY R.D.						
Binley Woods	1	2964	–	122	4	–
Ryton-on-Dunsmore	2	1941	–	140	3	–
(Wolston)	1	1819	189	113	3	–
Wolvey	1	1351	–	113	6	K2
Stretton-on-Dunsmore	1	1204	–	116	8	K2
Brinklow	1	1184	–	108	6	–
Shilton	1	689	–	108	3	–
Brandon	–	660	–	119	2	–
SHIPSTON-ON-STOUR R.D.						
Shipston-on-Stour	1	2773	1083	123	5	K1
SOUTHAM R.D.						
Southam	1	4506	918	135	5	K1
(Harbury)	1	2380	–	104	6	–
(Long Itchington)	2	1890	180	104	4	–
(Bishop's Itchington)	1	1840	–	100	5	K2
STRATFORD-ON-AVON R.D.						
Hockley Heath	1	3507	–	131	8	K2
Wellesbourne	1	3215	2100	116	6	K1
(Tanworth-in-Arden)	1	3193	–	83	6	–
Kineton	2	1806	123	124	3	K2
Henley-in-Arden	2	1577	273	141	2	–
WARWICK R.D.						
Bishop's Tachbrook	2	1679	–	112	4	–
Baddesley Clinton	–	181	–	109	4	–

Source: Jones (1974)

[1] Where existing commitments are less than 40 they are not indicated

settlements figured in the development potential short-list although they displayed considerable variation in land constraints scores. Of the eight second-tier key settlements, four demonstrated high development potential coupled with some existing commitments, and four were added to effect an adequate geographic spread of growth.

A vast amount of resources was used in the compilation of the Rural Settlements Report, but despite this deployment of time and manpower it is admitted in the report that 'it was only possible to make a very general assessment of each settlement's suitability for growth. The results of this analysis, therefore, can only be regarded as reliable where wide differences between settlements are indicated' (p. 2). Therefore, it is valid to question the use of this time-consuming yet imprecise technique in the selection of rural growth centres. This is far from being a general criticism of the careful application of urban and regional planning techniques to the smaller rural scale, which is an encouraging and fruitful trend. It is merely thought appropriate to question the particular application of this technique when detailed individual surveys in fewer settlements might have been more pertinent.

The report was compromised in the first place in that the target for reduced growth in the rural areas had to be equated with the level of outstanding planning commitments. Therefore, the report itself was largely reduced to the role of a retrospective examination of the appropriateness of planning decisions which had already been taken, in regard to individual settlements and their distribution around the county. Even so, this examination may not have been as impartial as it first appears. Jones (1974) noted that the entire selection procedure omitted the measurement of population or any other direct assessment of settlement size. Consequently, he undertook an analysis of the thirty-three short-listed settlements in relation to population. The results of this analysis are summarized in table 4.3. It is immediately evident that not only were the largest settlements generally being selected as key settlements, but also that there was a high coincidence between key settlement selection and settlements designated for limited expansion under the Interim Policy Statement of 1966.

Table 4.4 also offers a valuable insight into the efficiency of the final selection of key settlements in the various rural districts. The example taken here is Southam R.D., of which mention will be made below. Southam itself was the obvious choice for a first-tier

Table 4.4   Calculation of development potential in Southam

Values given by the Rural Settlements Report

	Strategy 1	Strategy 2	Strategy 3	Strategy 4	Mean
Bishop's Itchington	94	105	89.5	111.5	100.0
Harbury	94	98	119.5	103.5	103.8
Long Itchington	100	100	106.5	108.5	103.8

True values according to factor and weighting scores given in the report

	Strategy 1	Strategy 2	Strategy 3	Strategy 4	Mean
Bishop's Itchington	94	105	89.5	105.5	98.5
Harbury	94	99	95.5	103.5	98.0
Long Itchington	104	102	106.5	108.5	105.3

key settlement, but it was also decided that this area was under-represented in terms of future growth and so Bishop's Itchington was selected as a second-tier key settlement despite its low development potential and few commitments. Harbury and Long Itchington were discarded as candidates for key settlement status because of heavy recent growth and low development potential respectively. However, table 4.4 reveals inaccuracies in the report and it would appear that Long Itchington generally outscored its two rivals in development potential.

This example demonstrates the intricacy of granting key settlement status between various contenders. It is important to remember that on this decision depends the growth pattern of these various settlements for fifteen years. As it is, Long Itchington will now presumably be limited to the precommitted growth of 180 persons whilst Harbury, a settlement which many local planners recognize as being better-able than its competitors to fulfil the function of a key settlement, will be limited to small-scale growth according to local need.

The incongruities and theoretical doubts concerned with the selection procedures discussed above are likely to have a marked effect on the effective employment of the key settlements policy. In all fairness the first-tier key settlements in Warwickshire almost select themselves whatever selection procedure is utilized. Planning trends initiated under the Interim Policy Statement must be honoured under the Structure Plan policy and so it seems sensible that these preconceived growth centres should retain their role. However, the selection of second-tier key settlements is more dubious, especially in cases where more than one settlement appears to be suitable for growth, such as was seen in Southam Rural District. Here, a more thorough survey of the settlements in question might have aided the selection process. Therefore, there does remain a doubt that in using this technique with its admitted low degree of sensitivity, the decisions made as to the designation of certain key settlements (especially of the second tier) may have been wrong ones, thereby introducing growth into certain settlements when other settlements in the area may have a greater suitability for such growth. Where this has happened, planners may find it difficult to resist the pressures for growth in the more suitable settlement and, any compromise, however small, in this direction could lead to the eclipse of the designated key settlement.

4.2   *Public Service Policies*

The Warwickshire key settlement policy has been described above as a comprehensive and all-embracing policy whereby all facets of the planned rural system can be coordinated around the growth settlements. However, whether such a policy can actually be made to work effectively when it is translated from the pages of the Structure Plan into local-scale planning decisions, is a matter for careful scrutiny. In order to realize the comprehensive aims of the key settlement policy, extensive cooperation between different county-department policies is necessary. After all, the multiple roles in areas of housing, employment and services which have been attributed to the key settlements according to the Structure Plan, are dependent on the concomitant planning of public resource allocation to services and infrastructure. In effect, the strategies drawn up for the provision of these services form an integral part of the key settlement policy.

Three examples are selected here to assess the compatability of public service policies and the overall settlement policy. Education and sewage-disposal services were selected for investigation since a lack of these services will invariably result in an embargo on further growth in that particular settlement. The investigation of health service policy represents an attempt to monitor the cooperation between public and private resources in the provision of this facility.

Education

Education is perhaps the least flexible of the public services provided in rural areas, in that children of school age are compelled to attend an educational establishment whatever its location. Because of the rigidity of this system, the Warwickshire policy for replacement or new schools is dependent strictly on there being a demonstrable need for school places within a certain catchment area. Therefore, education policy is only allied to the key settlements policy in so far as most future growth in rural settlements will fall in the key settlements and so it is more likely that new or replacement schools will be sited there. This is not to say that a required new school will automatically be built in a key settlement rather than a non-key settlement. Indeed, the need to provide educational facilities for isolated groups of villages may be more desirable at any one time.

Any discussion of the link between education policy and key settlements must concentrate on present and future policy since the established pattern of educational facilities precedes the Structure Plan key settlements policy. Indeed, the selection procedure for key settlements took account of the presence or absence of primary and secondary schools as a major contributory factor in the suitability of a settlement for further growth. Therefore, it is likely that the selected key settlements will be well endowed with educational facilities. In fact, all nineteen key settlements have primary schools and thirteen also offer secondary education facilities. By contrast, only Wolston and Henley-in-Arden of the non-key settlements have secondary schools.

Future education policy would seem to revolve around a combination of population thresholds and distance barriers. The County Education Department report that there is no cost difference in the building of new schools in key and non-key settlement sites, but there is obviously a locational bias in the decision where to build, in that a suitable demand for school places must be proved to exist within the selected settlement and its catchment area. The *Manual of Guidance for Schools* (Ministry of Education, 1960) recommends that primary schoolchildren should travel no more than six miles, and secondary pupils no more than ten miles to school. These limits are followed in Warwickshire, with a few exceptions caused by school closures, although travelling times of forty-five and seventy-five minutes respectively are found to be more realistic travel parameters.

Within this framework, the ideal population size to warrant a primary school has been found to be 4500-6000, although units of half this size are satisfactory. The minimum population warranting a secondary school is theoretically 10,000-12,500, although again this is not always achievable within the above travel parameters. Theoretically, the entire educational needs of the rural areas could be served by the key settlements, since there are very few rural settlements in Warwickshire which are more than six miles distant from a key settlement. Obviously, this would be an extremely undesirable situation, not only from the point of view of the wastage of present school buildings in the non-key settlements and of the unacceptable level of school transport necessitated by such a policy, but also because of the social function that a school often adopts at the centre of a rural community. Primary school units serving catchment populations of 2500-3000 have been found to be suitable in rural Warwickshire, and such a threshold can easily be met by the grouping of non-key settlements into one catchment area.

All in all, little fundamental change can be expected in the provision of educational facilities under the recent key settlements policy, even taking the conversion to first and middle schools in primary education into account. Certain closures of the smaller under-subscribed primary schools have been taking place and no doubt will continue to do so in the future as larger units become increasingly desirable. Education policy does not conflict to any great extent with the objectives of the key settlement policy and does offer one avenue whereby the smaller rural communities can maintain a social base. However, it is to be expected that future education policy will be more closely related to the channelling of population growth into the key settlements, even though this may lead to school closures in the non-key settlements.

Sewage disposal
The new strategy for the planning of rural Warwickshire was similarly presented with an ongoing policy for sewage-disposal provision, although the provision of this facility requires a continuous locational decision-making process, and so priorities for resource allocation are more easily diverted to meet new policy

requirements, at least in the medium term. In that the provision of sewerage and sewage disposal is not statutory, a decision has to be made as to where available resources should be allocated. As demand invariably exceeds supply in this case, the decision is made on a Benthamite basis of the greatest good for the greatest number.

Section 16 of the 1973 Water Act allows that property-owners, developers or local authorities may requisition sewerage but not sewage-disposal facilities, but the Severn-Trent Water Authority has adopted the standard policy whereby it will normally only consider the provision of first-time sewerage in rural areas on receipt of a requisition from the appropriate local authority. Therefore, the planners might expect some degree of control over the locational decision-making process for the provision of this utility service. Ultimately, however, the financial constraint is the overriding one.

In fact, the water authority clearly states that its policy for programming sewage works extensions is dependent on factors other than development proposals. Very often such factors are concerned with the maintenance of particular effluent standards. Therefore, the allocation of this service is, as was education, based principally on the relative urgency of particular situations. No priority treatment is given to key settlements merely because of their planning status, neither is there any cost differential in the building of new sewage-disposal systems between key and non-key locations. Theoretically, then, if the sewage-disposal system serving a key settlement reached its capacity but did not contravene the critical effluent standards, a sewage embargo on further development could be imposed on that settlement while more pressing problems in non-key settlements could be dealt with.

This situation is unlikely to occur for three reasons. Firstly, the selection procedure for key settlements took particular note of sewage-disposal facilities, and those settlements with spare capacity in their systems scored highest in that part of the development potential index. Consequently, the selected key settlements were likely to have sewage-disposal systems with some spare capacity of varying degrees, although Southam was an exception. Secondly, it is likely to be the larger centres of population and settlements with high rates of population increase where the major problems of sewage disposal in the rural area will occur, and so effort may well be concentrated on the key settlements in this respect. Finally, more benefit in terms of population served can be perceived from the less expensive process of expansion of existing schemes rather than the financially crippling process of building entire new systems, and again the key settlements are favoured in these terms. Moreover, a local authority is unlikely to requisition new sewage-disposal systems in non-key settlements when development in key settlements is held up by a sewage embargo.

The general future policy for the provision of sewerage and sewage-disposal facilities would seem to be in line with the key settlements policy. Once the awkward stage of policy transition has been accounted for, it seems likely that existing works will be improved to provide acceptable effluent standards and, as far as possible, to meet the needs of planned development. The limited amount of finance which is likely to be available in the foreseeable future will lead to an inevitable selection of areas for priority treatment and the recommendation that development be restricted in those areas where treatment facilities remain inadequate. Certainly the outlying houses, farms and hamlets at present using cesspools and septic tanks have little hope of obtaining mains drainage unless substantial pollution occurs, although there is no apparent reason for refusing the development of a few houses with septic tanks in these non-key areas.

Although there is no cost variation between key and non-key settlements as locations for new works, it is presumably the case that the marginal cost of sewerage decreases with increasing population size and so it will be more economical to provide sewage-disposal facilities in larger units. For this reason, investment in new sewerage is likely to correspond with new housing development in the key settlements while non-key settlements will receive only residual investment for the improvement of sewage treatment. Thus, so long as short-term phasing problems can be ironed out and full cooperation is maintained between planning and water authorities, there seems to be little reason why the strategy for provision of sewerage and sewage-disposal facilities should in any way hinder the key settlement policy.

Health services

Health service provision policies, other than those concerning hospitals, are quite different from those of education or sewage disposal in that the initiative to provide the service comes from the individual (i.e. the doctor) and the location of the service receives varying degrees of guidance from the Family Practitioner Committee and the Area Health Authority. Once again, the rural settlement policy of the Structure Plan was preceded by an established system of health services which had the capability of meeting the needs of the rural population. Health services were another important factor in the calculation of the development potential of rural settlements, and although child health clinics were the variable used in this measurement, it is probable that these coincide largely with the distribution of health centres and doctors' surgeries. Therefore, it is to be expected that key settlements will be well supplied with these health facilities.

As is the case with other services, the building of health centres in rural Warwickshire is based on the premise of fulfilling a need rather than solely concentrating on the key settlements. However, it is admitted that if the need can be fulfilled equally from a key or non-key location, then the key settlement will be favoured even though the building cost will be the same in each case, varying only with the number of doctors using the centre. In fact, the use of health centres as opposed to mere doctors' surgeries is very much dependent on the size of the catchment population and on the availability of community health services. Thus, even of the key settlements, only Kingsbury has a health centre, although two more are planned at Bidford-on-Avon and Studley. None is situated in any of the non-key settlements.

The distribution of doctors' surgeries is more likely to represent the spatial element in health service provision in the rural areas. According to the Warwickshire Area Health Authority, 1500 is the minimum threshold population to warrant the full-time services of a doctor, although this figure does vary according to the scattered nature of the population and the effect of the doctor having to supply medicines because of the absence of a pharmacist. Allied to this population threshold is the ideal situation that there should be a maximum distance of five miles between a doctor and his patient. Although doctors have not officially been directed to practise from any particular location, the above parameters have ensured that every key settlement has a doctors' practice operating from it and, although the non-key settlements also contain practising doctors, it is clear that the key settlements constitute the hub of local health services for most of the rural area. This trend is perpetuated by the increasing incidence of two-, three- or even four-doctor practices which need a larger threshold population to support them. Furthermore, the present position in rural Warwickshire is that there are already sufficient doctors for the numbers of prospective patients, and the opportunities for a doctor to set up a new practice in such areas are therefore very limited. Thus any future practice will be steered into areas of new population, that is the key settlements.

These three examples suggest that the provision of public or semi-public services and facilities is fairly well-attuned to the needs of the key settlement policy. However, they also highlight the difficulties arising from any potential lack of cooperation between various public bodies. Education, water and health authorities each perceive their decision-making according to specific subject-related criteria, and very often the decisions made by these authorities will conflict with the overall plan which has been produced by a quite separate body, namely the County Council. In Warwickshire there are, at least in the short term, infrastructural problems affecting the immediate development of the key settlements. These arise from the difficulties encountered by the various public authorities in readjusting their strategies so as to make them compatible with the Structure Plan proposals for rural settlements. Priorities for the provision of new facilities have had to be altered and although most authorities have to base their allocation on the relative need for a particular service, presumably the relative needs of a settlement become more important when it is selected for considerable development. This would certainly be the attitude adopted by the planners.

Some time-lag between the different sets of priorities is bound to occur, as in Southam where development was halted for three years after it was originally classified as a key settlement, in anticipation of further sewage-disposal facilities. However, it is likely that the key settlement policy will not be compromised by incompatible strategies for public service provision once the discrepancies due to time-lag are overcome.

4.3   *The Policy in Practice*

Analysis of the written word of key settlement policies does allow the understanding of rural planning objectives and of the mechanisms with which these objectives are to be achieved. However, it is the effect of these policies as they take shape on the ground which is the crucial test of success or failure. Therefore, the questions raised in the discussion of theory and written policy relating to key settlements will be used as hypotheses on which a ground-level evaluation of the key settlement policy in Warwickshire will be based (table 4.5).

Table 4.5   Initial hypotheses

---

1   A key settlement policy is able to effect a successful polarization of infrastructure and service provision into selected centres (Chapter 1), and this provision in rural areas as a whole bears a direct relationship with population thresholds (Chapter 2).

2   Some form of settlement hierarchy does exist in pressured rural areas on which the promotion of selected key settlements may be founded (Chapter 2).

3   Key settlements perform two major growth centre functions:
    (a) the centrifugal spread of development and prosperity to the periphery.
    (b) the centripetal movement of population from within as well as from outside the rural area (Chapter 2).

4   A key settlement allows the conservation of settlements whose environmental quality is such that further large scale growth would be inappropriate (Chapter 1).

5   An inflexible attitude towards growth in non-key settlements, especially when linked to inappropriate key settlement selections, can cause physical and social hardship to healthy communities (Chapters 3 and 4).

6   Planning authorities are able to adhere to stated key settlement policy guidelines in everyday decision-making when faced with opposing social, economic and political pressures (Chapter 4).

In order to test these hypotheses, data were collected from a number of different sources. By far the greatest part of the information stemmed from a questionnaire survey sent to every parish clerk in Warwickshire. The questionnaire requested information concerning growth and decline in the provision of services, new housing and new employment in each parish between 1965 and 1975, while the opportunity was also taken to examine the knowledge and attitudes of parish clerks towards the key settlement policy in general. Thus, the survey provided a vehicle through which a catalogue of the infrastructure needed for rural living in Warwickshire could be compiled. Following a high response rate to the questionnaire (83 per cent), information concerning non-respondent parishes was obtained either through the auspices of the local District Council planning department, or by personal visit. In this way a complete data set was achieved, covering every civil parish in Warwickshire.

Questions immediately arise as to the validity of data collected in this manner, particularly concerning the accuracy with which a parish clerk is able to answer the questions included in the questionnaire. In order to test this accuracy, planning offices were asked to supply information for a random sample of parishes about which replies had already been received from parish clerks. Comparison of the two sets of data revealed a 92 per cent correspondence, and any deviations that did occur tended to reflect the timing of change rather than the physical presence or absence of any particular phenomenon. Bearing in mind the fact that information of this kind is not likely to be faultless even when supplied by planning offices, it was considered that the data set was sufficiently precise for the purposes of this study. Indeed, it is difficult to imagine a more profitable source of such information. Partial evidence is available from planning permission, rateable value and employment office data but, *in toto*, the catalogue for each parish is best compiled by someone with local knowledge of that parish. Another problem arising from the survey was the use of the civil parish as the areal unit of study. There is an inherent danger that two or more discrete settlements may occur within any one parish, in which case any internal variations, for example in housing or service development, will be masked by analysis on a parish basis. However, where this situation has occurred, parish clerks have usually been careful to outline differing levels of development between settlements within the parish and so this difficulty has largely been overcome.

Aside from the questionnaire, planning permission and public service provision data were obtained directly from the County and District Councils concerned, and socio-economic and household facts were provided by the Ward Library and County volumes of the census. Other criteria were measured from the County Structure Plan (Warwickshire County Council, 1973a, b).

Analysis of the Warwickshire key settlement policy is hampered by the fact that the Structure Plan of which it is part was not officially accepted by the Secretary of State until 1975 (Warwickshire County Council, 1975). Unofficially, however, the main tenor of the key settlement policy has been followed by the planners since the publication of the Coventry-Solihull-Warwickshire Sub-Regional Study (Coventry City Council *et al.*, 1971), and so the period from 1971 to the present day can reasonably be expected to reflect the commencement and continuing use of this type of policy in pressured rural areas. Though not ideal, the decision to study a newly-instigated key settlement policy does allow an insight into difficulties caused by a radical policy changeover in the countryside (cf. the long-established policy in Devon – see Chapter 5).

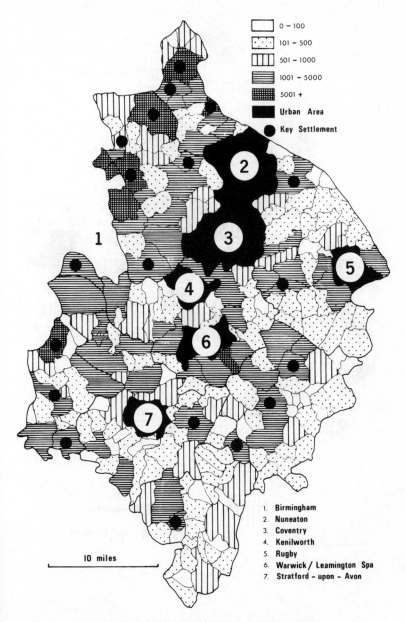

☐	0 - 100
☐	101 - 500
☐	501 - 1000
☐	1001 - 5000
☐	5001 +
■	Urban Area
●	Key Settlement

1. Birmingham
2. Nuneaton
3. Coventry
4. Kenilworth
5. Rugby
6. Warwick / Leamington Spa
7. Stratford - upon - Avon

10 miles

Fig. 4.2 Population distribution in rural Warwickshire, 1971

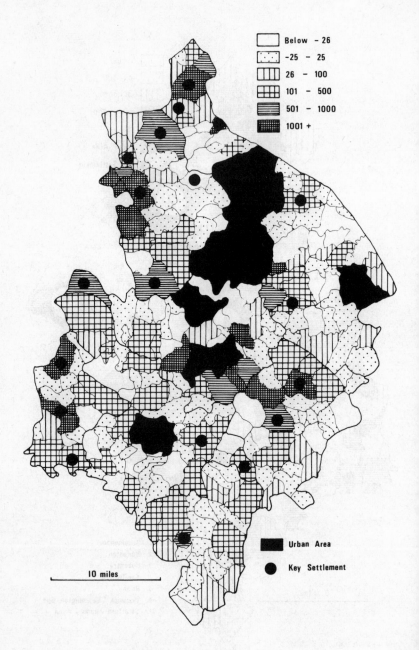

Fig. 4.3 Population change in rural Warwickshire, 1961–71

Below – 26
-25 – 25
26 – 100
101 – 500
501 – 1000
1001 +

Urban Area

Key Settlement

10 miles

The following analysis of the Warwickshire policy is divided into systematic themes, each reflecting one particular planning aspiration of the key settlement technique.

4.4 *Population*

The first topic for evaluation is of necessity the effect of the key settlement policy on population patterns, since the policy is to be viewed first and foremost as a mechanism for attracting or stabilizing population movement. Figure 4.2 shows the pattern of population distribution in 1971 at the starting point of the key settlement era in Warwickshire. It is apparent that the settlement pattern includes a large number of parishes of over 1000 population both in the north-west between the Birmingham and Coventry conurbations, and surrounding the smaller urban centres of Rugby, Leamington Spa/Warwick and Stratford-upon-Avon. As distance from these urban nodes increases, the occurrence of large centres of rural population becomes less frequent. In these more peripheral areas, the dominant population composition is one of sectors or channels of highly populated parishes (e.g. between Coventry and Rugby, and south-eastwards from Warwick-Leamington Spa) interspersed by areas of lower population usually in the 100-500 category.

All but one of the selected key settlements have populations over 1000 but it is noticeable that there are two distinct patterns of key settlement distribution. Nine key centres are clustered in the highly populated north-west buffer zone between Birmingham and Coventry. The remainder are more widely scattered amongst the rural hinterland to the south and west of the county. There may well be an interesting division of roles between these two groups, as the needs of a highly populated and highly protected rural green belt area differ considerably from those of the less restrictive peripheral rural areas.

The settlement size structure demonstrated by figure 4.2 forms the framework on which the following analysis of systematic topics is based. However, the assertion in Hypothesis 2, namely that some form of settlement hierarchy does exist in pressured rural areas, would seem to be corroborated at least in part by the spatial patterns of population distribution, with the selected key settlements often forming peaks in the hierarchy.

Population change, 1961-71
Population change is an important indicator of the relative effectiveness of the key settlement policy in channelling growth into
selected settlements. Planning documentation tends to treat population change in absolute rather than percentage terms, and as we
are mainly interested in the distribution of total population
increase in Warwickshire, this analysis adopts a similar absolute
numerical approach. In the pre-key settlement years of 1961-71,
three distinct types of population change are evident (figure 4.3).
Firstly, rapid population growth occurred in three zones:

(1) On the fringes of the Birmingham conurbation.
(2) In parishes surrounding Warwick/Leamington Spa, especially
     the south-east sector.
(3) In scattered centres including some later to become key set-
     tlements, e.g. Shipston-on-Stour, Alcester, Studley and
     Southam, and some not so selected, e.g. Harbury.

Secondly, intermediate growth trends can be distinguished in
parishes scattered throughout the county. These areas are particularly interesting because the key settlement policy plans to restrict
growth in non-key settlements to below this level (except where
outstanding planning permissions dictate otherwise). Although
several present-day key settlements fall into this category, there are
a large number of other settlements, particularly in the southern
half of the county, which face a much restricted scale of growth
from that experienced prior to the key settlement policy.

The third category encompasses parishes displaying moderate
growth, stability or even decline in population levels. Settlements
located within green belt restrictions are well-represented in this
category, but the lower end of this population growth continuum
is largely taken up by the smaller agricultural parishes in the south
and east of the county.

Population change, 1971-5
Against this background of widespread population growth, an
analysis of change between 1971 and 1975 is shown in figure 4.4.
The population figures for 1975 are taken from Warwickshire
County Council's unofficial population estimates. There are several restrictions imposed by the nature of this data, as is pointed
out by the County:

Because of the difference between methods of collecting census
information on population and methods of calculating home

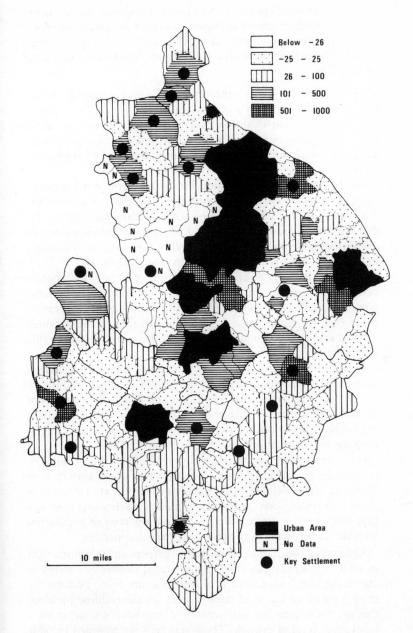

Below − 26

−25 − 25

26 − 100

101 − 500

501 − 1000

Urban Area

N   No Data

Key Settlement

10 miles

Fig. 4.4 Population change in rural Warwickshire, 1971–5

population since the census, the difference within any parish or
district between the census figures and the estimates figure does
not necessarily represent the growth or decrease in population
within that parish or district. (Warwickshire County Council,
1976, 1)

However, there being no other source of information concerning
post-key-settlement-policy population levels, the 1975 estimates
have been used with caution to give some indication of broad
trends in population growth and decline. Small-scale changes, on
the other hand, are unreliable and are not accounted for in the
analysis.

Further difficulties arise from the local government boundary
reorganization of 1974, as a result of which, parts of north-west
Warwickshire (including two key settlements) were annexed by
the West Midlands Metropolitan County. Population estimates
are not available for these parishes and so they have been omitted
from figure 4.4. Despite the approximate nature of the 1975
population data, some general indication of population change
under the key settlement policy is given by figure 4.4. The same
categories are used as in figure 4.3, although it must be remembered that the time-period involved is half that of the previous
analysis and so any comparison between the two should take this
into account.

It would appear from figure 4.4, that in terms of population
growth, the key settlement policy has so far been rigorously
applied in the southern half of the county. Here, the only major
growth points coincide with the key settlements, and the remaining parishes have been restricted to a level of growth which is in
keeping with the objectives of the Structure Plan. Contrary to
expectations, however, are the indications that certain non-key
parishes in the more urbanized northern half of the county have
displayed high levels of population growth despite the influence of
green belt restrictions. Moreover, some key settlements (particularly in the south) are recorded as having low rates of population
increase which again may not be the expected pattern.

Changes in population between the two periods are summarized
in table 4.6 with figures here again stated in absolute terms to
match the stated expectations of the Structure Plan. Perhaps the
most interesting aspect of these figures are the residual parishes;
that is, those non-key settlements which have not achieved a
substantial level of growth. These residuals are recorded in table

Table 4.6 Population change in rural Warwickshire[1]

Population size	Total	Population change 1961–70						Population change 1971–75						
		More than −25	−24 to +25	26 to 100	101 to 500	501 to 1000	More than 1000	More than −25	−24 to +25	26 to 100	101 to 500	501 to 1000	More than 1000	No data
0–100	42	3	39						42					1
101–500	96	24	55	16	1			5	64	24	2			2
501–1000	32	4	6	9	8	5		5	12	11	2(1)			5(2)
1001–5000	53	7	3	4	25	8	6	3(1)	7	19(3)	14(4)	5(3)		5(2)
5000+	9					1	8				5(4)	1(1)		3
Total	232	38	103	29	34	14	14	13	125	54	23	6		11

Source: Census 1961, 1971; and Warwickshire County Council

[1] The table details the number of parishes of a given population size experiencing similar rates of population change. For example, eight out of nine parishes of over 5000 population demonstrated population increases of more than 1000 between 1961 and 1970. Key settlement parishes are shown in brackets.

Table 4.7   Rural Warwickshire population residuals, 1971-5[1]

	1971-5
ALCESTER R.D.	
Bidford-on-Avon	48
ATHERSTONE R.D.	
Ansley	196
RUGBY R.D.	
Binley	106
Dunchurch*	607
Long Lawford	108
Princethorpe	201
Stretton under Fosse	212
Wolston	111
Stretton-on-Dunsmore	-34
SOUTHAM R.D.	
Long Itchington	150
Bishop's Itchington	70
STRATFORD R.D.	
Tanworth	247
Kineton	44
WARWICK R.D.	
Bishops Tachbrook	221
Budbrooke	113
Leek Wootton	170
Radford Semele*	103
Stoneleigh	572
Whitnash*	411

[1] Low-growth key settlements are given in italics and high-growth non-key settlements appear in ordinary type.
* These parishes form part of Urban Structure Plan Areas.

4.7. Some of the unexpected population increases might be explained by outstanding planning permissions. In fact, only two of these parishes (Ansley and Wolston) are named as having outstanding commitments equivalent to 100 or more persons. Other increases have occurred in parishes which form part of Urban Structure Plan areas and are thus not affected by the key settlement policy. For the remainder it must be concluded either that a very high rate of natural increase is in evidence or that a large intake of institutional population has occurred, or else that the key settlement policy has been unable to withstand pressures for commuter migration into certain of the larger non-key rural settlements. This last reason may particularly be the case where the settlement concerned was earmarked for growth during the Interim Policy period and had therefore gained a growth impetus.

Four low-growth key settlements are identified, with one – Stretton-on-Dunsmore – actually demonstrating a loss of population. This could be interpreted as a reflection of these settlements' ability to perform key settlement functions, although further evidence is needed to substantiate any such interpretation.

This investigation of population change in Warwickshire has highlighted three questions. Firstly, is it practicable or even desirable to channel the major proportion of rural population growth into a small number of key settlements when other settlements demonstrate an undeniable impetus for growth? Secondly, can a restrictive key settlement policy be fully enforced on a highly pressured rural buffer zone, even with the aid of a concomitant green belt strategy? Lastly, does the bestowal of key settlement status necessarily ensure the attainment of policy objectives such as an increasing population? The evidence of population change in rural Warwickshire would appear to offer a negative answer to each of these questions.

4.5 Housing

Tables 4.8 and 4.9 represent parishes of different population sizes falling into differing categories of new housing between 1965-70 and 1971-5. It is evident from table 4.8 that some settlements of more than 500 population exhibited large-scale development of both private and council housing and that substantial amounts of new housing were built in most settlements over 1000 population during the period 1965-70. The situation under five years of key settlement policy (table 4.9) appears to be very similar. New

Table 4.8 New housing in rural Warwickshire, 1965–70[1]

Population size	Private housing							Council housing						
	Total	0 to 10	11 to 30	31 to 50	51 to 100	More than 100	No data	0	1 to 10	11 to 30	31 to 50	51 to 100	More than 100	No data
0–100	42	42						42						
101–500	96	86	9		4		1	85	5	4	1			1
501–1000	32	21	5	1				25	2	2	2			1
1001–5000	53	7	10	12	8	8	8	19	5	8	2	8	3	8
5000+	9				1	6	2	4		1			2	2
Total	232	156	24	13	13	14	12	175	12	15	5	8	5	12

[1] This table demonstrates the number of parishes of a given population size where similar rates of new housing have occurred.

Table 4.9 New housing in rural Warwickshire, 1971–75[1]

Population size	Total	Private housing					Council housing					
		0 to 10	11 to 30	31 to 50	51 to 100	More than 100	0	1 to 10	11 to 30	31 to 50	51 to 100	More than 100
0–100	42	42					42					
101–500	96	93	3				90	5	1			
501–1000	32	22	7		2(1)	1	23(1)	3	4	1	1	
1001–5000	53	12(1)	16	12(6)	10(4)	3(2)	30(5)	5	14(5)	2(2)	1	1(1)
5000+	9		1(1)	2(1)	2(1)	4(2)	2		3(3)	2(1)		2(1)
Total	232	169	27	14	14	8	187	13	22	5	2	3

[1] The total number of parishes of a given population size experiencing similar rates of new housing are shown in the main body of the table, with a concurrent analysis of key settlements alone appearing in brackets.

house-building in parishes under 500 population has been slightly more restricted during this later period, but three settlements of between 501 and 1000 population exhibit corresponding distributions of new housing both before and after the instigation of a key settlement policy. Only in the largest settlements are there signs that building rates have been cut, particularly in the public housing sector.

A synopis of these trends is presented in table 4.10, which compares building rates in all parishes over the two periods in question. It can be seen that the differences in rural housing brought about by the key settlement policy occur at the extremes of the building scale. Large numbers of parishes have been confined to little or no new housing whereas fewer parishes have been allowed to accommodate substantial development. These figures would appear to support the claim that the aims and objectives of the Warwickshire key settlement policy are being effectively achieved.

However, when new private and council housing are placed in the spatial context it is again apparent that there are some important anomalies to the expected patterns of concentration of new houses into the key settlements. In the case of new private housing between 1971 and 1975 (figure 4.5), considerable development has occurred in non-key settlements in the Warwick/Leamington

Table 4.10 Comparison of parish building rates, 1965-70 and 1971-5 (by numbers of parishes)

	1965-70	1971-5
New private housing		
0-10	156	169
11-30	24	27
31-50	13	14
51-100	13	14
101+	14	8
No information	12	-
New council housing		
0	175	187
1-10	12	13
11-30	15	22
31-50	5	5
51-100	8	2
101+	5	3
No information	12	-

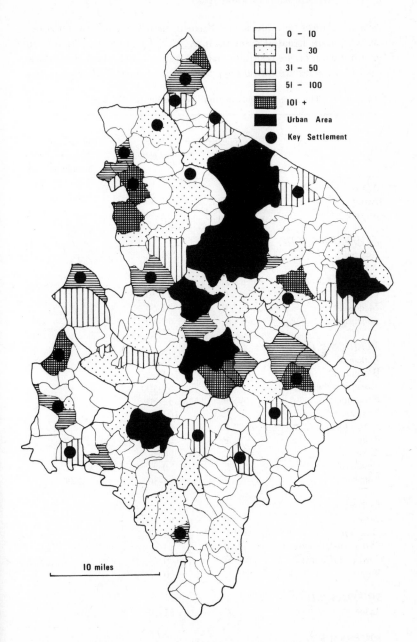

10 miles

Fig. 4.5 New private housing in rural Warwickshire, 1971–5

Spa commuter belt and in the Birmingham/Coventry buffer zone, as well as in isolated cases such as Welford-on-Avon. Again, an examination of the residual parishes (table 4.11) reveals that these inconsistencies are not always the result of outstanding planning

Table 4.11   Housing residuals in rural Warwickshire, 1971-5[1]

	Housing type[2]	Growth category	Outstanding planning permissions
ALCESTER R.D.			
Aston Cantlow	C	11-30	
Salford Priors	C	11-30	
ATHERSTONE R.D.			
Austrey	P	101+	
Austrey	C	51-100	
Baddesley Ensor	C	11-30	
Grendon	C	11-30	
Mancetter	P	31-50	
Shuttington	C	11-30	
MERIDEN R.D.			
Berkswell	P	31-50	
Bickenhill*	P	101+	
Castle Bromwich*	P	51-100	
Kingshurst*	P	31-50	
Kingshurst*	C	101+	
Water Orton	P	51-100	
Arley	P	0-10	400
Arley	C	0	
Curdworth	C	0	
Kingsbury	P	11-30	524
RUGBY R.D.			
Binley	P	51-100	
Dunchurch*	P	31-50	
Stretton-on-Dunsmore	P	11-30	
Stretton-on-Dunsmore	C	0	
Wolvey	C	0	
SHIPSTON R.D.			
Tysoe	C	31-50	
SOUTHAM R.D.			
Fenny Compton	C	11-30	

permissions as listed by Warwickshire County Council (table
4.12), although some are accounted for by parishes falling within
Urban Structure Plan areas. Overall there is some correspondence
with those parishes regarded as residual to the population analysis,

Table 4.11 Continued

	Housing type[2]	Growth category	Outstanding planning permissions
Long Itchington	P	51-100	
Long Itchington	C	11-30	
Stockton	P	51-100	
Stockton	C	11-30	
Bishops Itchington	C	0	
STRATFORD R.D.			
Beaudesert	C	11-30	
Claverdon	P	31-50	
Hampton Lucy	C	11-30	
Henley-in-Arden	P	31-50	91
Tanworth	P	31-50	
Ullenhall	C	31-50	
Welford-on-Avon	P	51-100	
Kineton	C	0	
WARWICK R.D.			
Bishops Tachbrook	P	101+	
Bishops Tachbrook	C	51-100	
Bubbenhall	C	11-30	
Budbrooke	C	11-30	
Leek Wootton	P	51-100	
Radford Semele*	P	51-100	
Radford Semele*	C	11-30	
Whitnash*	P	101+	
Whitnash*	C	31-50	

[1] Two forms of parish which may be described as residual to the analysis of new
housing are shown in this table. Key settlements exhibiting lower growth than
expected are given in capitals, and non-key settlements with higher than expected
growth patterns are listed in ordinary type. Parishes marked with an asterisk are
included within Urban Structure Plan areas.

[2] P = private
C = council

but it is also clear that some new private housing has been built which is masked in the population data.

The distribution of new council housing in Warwickshire parishes during the key settlement period is set out in figure 4.6. Patterns of new buildings in this instance are more in line with the anticipated rationalization into key settlements. There are, however, examples of council house-building in non-key settlements which oppose the objectives of the key settlement policy. It is interesting to note that six key settlements did not accommodate any new council house-building during the period 1971-5 and that of these, Bishops Itchington, Kineton and Stretton-on-Dunsmore were also found to have low population growth over the same period.

These housing trends lend support to some of the conclusions drawn from the analysis of population change. It seems clear that the key settlement policy has found it difficult to restrict increases in population and housing in settlements where an impetus for growth has already been established, particularly when this momentum has been supported by previous settlement policies (note the Interim Policy status of many of the residual parishes in table 4.11). This conclusion is borne out by a detailed study of planning permission statistics for Southam R.D. (table 4.13) which demonstrates that housing growth in non-key settlements has often not been strictly controlled, and that the key settlement policy has not been able to channel growth solely into the two key settlements of Southam and Bishops Itchington. Indeed the proportion of planning permissions accounted for by key settlements after 1971 is little different from that under the previous policy, although the rate of refusals would appear to have increased substantially.

A note of caution should, however, be introduced at this point. The time-period under observation is comparatively short, and the data obtained from parish clerks are at best liable to discrepancies. Moreover, there are invariably some teething troubles both in administration and in policy decision-making in the various local government departments, particularly when administrative boundary changes have also occurred. However, taking all these criteria into account, doubt must be cast on Hypothesis 6 (table 4.5). The indications are that planning authorities are not able to adhere strictly to stated policy guidelines when faced with opposing social, economic and political pressures.

Table 4.12   Land committed for development in rural Warwickshire

	Population equivalents	Dwellings
Atherstone	4500	1500
Wellesbourne	2100	700
Alcester	1752	584
Balsall Common	1740	580
Kingsbury	1572	524
Arley	1200	400
Bidford-on-Avon	1137	379
Studley	1092	364
Shipston-on-Stour	1083	361
Southam	918	306
Polesworth	654	218
Henley-in-Arden	273	91
Warton	270	90
Coleshill	240	80
Dordon	240	80
Ansley	231	77
Curdworth	231	77
Wolston	189	63
Long Itchington	180	60
Pailton	159	53
Kineton	123	41
Alcester R.D.	93	31
Atherstone R.D.	270	90
Meriden R.D.	204	68
Rugby R.D.	303	101
Shipston R.D.	480	160
Southam R.D.	429	143
Stratford R.D.	813	271
Warwick R.D.	102	34

Source: Warwickshire County Council

4.6   *Conservation*

It has been hypothesized that a key settlement policy allows the conservation of settlements whose environmental quality is such that further large-scale growth would be inappropriate. Matters of conservation were certainly given due emphasis in the selection of key settlements (Warwickshire County Council, 1973b), with the inclusion of both landscape and townscape as variables in the Development Potential equation and with two of the four weightings of the index being devoted to the protection of good-quality environments.

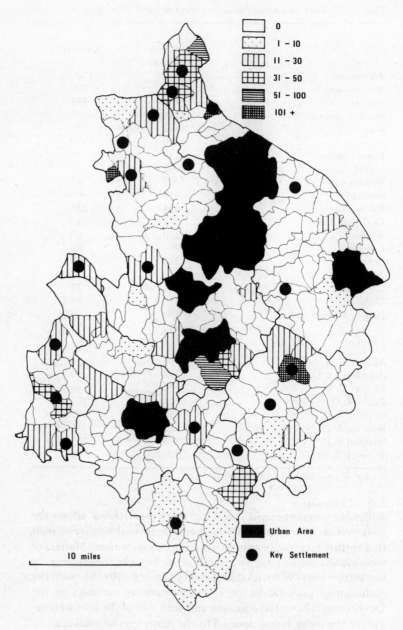

☐	0
⣿	1 – 10
⫼	11 – 30
⊞	31 – 50
☰	51 – 100
■	101 +

■ Urban Area

● Key Settlement

10 miles

Fig. 4.6 New council housing in rural Warwickshire, 1971–5

Table 4.13   Planning permissions in Southam R.D.[1]

	1965-70		1971-5	
	Permissions	*Refusals*	*Permissions*	*Refusals*
Key settlements	42.1	36.9	44.0	50.2
Non-key settlements	57.9	63.1	56.0	49.8

[1] Figures refer to the percentage of the total number of dwellings permitted and refused within Southam R.D. between 1965 and 1975.

The measurement of townscape was done by assigning a score from 0 to 5 to each settlement, where 5 represented no detrimental effect and the greatest potential for development, and 0 serious effect and hence least potential for development. A similar indication of landscape was included, with an identical inverse scoring system whereby the maximum landscape value scores reflected the best landscape and the least suitability for development on conservation of landscape objectives.

It is interesting to compare these landscape and townscape scores for those settlements selected as key settlements and for those in which Conservation Areas have been designated. This comparison is undertaken in table 4.14. As might be expected, the group of key settlements which do not encompass Conservation Areas score highly on both measurements, although it would seem that greater account is taken of townscape than of landscape for the purposes of allowing development. A greater degree of variation is apparent when the scores appertaining to parishes with Conservation Area status are investigated. Again, the higher scores are associated with the townscape index (with an average score of 2.1 compared with 1.3 for landscape), which suggests that better-quality landscapes than townscapes are being conserved under the key settlement policy.

However, these averages are misleading since they include the high scores attributed to those key settlements of which only parts have been designated as Conservation Areas. The distinction has to be made here between, on the one hand, a Conservation Area in a large settlement where development in one sector will not be detrimental to the conservation status of another, and on the other hand, a small settlement where any development would detract from the scenic or architectural character of the entire location. The former situation explains why ten key settlements appear in the list of Conservation Areas as part of a policy to preserve

Table 4.14 Conservation Area characteristics in rural Warwickshire

	Interim policy status	Landscape	Townscape
ALCESTER R.D.			
Alcester*	1	2	4
Arrow		0	1
Aston Cantlow(2)	2	2(2)	0(1)
Bidford-on-Avon* (2)	1	3(–)	3(–)
Coughton		1	2
Great Alne	2	2	2
Haselor		2	0
Morton Bagot	–	–	–
Salford Priors	2	3	0
ATHERSTONE R.D.			
Atherstone*		0	4
Mancetter		2	4
MERIDEN R.D.			
Balsall*	1	3	5
Barston	–	–	–
Berkswell		1	2
Coleshill**		3	5
Fillongley	1	1	2
Hampton-in-Arden	2	2	1
RUGBY R.D.			
Brinklow	1	2	3
Dunchurch	1	–	–
Monks Kirby	2	1	2
Stretton-in-Dunsmore**	1	1	3
Thurlaston	2	2	0
Wolston	1	3	3
SHIPSTON-ON-STOUR R.D.			
Barton-on-the-Heath		–	–
Brailes (2)	2	0(–)	2(–)
Cherington	2	0	1
Great Wolford		–	–
Halford	1	1	0
Honington		–	–
Ilmington		0	2
Little Compton		1	1
Long Compton	2	0	1
Oxhill		2	5

Table 4.14 Continued

	Interim policy status	Landscape	Townscape
Shipston-on-Stour*	1	1	5
Stourton	2	1	1
Stretton-on-Fosse	2	1	0
Sutton-under-Brailes		–	–
Tredington	2	1	0
Tysoe (2)	2	0	1
Whichford		0	3
SOUTHAM R.D.			
Avon Dassett		–	–
Farnborough		0	0
Fenny Compton	2	1	2
Lighthorne		3	2
Long Itchington	2	3	3
Priors Hardwick		2	2
Priors Marston		2	3
Radway		3	2
Ratley		0	2
Shotteswell		0	2
Southam*	1	2	5
Warmington		1	2
Wormleighton		–	–
STRATFORD-UPON-AVON R.D.			
Bearley	2	1	0
Beaudesert	1	–	–
Charlecote		2	2
Claverdon	2	0	2
Clifford Chambers		2	2
Combrook		–	–
Compton Verney		–	–
Hampton Lucy		2	3
Henley-in-Arden	2	2	3
Kineton**	2	2	4
Moreton Morrell	2	1	0
Quinton	2	–	–
Snitterfield	2	1	3
Tanworth-in-Arden	1	0	0
Temple Grafton		0	2
Welford-on-Avon	2	1	0
Wellesbourne*	1	4	4
Wootton Wawen	2	0	1

Table 4.14 Continued

	Interim policy status	Landscape	Townscape
WARWICK R.D.			
Ashow		–	–
Barford	2	2	2
Cubbington		–	–
Lapworth	1	1	4
Leek Wootton	1	–	–
Offchurch	2	0	2
Sherbourne		–	–
Stoneleigh	2	–	–
OTHER KEY SETTLEMENTS			
Arley		1	5
Bishops Itchington		4	4
Curdworth		5	5
Dordon		3	5
Hockley Heath		3	5
Kingsbury		5	4
Polesworth		3	4
Studley		3	4
Wolvey		3	3

Source: Warwickshire County Council
*   1st-tier key settlement
** 2nd-tier key settlement

worthwhile environments. Indeed, it may well be seen as beneficial in a social sense to concentrate population into a pleasing situation if the former may be carried out without the ruination of the latter.

The designation of Conservation Areas in Warwickshire may be viewed in the spatial context in figure 4.7. This distribution demonstrates that those clashes between key settlement designation and Conservation Area status occur mainly in the less densely populated south and east of the county, and that six of the key settlements within the northern buffer zone are noticeably lacking in officially planned conservation. Also apparent is that the highly developed suburban parishes surrounding the major urban centres are also considered as low in the list of conservation priorities.

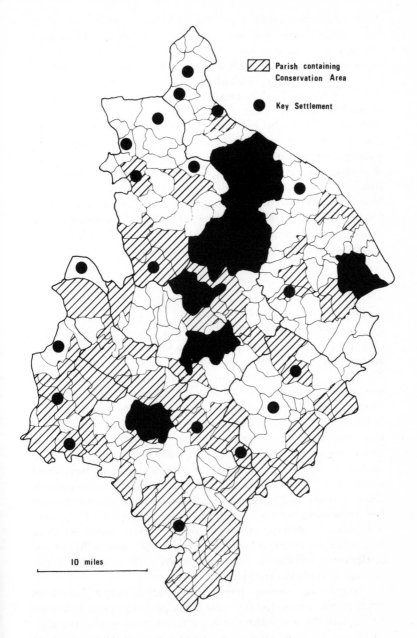

Key:
- Parish containing Conservation Area
- Key Settlement

10 miles

Fig. 4.7 Conservation Areas in rural Warwickshire

All in all, the fourth hypothesis would seem to be upheld, at least in the example of Warwickshire. Smaller settlements of high environmental quality have not been selected for development, and attempts have been made to introduce sectoral housing growth into larger settlements of similar quality, so that the excellence of any desirable physical milieu will not be belittled. In terms of *physical environment*, then, the key settlement policy appears to exert a beneficial influence, but what of the *social environment*? The question of whether a settlement is socially able to accept large-scale growth is not broached in the selection procedure for the Warwickshire key settlements, presumably because it is a factor that is not easily quantified. However, the predilection with physical matters in rural planning (new houses, industrial estates, Conservation Areas, etc.) has often led to a neglect of social aspects and this may be one reason for the apparent 'lack of humanity' recognizable in many key settlement policies.

4.7 Services

Patterns of service change

One of the principal justifications for any key settlement policy is that it is economically unviable to provide services and infrastructure in every village and town in a scattered settlement hierarchy. Therefore, it is postulated in the first hypothesis that a key settlement policy is able to effect a successful polarization of infrastructure and service provision into selected centres.

Once again, matters of infrastructure and service provision were built into the key settlement selection procedure in the form of factors representing accessibility to shops and spare capacity of sewage works. In effect, the chosen key settlements were those which already possessed the highest levels of shops and services in the rural areas, and those whose infrastructural capabilities either had preexisting additional capacity or could be expanded. Thus the objective of the key settlement policy was to build up these centralized facilities in order to service the various hinterland settlements, and therefore inherently look to the rationalization of services in outlying parishes.

Changes in service levels are predominantly long-term phenomena, and so the five-year study period presents some difficulties in the monitoring of any alterations to service patterns. Moreover, the streamlining of rural service distributions has been

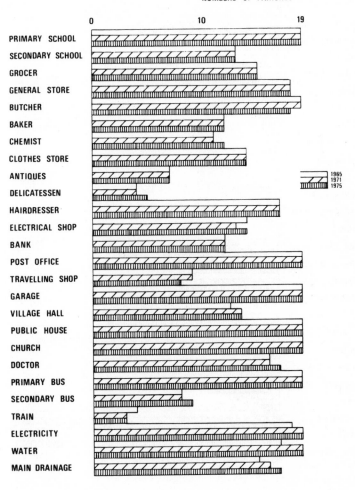

Fig. 4.8 Service provision in Warwickshire key settlement parishes

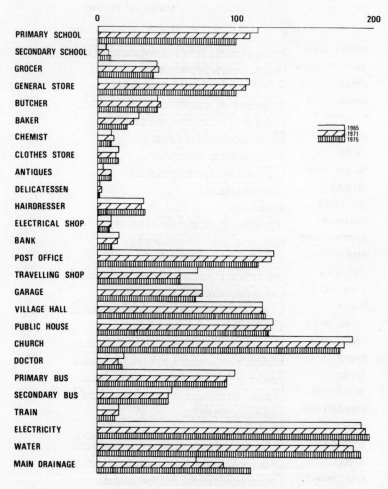

Fig. 4.9 Service provision in Warwickshire non-key settlement parishes

an ongoing occurrence over very many years and it is difficult to isolate any particular outworking of key settlement policies from the overall trend. Nevertheless, the service and infrastructure data obtained from the survey of parish clerks are catalogued in figures 4.8 and 4.9 in the hope that some general patterns of increase or decline in services may be distinguished. The information presented here is concerned with the presence or absence of particular services rather than any multiplicity of provision, and so withdrawal or introduction in any particular category will have an important influence on the settlement involved.

Service levels in key settlements (figure 4.8) have remained reasonably stationary over the last ten years, although numerically some retail categories have increased contiguously with housing and population growth. Singular increases have occurred in the health service classes of chemist and doctor's surgery and also in the provision of public infrastructure. Similar trends are apparent in the private sector with all first-tier key settlements possessing a considerable range of retail, community and service facilities.

The pattern of provision in non-key settlements shows a definite trend of decline or stability in most retail and public services, but a gradual increase in the distribution of public infrastructure such as electricity, water and mains drainage. Particular recessions can be seen in the location of primary schools and general store/post offices in non-key areas, these two being important factors in local community life. Remarkably the analysis shows that bus services have remained stable over this period, although frequency of buses may well have deteriorated.

Against this background, the service changes during the key settlement period (1971-5) are not contrary to expectation. The raw figures are presented in table 4.15. Under the influence of the key settlement policy, the numbers of primary schools and foodshops in non-key parishes have decreased at a faster rate than in the previous decade. Elsewhere the general pattern of steady rationalization has continued apart from some unconformities due to the transient nature of delicatessen, antiques and hairdressing enterprises, which are very responsive to the ebb and flow of demand and fashion. Another departure from the overall trend is the travelling shop, on which many hopes for the servicing of remoter rural areas are pinned. The threshold between profit and loss in this particular undertaking is also precarious, as is shown in its multiple introduction and withdrawal in various parishes. Table 4.15 also shows that levels of public transport have actually increased

Table 4.15   Service changes in rural Warwickshire, 1971-5

		Introduced	Withdrawn
P	Primary school		10
GR	Grocer		4
G	General store		7
B	Butcher		3
BA	Baker		4
C	Chemist	1	1
CL	Clothes store	3	1
A	Antiques shop	3	3
D	Delicatessen	1	1
H	Hairdresser	3	1
E	Electrical and T.V. Shop	1	1
BK	Bank	1	4
PO	Post office		5
TS	Travelling shop	5	6
GA	Garage		3
V	Village hall	3	
PU	Public house	1	2
CH	Church		2
DO	Doctor's surgery	3	
1	Primary bus service	2	1
2	Secondary bus service	3	2
ED	Electricity to all dwellings	1	
W	Piped water to all dwellings	4	
M	Mains drainage to all dwellings	24	

during this period, although the benefits from this increase have only been gained in two individual parishes.

Figure 4.10 shows the rural locations where service gains and losses are encountered over the key settlement period. As previously indicated, the key settlements already possess the highest levels of service provision in the rural areas. However, there is some evidence that second-tier key settlements have attracted vital services. For example, Bishops Itchington has gained a chemist, a doctor's surgery and an electrical and television shop within the first few years of its key settlement status. Service losses in key settlements are restricted to transient food and luxury retail facilities in locations where competition from urban centres is very high.

Reductions in service provision in non-key settlements are greatest in the less-pressured southern and eastern sectors of the

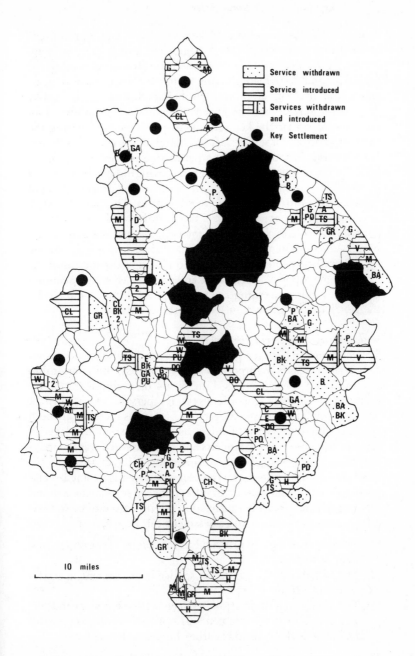

Fig. 4.10 Service changes in rural Warwickshire, 1971–5

county. It is in areas such as Rugby, Southam and Shipston-on-Stour Rural Districts where villages are losing their primary school, post office and food shop which are all so important to the life of a rural settlement. Gains in infrastructure have occured where the backlog of projects is being cleared in the policy changeover period, but the general conclusion to be drawn from this picture is that the key settlement policy is exacerbating the 'natural' processes of service rationalization in the countryside, and is promoting, through planning permission restrictions, through public service policies and through the changing of market forces by the polarization of housing development, the concentration of rural facilities into the selected growth centres. This part of the key settlement policy appears to be successfully fulfilling its stated aims and objectives, but what of the ramifications of service losses in non-key settlements? Is social upheaval a suitable price to pay for economic expediency? Once again the apparent success of the key settlement policy in economic and physical aspects of planning raises questions concerning the social upheaval brought about by the restriction of growth in parts of the countryside.

Settlement size and service thresholds
The relationship between population thresholds and service provision in rural areas is an important one. In the past, this relationship has invariably been expressed in terms of a simple ratio, for example one primary school for every 500 persons, or one chemist for every 3000 persons (see Green, 1971). It has increasingly been the case, however, that planners have emphasized the level of services in individual settlements and then explored ways of making these services available to hinterland villages through the medium of public transport. Therefore, a more important association in modern rural planning is that between settlement size and service provision. If such a correlation can be proved to be statistically significant, then some assessment can be made of:

(1) The response of particular services to changes in the population sizes of settlements.
(2) The likelihood of a particular service being present in settlements of certain sizes.
(3) The strength of association between settlement sizes and service levels in key settlements as opposed to non-key settlements at various distances from higher-order centres.

These factors may be evaluated using a standard asymptotic regres-

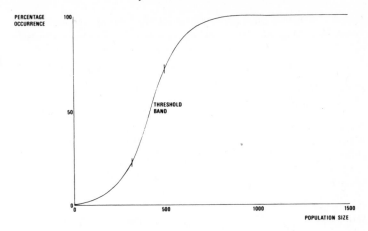

Fig. 4.11 Service threshold by regression

sion curve where changes of slope are used to delimit a threshold band below which the service is unlikely to be present, but above which it is statistically probable that the service will occur (figure 4.11). Naturally, the width of the threshold band depends on the quality of fit of the regression line, but this very width is able to distinguish varying patterns of service centres. For example, a narrow threshold band would suggest regularly-sized service centres, whereas a wider band might indicate that some smaller settlements were displaying a higher level of centrality than would be expected from settlements of that size.

Table 4.16 shows the results of this analysis as applied to all parishes in Warwickshire. No significant regression line could be constructed for certain services. This in itself highlights the fact that the distribution of publicly provided or sponsored facilities such as secondary schools, fringe public transport services and the important chemist's shop depend more on spatial location (whether this be geared to an even spatial distribution of education and health centres, or to transportation routeways) than on settlement size. Those retail services previously described as transient are also insufficiently related to the size of the settlement in which they are located. Finally, it was found that infrastructural facilities are based on discrete locational systems consisting of a range of settlement sizes rather than one particular size group.

However, good regression fits were obtained for the remaining

Table 4.16   Warwickshire settlement service thresholds by regression (total)[1]

	R^2	Threshold band
Primary school	0.7957	250-700
Secondary school		
Grocer	0.6198	1200-2000
General store	0.6078	300-700
Butcher	0.8452	900-1500
Baker		
Chemist		
Clothes store	0.9138	2500-3500
Antiques shop		
Delicatessen		
Hairdresser	0.9128	1500-2000
Electrical and T.V. shop		
Bank	0.8285	3000-4500
Post office	0.4555	200-400
Travelling shop		
Garage	0.7298	500-1000
Village hall		
Public house	0.7613	0-300
Church		
Doctor's surgery	0.6574	1750-2500
Primary bus service	0.8078	300-800
Secondary bus service		
Train		
Electricity		
Piped water		
Mains drainage		

[1] The threshold band represents a critical level of settlement size below which the service in question is unlikely to occur but above which there will be a high probability of occurrence. The R^2 value indicates the strength of those regressions which were found to be significant.

services in table 4.16. Thus it is clear that settlements of 700 or so population are likely to possess a primary school, general store/ post office, public house and perhaps some access to public transport, whereas higher-level food-shops, luxury retail services and professional services are all centralized into increasingly larger centres. These threshold bands give further credence to the rationalization of services in rural areas, and to the part played by the key settlement policy in the acceleration of this process.

Table 4.17 Warwickshire settlement thresholds by regression (including distance factor)[1]

	Key settlement		2 miles		5 miles		10 miles	
	R^2	Threshold	R^2	Threshold	R^2	Threshold	R^2	Threshold
Primary school	0.8736	100%	0.7611	100%	0.7573	250–600	0.5953	300–500
Secondary school*	0.8384	2000–2750						
Grocer	0.9023	1500–1750	0.8397	1200–2000	0.6323	1200–3000	0.5434	1000–1750
General store	0.6617	900–1500	0.2925	700–1000	0.6485	200–700	0.5503	300–500
Butcher	0.5962	1100–1500	0.4151	2250–4000	0.8352	1200–2000	0.8210	500–700
Baker*	0.5237	2000–2500						
Chemist*		1750–2250						
Clothes store			0.7265	1200–1800	0.8183	1750–3000	0.4841	900–1200
Antiques shop*								
Delicatessen*								
Hairdresser	0.7782	1100–1500	0.3959	600–900	0.7058	3250–4500	0.8024	800–1000
Electrical & T.V. shop	0.4682	1800–2500	0.8243	900–1300	0.5771	100–400	0.5733	400–550
Bank	0.5962	2000–2750	0.4641	300–650	0.3729	600–1200	0.4993	350–550
Post Office		100%	0.6559	225–550	0.4876	100–300	0.2406	300–550
Travelling shop*								
Garage		100%	0.3114	0–100	0.6621	100–400	0.6079	250–450
Village hall*								
Public house		100%				100%		100%
Church*		100%						
Doctor's surgery	0.7258	1200–1750	0.5774	2250–3500	0.7078	200–650	0.4563	700–1000
Primary bus service		100%					0.2673	250–500
Secondary bus service*								
Train*		100%						
Electricity*		100%						
Piped water*		100%						
Mains drainage*		—						

— straight line regression   * no regression response for total parishes

[1] The table shows a similar analysis of service thresholds as in table 4.16 except that total service levels have been divided into those occurring in key settlements and those in non-key settlements at distances of 2, 5 and 10 miles from a key settlement. Services marked with an asterisk did not exhibit a significant regression line on the basis of total service occurrence data.

A further regression analysis was carried out on Warwickshire parishes divided into key settlements and non-key settlements of varying distances from higher-order centres (table 4.17). The threshold bands in the first column reaffirm the strong relationship between service levels and the generally high population sizes of the key settlements. Only the most location- or fashion-conscious facilities fail to occur regularly in key settlements.

Those settlements situated within two miles of a higher-order settlement tend to display high minimum values for the threshold bands of various services. It seems logical that small settlements adjacent to larger centres are less likely to possess services of their own, and the relatively high maximum figures for threshold bands represent the fact that a greater population size is required at this distance to achieve similar service levels to those in key settlements.

Both the minimum and maximum figures are lower for the next distance category (more than two but less than five miles distant). Here there is a greater need particularly for the provision of lower threshold facilities as the distance from larger centres increases. In the case of the most isolated parishes, certain higher-order threshold bands (particularly grocer, hairdresser and doctor's surgery) are significantly reduced, although it must be remembered that very few rural settlements in Warwickshire do, in fact, occur at distances of ten miles from a recognized centre and so this trend should not be overemphasized. Nevertheless, table 4.17 does give some indication of the manner in which key settlements dominate the service patterns in those parts of rural Warwickshire which are beyond the reach of the major urban centres.

The relationship between settlement size, threshold bands and servicing levels is a vast topic which demands further study. This level of analysis does, however, suggest that the concept of the threshold band in general may be more meaningful than a single threshold figure, and that service provision in pressured rural areas does bear a direct relationship with population thresholds and particularly with key settlements.

4.8   *Employment*

One final topic which is an essential part of any rural settlement policy, and is particularly crucial to the key settlement policy, is that of employment provision. The situation in a pressured rural area is very different from that in its remoter counterpart, in that by definition the pressured areas are located adjacent to the centres of employment provided in the major urban centres. The Warwickshire policy on employment in rural areas is plainly stated:

> Manufacturing and service employment cannot generally be encouraged in rural areas unless the proposals are essentially for the benefit of the rural community. Where there are appropriate developments, it is intended that in general they should be located within the key settlements, although limited expansion of existing small businesses will not automatically be precluded providing they are in satisfactory locations. (Warwickshire County Council, 1973a, 28)

There would appear, therefore, to be two strands to the question of rural employment in Warwickshire. Firstly, if manufacturing and service employment are generally to be restricted to the urban centres, then the problem of accessibility to these centres becomes paramount. Secondly, and of equal importance, if any regional imbalance of accessibility occurs, the policy response in terms of attracting employment into deprived areas becomes a matter of urgency.

Accessibility to employment
Accessibility to employment was one of the criteria measured as part of the key settlement selection procedure (Warwickshire County Council, 1973b). An index was interpolated from the formula

$$A_i = \Sigma_j \ \frac{0_j}{D_{ij}C_j}$$

where A_i = job accessibility of settlement i,
O_j = number of jobs in Employment Area j,
D_{ij} = travel cost from settlement i to Employment Area j,
C_j = competition for jobs in Employment Area j from all other settlements.

One criticism of this index is that it does not take sufficient account of local jobs, but this factor does not greatly detract from the overall pattern of employment accessibility. Once again scores from 0-5 were produced, and the resulting distribution is shown in figure 4.12. Settlements of below 200 population were discarded

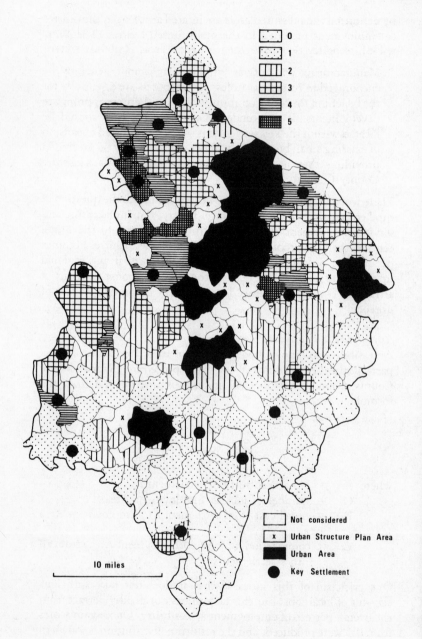

Legend:
- 0
- 1
- 2
- 3
- 4
- 5

- Not considered
- x Urban Structure Plan Area
- Urban Area
- ● Key Settlement

10 miles

Fig. 4.12 Job accessibility index for rural Warwickshire

from the Structure Plan analysis as being too small to act as centres, but some indication of their accessibility can be gleaned from the scores of the surrounding settlements, except that the smaller parishes are less likely to be served by reasonable public transport services. At the other end of the scale, parishes included in Urban Structure Plan areas and those adjacent to the major urban centres are also excluded, but these may be assumed to have high levels of job accessibility.

Figure 4.12 shows a distinct regional imbalance of accessibility to employment. It is clear that the southern areas of the county have far less opportunity than those in the north so far as employment is concerned. This in itself is neither surprising nor disturbing since it has already been established that the major concentrations of rural population occur in the north and west of the county. Moreover, distances within the county are not great and so accessibility from the south, although low in relative terms, remains at a higher level than in some other pressured rural counties.

The Structure Plan suggests that 'younger people tend to settle in those settlements closest to the main towns, whilst retired people prefer the more remote areas in the south of the County'. (Warwickshire County Council, 1973b, 12). This statement would, however, appear to be too great a generalization. If key settlements are to be established in the south and east of the county in order to concentrate housing, service and population growth, these centres will inevitably attract people with some expectation of local employment. Figure 4.12 clearly shows that the key settlements in the south of the county offer a low degree of job accessibility and would seem to require some responsible policy response concerned with the attraction of new employment to these locations.

Location of new employment
The Warwickshire Structure Plan clearly outlines the expected increases in employment over the plan period, and naturally the widespread problems of unemployment in the major conurbations occupy the major emphasis of employment policy. The difficulties involved with the decline of mineral-related and heavy industries are enormous and entirely overshadow the plight of the rural minority who might wish to see some employment centred in the key settlements. Consequently, the key settlements are given the promise of job increases only in the ubiquitous 'rural services' category, or not at all.

This problem is clarified by the information collected from parish clerks concerning new employment in Warwickshire parishes. Since this sector of rural life is the one of which clerks are likely to have the least perfect knowledge, they were simply asked whether any new jobs had been created in their parishes between 1965-70 and 1971-5. Their response indicates small amounts of new jobs in a few parishes, mostly from specific enterprises and projects in the northern half of the county (figure 4.13). The distribution for 1965-70 is very similar to that for 1971-5, and there is no indication that the key settlement policy has caused any changes in employment policy. Therefore, the situation remains that small industrial estates, each with additional land available, have been built in the southern centres of Southam, Shipston-on-Stour, Alcester and Bidford-on-Avon, and yet of these only Alcester has received any expansion of employment during the key settlement period.

There would appear to be fundamental discrepancies in a policy which concentrates housing and services into key settlements with low employment accessibility and this rural sub-system may well be a candidate for the constant monitoring and reviewing of the key settlement policy that was promised in the Structure Plan.

4.9   *Conclusions*

Clusters of Warwickshire parishes

So far, the analysis of the outworkings of the Warwickshire key settlement policy has taken the form of investigating distributions of raw data and descriptively measuring the influence of the key settlements on these various patterns. Indeed, several interesting conclusions have arisen from this process. The need is apparent, however, to present some significant statistical corroboration for the trends and relationships discovered above. It is relatively simple to demonstrate that significant associations exist between key settlements and the concentrations of population, housing, services and employment by using the Chi^2 technique. The Chi^2 associations shown in Table 4.18 form a backcloth to the more descriptive analysis of relationships between key settlements and the various sub-systems, and indeed fully justify the above attempts to explain such relationships. There nevertheless remains the need for some form of spatial analysis which is able both to juxtapose the various strands of life in rural settlements, and to

Table 4.18   Warwickshire key settlement associations with rural sub-systems[1]

	Chi^2	Degrees of freedom	Significance
Population			
Population, 1971	87.3719	8	.0000
Population, 1971-5	73.7200	8	.0000
Housing			
Private housing, 1971	76.5203	8	.0000
Council housing, 1971	90.4325	8	.0000
Services			
Primary school	15.5999	2	.0004
Secondary school	73.9454	2	.0000
Grocer	38.5667	2	.0000
General store	15.5999	2	.0004
Chemist	93.4011	2	.0000
Bank	78.5600	2	.0000
Post office	11.7559	2	.0028
Doctor's surgery	78.6742	2	.0000
Primary bus service	24.3048	2	.0000
Employment (new jobs)			
Factory employment, 1971-5	71.3571	2	.0000
Office employment, 1971-5	60.7911	2	.0000
Service employment, 1971-5	59.9353	2	.0000

[1] The Chi^2 test enables a very broad statement of statistical association between two or more variables. The association between key settlement designation and high levels of population, housing, service and employment growth is asserted by the high levels of significance pertaining to the Chi^2 statistic in each case.

allow some assessment of the degree to which certain types of parish are affected by the key settlement policy.

The technique which comes nearest to fulfilling these requirements is cluster analysis, and little needs to be said of this statistical tool which has received standard usage in spatial and locational analysis in the fields of geography and planning. In this case, clusters of Warwickshire parishes were produced so that intra-

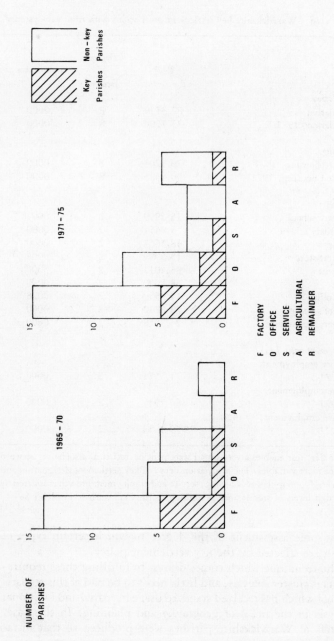

NUMBER OF PARISHES

15

10

5

1965 – 70

F   O   S   A   R

15

10

5

0

1971 – 75

F   O   S   A   R

F   FACTORY
O   OFFICE
S   SERVICE
A   AGRICULTURAL
R   REMAINDER

Non – key
Parishes

Key
Parishes

Fig. 4.13 Provision of new employment in Warwickshire parishes

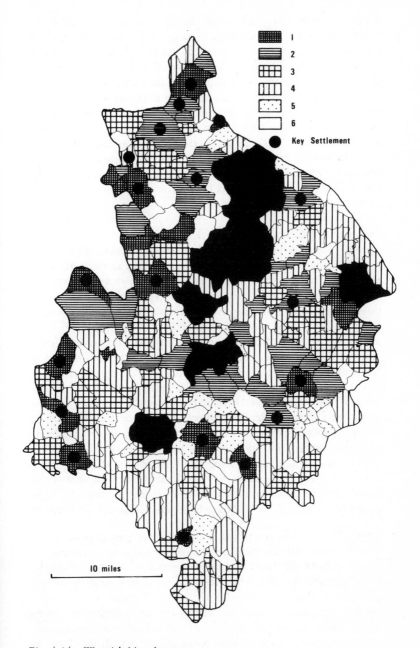

Fig. 4.14 Warwickshire clusters

cluster similarities and inter-cluster differences might be examined and the relationships between each cluster and the key settlement policy might be analysed. All the Warwickshire parish questionnaire data under the headings analysed above were used in the clustering process, with two important exceptions. No measures of population size or key settlement status were included, since it has been established that significant causal relationships exist between these two factors and the service, housing and employment variables which form the major proportion of the data to be clustered. Considerable auto-correlation would have occurred had these two causal factors been included. Indeed, cluster analysis was used in this case to suggest lateral similarities other than mere groupings of similar population size.

The analysis produced six clusters (figure 4.14).
Cluster 1 with a very high level of internal correlation (0.38) includes nine first-tier and three second-tier key settlements along with six other parishes. Settlements included in this cluster are characterized by the highest level of service provision, typically possessing primary and secondary schools, food-shops, chemist, bank and doctor's surgery, plus a full complement of infra-structural facilities. New housing, both public and private, is also concentrated in these settlements, along with new factory employment in some locations. It is apparent that this cluster represents either those settlements which have received some definite benefit from the key settlement policy or those which are self-sufficient enough to act as rural or suburban centres without the aid of key settlement status. The latter group have been found to be well-represented in the list of residual parishes from the population-change and housing analyses. All in all, this cluster constitutes high-centrality key settlements and those parishes which, but for their suburban locations or their excessively rapid past rates of growth, would have been selected as key settlements.

Cluster 2 is spatially restricted to the northern part of the county, and this locational bias indicates that the settlements concerned are heavily reliant on the major urban centres of north and central Warwickshire. In fact, the cluster is an agglomeration of two sub-groups. The first includes six key settlements along with a number of other settlements which are not adjacent to urban nodes, while the second consists of large suburban and commuter centres. Both groups have high levels of services (although not as

high as in Cluster 1), of which the presence of the primary school
and a wide range of food-shops is symptomatic. Private house-
building rates have been high and there has also been some
building of new council houses. Some new employment has also
been attracted.

The overriding factor in this cluster is the excellence of transport
links. A high ratio of train services is linked with good primary bus
services, and together these variables suggest that Cluster 2 settlements are very attractive to the commuter. This one factor
transcends a wide range of population sizes.

As for the future of settlements in this cluster, many of the
suburban sub-group are bound up in Urban Structure Plan areas,
while those people living in the key settlements will also be
reaping the benefits of Structure Plan policies. Of the remainder,
those situated away from the urban centres will suffer from the
restrictions on all but the smallest amounts of housing growth.
The high quality of transport links will ensure good access to urban
facilities but there may be a case for allowing greater flexibility in
fulfilling local housing needs in these settlements.

Cluster 3 contains parishes with small villages typified by the
presence of a primary school, general store/post office, public
house and church. There is a high incidence of travelling-shop
occurrence, and further proof of the isolated nature of these
parishes is instanced both by the greater proportion of secondary
rather than primary bus services, and by the low level of mains
drainage facilities. Some new private housing has been scattered
amongst these parishes but there is little or no indication of new
employment.

Thus, with locations often detached from key settlements and
larger centres, and with poor lines of communication, these settlements are at some disadvantage from the key settlement policy.
Only minimal growth will be allowed in such places and so there is
little hope that further facilities will be attracted. Indeed, service
losses may continue to occur in these parishes. Furthermore,
imperfect transport services present some difficulties in reaching
centralized services, and so some improvement in these linkages
would seem to be the minimum requirement for the parishes
represented by this cluster.

Cluster 4 settlements are broadly similar to those in Cluster 3
except that they often have a larger population size and that in the

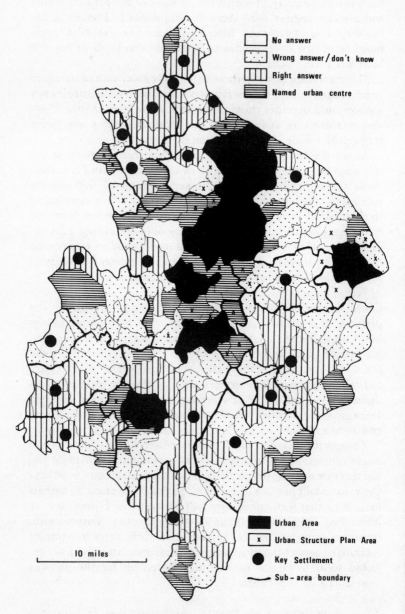

Legend (top):
- No answer
- Wrong answer / don't know
- Right answer
- Named urban centre

Legend (bottom):
- Urban Area
- X Urban Structure Plan Area
- ● Key Settlement
- Sub-area boundary

10 miles

Fig 4.15 Key settlement sub-areas and parish clerks' perception in Warwickshire

past there has been considerable private and council housing growth. Specific servicing differences from Cluster 3 are vital in the interpretation of this grouping. For instance, there is a very high incidence of primary public transport facilities which, together with the cluster distribution shown by figure 4.15, suggests that these parishes tend to straddle the main lines of communication. The reasonably high levels of mains drainage fit into this pattern, while the smattering of antiques and hairdressing establishments suggest that some Cluster 4 settlements prove fashionable to some affluent sections of the commuting population.

One interesting member of this cluster is Curdworth, which is the key settlement with the lowest levels of servicing and employment. It does, however, comply with the criterion of high rates of past housing growth. Even apart from Curdworth, the settlements in this chapter are fairly well-served by the key settlement policy. With a high degree of public transport services, they are better-able than many rural settlements to use the services provided in the key settlements, although being on good lines of communications, there will always be the tendency to ignore key settlement facilities in favour of links with the better opportunities presented by the major urban centres. Also, the largest Cluster 4 settlements might consider themselves well suited to accept further growth (particularly in the housing sector) but are restricted in this respect by the key settlement policy.

In *Cluster 5* the dominant factor is the lack of services and facilities of any description. Such settlements occur in two types of location. Firstly, ten parishes are included which are situated adjacent to major urban centres, and thus have few facilities of their own because of the proximity to urban services. These parishes vary in population size but often contain intensive agricultural areas and are covered by green belt restrictions. The second sub-group may be interpreted as small unserviced hamlets serving agricultural areas which form the green wedges between the channels of more densely populated parishes in the southern part of the county. Thus, although both types of settlement in this cluster are physically close to the opportunities provided by key settlements and major urban centres, the lack of public transport means that private transport is required to take advantage of these opportunities.

Cluster 6 is akin to the fifth category in that it consists of relatively unserviced suburban settlements within the northern green belt zone along with similar but smaller settlements in the southern parts of the county. Cluster 6 differs in that there are some communications with higher-order settlements (about half of the parishes possess public transport facilities) and that there is a greater incidence of past housing growth and pockets of new employment. These parishes again tend to be situated within the green wedges, and their opportunities under the key settlement system differ from Cluster 5 only on the strength of greater public transport facilities.

Cluster analysis provides an efficient summary of the relationships between the key settlement policy and the rural settlement hierarchy. In particular the analysis has highlighted the fact that only a small minority of settlements receive positive benefits from the key settlement system. Linking the cluster diagnostics with the various analyses of housing, services and employment, we get a clear picture of the implications of key settlement policy for the residents of villages which have been positively discriminated against. It is obvious that some non-key settlements are continuing to receive some new housing development, without the benefit of concurrent service and employment growth. This has led to an influx of affluent commuters, resulting in difficulties of physical and social integration in those villages. In smaller settlements where no additional housing has been permitted, problems of social stagnation and decline are occurring. The steady withdrawal of services, particularly in the transport sector, has prohibited the in-migration of young families, and therefore a gradual imbalance of social structure is taking place. These transport deficiencies are of paramount importance. For the key settlement policy to be democratic and wide-ranging, linkages are required between key settlement and hinterland on a scale that is not evident at present. The situation revealed by the cluster diagnostics is further supported by evidence of parish clerks' perception of key settlements.

Key settlement perception

In answer to the question 'Do you know which is the nearest key village to your parish?' only sixty-nine of the 196 parish clerks who responded to the questionnaire were able to name the key settlement correctly (table 4.19). Of the remainder, thirty-nine named an urban centre rather than a rural settlement, and the other eighty-eight either named a non-key settlement or had no knowledge of key settlement at all. Perhaps even more surprising than

Table 4.19   Key settlement perception in Warwickshire[1]

		Key parishes	Non-key parishes
1	No response	4	32
2	Correctly named key settlement	12	57
3	Named larger urban centre	-	39
4	Named incorrect village/ don't know	3	85

[1] Parish clerks were asked to named their nearest key settlement; their replies have been categorized according to the number of correct answers and to the type of incorrect answer proffered by the remainder.

these statistics is that three parish clerks representing key settlement parishes did not know that their parish contained a key settlement.

Bearing in mind that parish clerks are more likely than most other rural settlement residents to have encountered the Structure Plan and its key settlement policy, there would appear to have been some lack of penetration in the way that the policy was presented to the rural populace, and to the officials who administrate rural community affairs. Another explanation for this low level of policy perception could perhaps be attributed to the choice of boundaries for key settlement sub-areas. If a settlement is placed within the hinterland of a distant key settlement but is located adjacent to another centre, then it would not be surprising if the parish clerk or indeed any of the residents did not know of the key settlement policy's influence on their particular parish.

Figure 4.15 places parish clerks' perception and the key settlement sub-areas in the same spatial perspectives. Two points arise from these distributions. Firstly, the spheres of influence are extremely variable and seem to take little account of linkages between key settlement and hinterland. Some boundaries defy all understanding. For example, the parish of Chesterton and Kingston is included in the Southam sub-area despite the fact that it is cut off from Southam by the two parishes which comprise the Bishops Itchington sub-area. Furthermore some sub-areas (for example those of Wellesbourne and Balsall Common) include considerable tracts of suburban parishes which are inevitably closely linked with urban rather than rural centres. In these cases a rational decision might be taken to link certain semi-urban parishes into that particular urban system and to use the key settlement to service those parishes which are more divorced from the urban centres.

The second point arising from figure 4.15 is that the perception of some key settlements is extremely high, whereas in other cases it is almost non-existent. As a general rule, first-tier key settlements appear to be better-known than the second-tier group. Centres such as Atherstone, Alcester, Bidford-on-Avon, Wellesbourne, Shipston-on-Stour and Southam are well-known within many of the parishes which they serve, while the two second-tier centres in Rugby Rural District hardly make any impact whatsoever. These patterns would seem to indicate that the sub-areas surrounding some smaller key settlements are too expansive to be serviced efficiently, particularly when urban centres provide intervening or adjacent competition to the facilities of the key settlement.

If previous sections have demonstrated that key settlement policies need to forge links between key settlements and their hinterlands, then this analysis of parish clerks' perceptions has shown that it is equally important to forge public attitudes into the mould of the key settlement policy. This will not be achieved unless logical and rational selections of key settlements and their hinterlands are presented for thorough public discussion so that rural people understand the processes and objectives of the policy. Such an understanding is necessary to counteract public antagonism against the seemingly selective and restrictive local-scale policy ramifications, some of which will be reviewed later.

5
Key Settlements in a Remoter Rural Area: a Case-study of Devon

The selection of a remoter rural study area took account of the belts of extreme rurality exhibited in Chapter 1. Suitable size-limits for a study area, and the extent to which policies in other counties have been subject to previous study led to the choice of Devon (figure 5.1), which displays the highest aggregate index score for a county planned by a definitive key settlement policy and which encompasses a variety of terrain which makes it representative of many rural situations in Britain.

5.1 The Rural Settlement Policy

The rural areas of Devon reached a population peak around 1851, and since that time there has been a general pattern of declining rural population. Inter-war planning in Devon merely attempted to assess and preserve the scenic qualities of the county, and so it was not until the formulation of the County Development Plan (Devon County Council, 1953) that the problems afflicting the rural settlements were formally recognized. At this stage, a survey of rural facilities was undertaken, but the formulation of a positive rural settlement policy was delayed until a deeper study of rural community structure could be undertaken. As with many rural counties, the lack of adequate planning resources, when coupled with an underestimation of the problems pervading the rural areas, resulted in a lack of urgency when formulating rural settlement planning policies.

The First Review of the Development Plan (Devon County

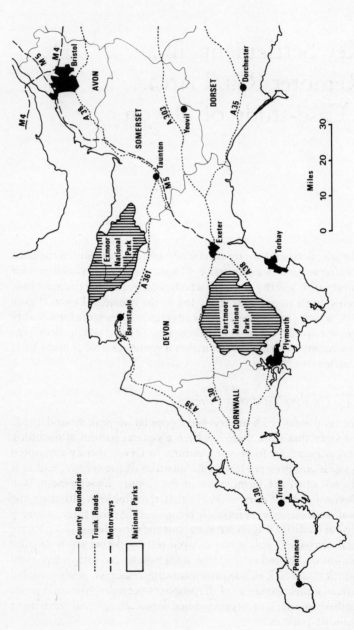

Fig. 5.1 The case study area (remoter)

Council, 1964) undertook an in-depth study of rural community structure and used the results as a basis for the formulation of a rural settlement policy. Information concerning a wide spectrum of rural life was gathered and several variables selected as being indicative of the social condition of a rural settlement, with the conclusion that a thriving rural community should possess the following facilities and services:

1 public utilities – mains water, electricity and sewerage;
2 social facilities – primary school, places of worship, village hall, and possibly a doctor's surgery;
3 shops, for day-to-day needs, and post office;
4 employment either in the village or conveniently situated nearby. (p. 45)

However, in order to create such thriving rural communities the planning of the rural areas had to be modified from the *laissez-faire* attitude adopted by the initial Development Plan. Up to this point, council house building had been in the form of small estates wherever an immediate need existed, and public utility services such as sewerage schemes had often been carried out in settlements that were unsuitable for further growth. Locational decisions such as these led to a spread of public investment right through the settlement pattern and created a precedent (especially in the case of sewerage schemes) for further development on a dispersal basis. The First Review decided that this form of investment failed to take full advantage of available resources, and so a rural settlements policy was proposed that would 'ensure that services, facilities and new development are provided or maintained in the most appropriate places and that these various efforts to improve the environment support each other' (p. 46).

The emergent policy consisted of the selection of sixty-eight key settlements which would be the only rural locations for major extensions of residential development and public utilities. Any appropriate industry requiring a rural location would be channelled into these key settlements, which would also act as centres for social services such as police and general-practitioner facilities. So, as with Warwickshire, the Devon policy aimed at a comprehensive role for its key settlements in the fields of housing, services, employment and (implicitly) conservation of settlements unsuitable for growth. As it was, the comprehensive nature of the policy was dependent on the availability of employment in or near the key settlements, and little indication was given at this stage as to the steps to be taken to attract new employment opportunities into the key settlements.

The key settlements themselves were simply one order in a growth centre hierarchy which also included higher-order suburban centres, coastal resorts, key inland towns and sub-regional centres. Of particular interest in the context of the key settlements are the key inland towns which were programmed for both residential and industrial growth and would thus serve as the centres for employment and non-essential shopping around which most of the satellite key settlements would revolve.

At the lowest level of the rural settlement hierarchy, all non-key settlements were classed together as being locations where 'further residential development should be restricted' (p. 48). Permission for development was only to be granted to relieve a particular need, and even then the decision was dependent upon criteria such as 'availability of public utilities and social services, the adequacy of approach roads and public transport together with their location in relation to key settlements and urban centres' (p. 48). On the face of it, this policy adopts a strict attitude towards the non-key settlements, as the criteria quoted are the very factors influencing the selection of the key settlements, and so those settlements not singled out as being suitable for growth are likely to be lacking in the infrastructural requirements for non-key settlement growth.

Selection of individual key settlements

Selection of key settlements was dependent on certain strict criteria (table 5.1). Considering the relative paucity of experience and expertise in the planning of key settlements that was available to planners at the time, this list of criteria appears to be a commendable attempt to account for all parts of the planned rural system in the selection of the key settlements. It cannot be stressed too often that the success or failure of any key settlement policy may be due to the wisdom of the original selection of the constituent growth centres. The First Review makes no mention of how the list of criteria in table 5.1 was translated into a decision for or against growth in any particular settlement. Whether the nine groups of variables were given equal emphasis or whether weighting procedures were used is not known. The extent to which the criteria were compromised in favour of an even geographical spread of growth centres is also unexplained.

A deeper investigation of selection procedures reveals some inconsistencies. For example, it was found that many of the

Table 5.1   Criteria for key settlement selection in Devon

(a)	Existing social facilities, including primary (and in some cases, secondary) schools, shops, village hall and doctor's surgery; and public utilities (gas, water, electricity, sewerage).
(b)	Existing sources of employment (excluding agriculture) in, or in the vicinity of, a village.
(c)	Their location in relation to principal traffic roads and the possibility that new development may create a need for a by-pass.
(d)	Their location in relation to omnibus routes or railways providing adequate services.
(e)	Their location in relation to urban centres providing employment, secondary schools (where not provided in the key settlement itself), medical facilities, shops and specialized facilities or services. A town will provide all services and facilities which one would expect to find in a key settlement. Key settlements are not appropriate near main urban centres.
(f)	Their location in relation to other villages which will rely on them for some services.
(g)	The availability of public utilities capable of extension for new development.
(h)	The availability and agricultural value of land capable of development.
(i)	The effect of visual amenities.

Source: Devon C.C. (1964).

discriminating variables in the Warwickshire key settlement selection procedure were positively associated with the population size of the individual settlements. As many of the variables used in the selection of Devon's key settlements were duplicated in the Warwickshire method, it would seem likely that population size would have been a significant factor in the Devon selection process. Figure 5.2 shows the population sizes of the key settlements selected under the Development Plan Review policy.

This patterns suggests that two distinct levels of reasoning can be seen behind the selection of Devon's key settlements. These might be described as the recognition of *existing resource locations* and *potential resource locations* in the rural settlements hierarchy. The selection of existing resource locations as key settlements for future growth is clearly demanded by the criteria on which key settlement selection depended, and this level of reasoning can be easily discerned from the parish population totals. Axminster, Bideford, Kingsbridge, South Molton, Tavistock and Totnes Rural Districts, all devote their quota of key settlement designations to those settlements with the highest populations. Few exceptions can be seen in these Rural Districts, but those which do occur are

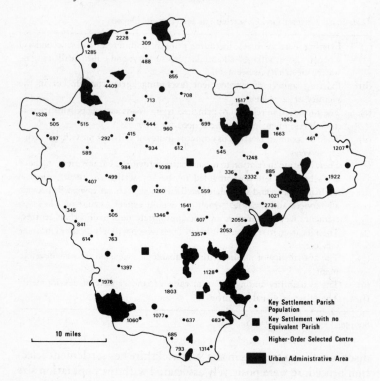

Fig. 5.2   Populations of Devon rural settlements, 1961

interesting in themselves. It might have been expected that settlements such as Parkham (Bideford R.D.), Buckland
Monachorum and Lydford (Tavistock R.D.) and Ugborough
(Totnes R.D.) would have been selected as key settlements under
the same reasoning. However, on further examination these settlements are situated adjacent to other growth centres and so were
passed over.

Potential resource locations were selected when the need for a
geographical spread of key settlements was not satisfied by larger
existing resource locations. This reasoning was hinted at by criteria
(f), (h) and (i) in table 5.1, and can be seen in the key settlement
selections in Crediton R.D. where the four largest settlements
were disregarded in favour of a more even spread of smaller key
settlements. More commonly, rural districts are found to exhibit a

combination of the two selection rationales. For instance, the three largest rural settlements in Barnstaple R.D., all over 1000 population, were selected as key settlements along with Bratton Fleming and Parracombe with populations of 488 and 309, respectively. Similar, if sometimes less extreme, differences are exhibited by the key settlements of Holsworthy, Okehampton and Tavistock Rural Districts.

Several important points are raised by these two differing locational types of key settlement. Firstly, the original Development Plan for Devon suggested 500 as the threshold population for a socially balanced and well-serviced local centre. However, it is noted in figure 5.2 that at least eleven key settlements do not meet this population threshold, the extreme example being Merton (Torrington R.D.) with a population of 292. Three possible explanations may be offered for this apparently contradictory situation. Either these settlements all had large existing planning-permission commitments, or it was hoped to build these smaller settlements up into higher-order service centres and thus fulfil their location potential, or else the association between population and the key settlement criteria is not as powerful as in pressured rural areas such as exist in Warwickshire.

No mention is made of any consideration of existing commitments but it is probable that some account may have been taken of this factor. However, it is quite possible that in isolated rural areas, a settlement of relatively small population size will have traditionally acted as a centre of services and facilities for a sizeable surrounding area, in which case the designation of key settlement status can only improve the situation in this rural system. On the other hand, it may be that key settlement status was inflicted somewhat indiscriminately on unsuitable small settlements so that a comfortably even distribution of rural growth centres could be seen on the map of Devon.

Another major theme to emerge from the population analysis concerns the wisdom of selecting some of the larger-size band of key settlements where existing resources were located. The extreme example of this size group is Fremington, with a population of 4409 in 1961, but it is noticeable that there are many key settlements with well over 1000 population. A suspicion arises that some of these settlements, having missed selection as key inland towns or coastal resorts, usually on the grounds of their proximity to other centres, had to be designated as key settlements in view of their size and consequent ability to create political pressure. The alternative classification for these settlements would have been as 'other towns', and this might have led to growth restrictions in the settlements at some later date, and perhaps would be seen as a less desirable title than the key settlement designation. Besides, 'other towns' were planned to serve a rural hinterland of 5000 population, and many of the large settlements in question do not meet this criterion. However, it is to be wondered whether large settlements which act merely as dormitory settlements for higher-order centres, and thus tend to have more upward than downward linkages within the settlement hierarchy, can successfully fulfil the role of key settlements.

The county pattern of key settlements

The number and geographical location of the selected key settlements has been one of the major criticisms of the Devon policy. Twelve years' planning experience of key settlements has tended to reach the intuitive conclusion that too many key settlements were originally selected and that consequently the intermediate distances between growth points were too small. It is important, then, to reach some conclusion as to a more suitable level of key settlement provision, but this can only be done by looking at the original decision and discovering whether changing circumstances have produced an outmoded key settlement pattern.

The First Review of the Development Plan gives no indication as to the reason for selecting sixty-eight key settlements or of the justification for the geographical distribution of these centres. Certainly, no rural population growth target is assumed, as in the Warwickshire policy. Indeed, the very nature of the policy suggests that key settlements were an unknown quantity, and so rather than limit them to a certain number, the decision seems to have been made to allow any settlement which was capable, or potentially capable, of acting as a service centre to be given the chance to prove itself.

Table 5.2 analyses the key settlement situation in each rural district. Clearly, the number of key settlements selected is related to both area and population size of the district. Those districts adjacent to centres of urban population and thus with relatively high rural populations have less key settlements per head of population than do the more problematical districts with low base populations at low densities.

Other variations are highlighted by the use of nearest-neighbour

Table 5.2 Nearest-neighbour analysis by key settlements

Rural Districts	Population	Density (population/hectare)	Key Settlements	Higher order settlements	Rurality index 1961	Nearest neighbour index	Z Score
Axminster	14,324	0.697	2	1	−3.7733	0.873	0.769
Barnstaple	25,073	0.478	5	1	−2.5061	1.225	0.962
Bideford	5,102	0.226	3	−	−6.8705	1.670	1.217*
Crediton	9,783	0.259	3	−	−2.9482	1.205	0.680
Holsworthy	8,468	0.215	3	1	−8.0555	2.049	3.474**
Honiton	7,070	0.285	2	−	−4.556	1.373	1.011
Kingsbridge	11,738	0.410	6	−	−3.5270	1.444	2.081*
Newton Abbot	25,921	0.693	4	−	−1.2451	1.381	1.460
Okehampton	11,994	0.224	6	1	−6.2182	1.588	2.757**
Plympton St Mary	12,192	0.530	1	−	3.6099	1.603	1.621
St Thomas	27,187	0.596	8	−	0.6166	1.726	3.924**
South Molton	11,173	0.224	6	1	−7.5281	1.447	2.096*
Tavistock	21,597	0.348	6	1	−1.8262	1.356	1.611
Tiverton	20,547	0.445	4	1	−3.0783	1.633	2.425*
Torrington	6,944	0.215	5	−	−6.6319	1.794	3.396**
Totnes	13,769	0.412	2	−	−1.6967	1.198	0.756

* significant at 5% level
** significant at 1% level

analysis on the pattern of key settlements within each rural district. The nearest-neighbour index scores range from 0.8 to 2.1, thus indicating the presence of a reasonably uniform level of key settlement distribution. Apart from Axminster R.D., where the two key settlements are clustered around the key inland town of Axminster, the scores represent the tendency towards an even spread of key settlements within each district to the extent that Holsworthy R.D. exhibits an almost perfectly even distribution. Other high scores are found in Bideford, Okehampton, Tiverton and Torrington Rural District, all of which were found to have high negative scores in the 1961 rurality index. Thus, in most of the remoter rural areas of Devon the highly even spread of key settlements mirrors the 'natural' central place hierarchy. High nearest-neighbour scores are also found in St Thomas and Plympton St Mary Rural Districts, which border Exeter and Plymouth respectively. Therefore, it is evident that great emphasis has been placed on the achievement of an even spread of key settlements in the most remote districts and also possibly in those districts under greatest urban pressure.

It is interesting to determine the probability that these distributions resulted from 'chance', through the calculation of a z score. Table 5.2 shows the distributions which were significant at the five- and one-per-cent levels and therefore can confidently be said not to have been derived by chance. It is again noticeable that the extreme rural districts, as well as St Thomas R.D., are those where a significant z score is attained, and this demands some explanation for such an even settlement pattern.

Analysis of the selection of Devon's key settlements both by population totals and by the nearest-neighbour technique suggest two general trends on which selection was principally based. Firstly, those rural settlements with the largest populations were selected as the natural service centres in each area. In addition, a number of smaller settlements were selected to fill in the rural spaces between the larger settlements. Nearest-neighbour analysis suggests a tendency towards a contrived even distribution of key settlements in many districts, and it is important to judge the performance of the key settlements policy in the light of this suggestion. Certainly, the above analysis allows the hypothesis that the selection procedure was heavily influenced by political pressure both from individual settlements for designation as key settlements, and from rural settlements in general (or more exactly from prestigious persons living within those settlements) for there to be a key settlement within easy reach. Any such pressure might have resulted in too many key settlements with relatively small population hinterlands. Thus public investment would have to be spread too thinly, and the key settlements policy would not be able to fulfil its desired objectives.

Key settlements reviewed

Six years after the instigation of the Devon key settlements policy, a Second Review was published (Devon County Council, 1970) which, amongst other things, presented the opportunity for a general reappraisal of the rural settlements policy. Over the interim period, population decline in north and central Devon was seen to have been retarded, while housing, service and industrial development in the key settlements was judged to be satisfactory. The Second Review considered that a strictly implemented key settlements policy was able to reverse rural depopulation, and in general the Devon policy was seen to have been successfully implemented and was fulfilling the aims expected of it:

> The Local Planning Authority selected sixty-eight key settlements in the First Review which appeared to be the right villages for further development as rural centres; the rapid subsequent decrease in the rate of rural depopulation indicates that the policy has made a comprehensive and correct selection of villages. (Devon County Council, 1970, 30)

Changes in key settlement designations were discussed, but in general any additions to the original sixty-eight settlements were seen to run the risk of 'dissipating the level of investment in key villages' (p. 30) and thus would weaken the policy, while deletions were generally avoided because of the consequent 'waste of investment and the misleading effect such changes will have on the public' (p. 30). If these explanations are taken at their face value, it would have been extremely difficult for the planners to reduce the number of key settlements even if this was thought to be desirable. Therefore, over the space of six years the selected key settlements had become firmly entrenched as the centres for rural growth, and existing investment and public opinion were able to perpetuate this situation. Some small-scale alterations were made to the policy, resulting in a net loss of three key settlements. Dunkeswell was added to the list, while Woolacombe and Chudleigh were moved up the settlement hierarchy, and Thurlestone and North-lew were moved down as they were not able to perform the required central place functions.

The Second Review did bring about an important modification of the key settlements policy in terms of the attitude adopted towards the non-key settlements. Between 1964 and 1970, twenty per cent of all new housing in Devon had been built in settlements of this category, and although this increase was due in part to longstanding planning permissions, it was decided to tighten up this part of the policy. This was done by altering the emphasis of the development specification in the non-key settlements from expansion to meet the immediate needs of the settlement, to expansion 'to an extent which will depend upon the character of the village or hamlet and the adequacy of services' (p. 31). The revised policy made it easier for planners to refuse development in non-key settlements, and in this way it was hoped to divert this pressure for growth into the key settlements themselves. However, by adopt-ing this stricter attitude, the planners laid themselves open to the criticism that they were thwarting natural growth in the smaller rural settlements.

The policy as set out in the Second Review has been maintained up to the recent formulation of the Structure Plan (1978) and therefore presents an opportunity to examine an established and longstanding usage of the key settlement technique in a remoter rural area.

5.2 *Public Service Policies*

A policy such as the one outlined above, which aims at the comprehensive planning of key settlements in the fields of hous-ing, services, employment and conservation, would need max-imum cooperation from public service provision strategies to ensure that the 'various efforts to improve the environment support each other' (Devon County Council, 1964, 46). Once again, public service policies should be viewed as an integral part of the overall key settlement policy.

Education
The general education policy for Devon is clearly set out in the First Review of the Development Plan, and makes special reference to the scattered rural settlement pattern, which it claims 'has been

a main factor in the formulation of the policy designed to secure an economic distribution of social services, one of the most important of which is education' (p. 81). In fact, the minimum provision of educational facilities was expected to be the placement of technical education facilities in regional centres; secondary education facilities in key inland towns, coastal resorts, suburban towns and 'other towns'; and primary and area school facilities in key settlements.

The emphasis placed on the key settlements as centres for primary education, especially where schools assume extramural functions as in the case of area schools, has led to changing patterns in rural education. Three thousand is considered by the Education Committee to be the minimum catchment population for a primary school, and thus a considerable area of scattered population may be covered by a key-settlement primary school. Consequently, the policy for education provision is likely to result both in the closure of some of the smaller primary schools in non-key settlements and in an increased level of school pupil transportation.

Five key settlements offered secondary education facilities during the Development Plan period, but the major concentration of secondary schooling was located in the higher-order settlements. Pupils were not expected to travel for more than $1\frac{1}{4}$ hours to reach their school, but this limit would appear to be one of expediency since a secondary school would need a threshold population of around 12,500 for it to remain viable.

The smaller-scale policy relationship between new housing and education provision in rural Devon would appear to have been a strained one over the Development Plan period. This was partly due to the planners' inability to restrict substantial new housing projects to the centres of primary education, namely the key settlements, and partly because of the overriding policy restrictions imposed on the Education Committee by the increasing curtailment of capital and revenue expenditure. Problems have been experienced concerning the timing and rate of development of new housing projects. The time within which planning permission can be given and acted upon is often shorter than the period required to include permanent school accommodation in a building programme and then to complete the building (even where the necessary site is already in hand). Differing rates of development produce a similar effect. Where rates are accelerated, the building programme cannot keep pace, yet where rates are slowed, the gradual growth in school catchment may be met by the provision of unsatisfactory temporary classrooms, as at no point in time is there a sufficient volume of growth to give the required priority to a new school or substantial extensions to the existing school.

Difficulties have also arisen from a lack of cooperation over the limits of development in a certain area. Obviously, when making a long-term plan for educational provision in an area it is necessary to have access to information concerning planning proposals for future population or housing increase. Any uncertainty as to the limits of this development, or subsequent changes in plans, can easily throw the longer-term educational planning out of joint. Thus in a policy where no growth targets or population change levels are set, a workable system of information exchange and cooperation is a prerequisite for compatible policy formation. That such a system has not been maximized in Devon is the fault of neither party in particular. Clearly the planners were faced with a situation where the location and rate of growth could not be predicted accurately, whereas the planning of educational facilities was necessarily long-term because of the perennial insufficiency of capital to meet school building needs in time. Priorities had to be established which invariably meant that adequate school accommodation followed some way behind housing development rather than being ready at the same time.

The Education Committee submitted the suggestion to the Structure Plan that educational facilities should be as important a consideration in the location decision for new housing development as sewerage requirements have been in the past. The very fact that education facilities have thus far lacked such consideration has given rise to the situation whereby the overall key settlements policy and the provision of education services have often been out of phase over the Development Plan period.

Sewage disposal
The First Review set out the major policy directions for the provision of sewerage and sewage-disposal facilities in the rural parts of the county. By 1964, most of the larger villages were reported to have water-borne sewerage systems and it was expected that 'water-borne sewerage will be extended to all but the smallest villages, and inadequate systems improved during the period of the plan' (p. 88). An important part of the policy was the provision

of spare capacity in systems serving the key settlements where residential expansion was to be expected.

Within this general framework, actual priorities for investment in capital programmes were decided by a points system which did not, as such, take into consideration the Development Plan designation of a village as a key settlement. However, such consideration was inherent in the awarding of points for factors such as the number of houses or industrial areas outlined in development plans for a settlement. Therefore, any priority given to key settlements was given only indirectly, and so, theoretically, if a non-key settlement was proved to have a greater need, then priority for investment would have been granted to that location. Sewerage schemes of differing size, and thus serving varying population thresholds, have been used in rural Devon. The First Review suggests that small schemes serving one or two villages were favoured despite the high per capita cost, but as the Development Plan period progressed there was a noticeable trend towards larger schemes with their accompanying economies of scale. Consequently, there has been a corresponding decrease in the likelihood of non-key settlements obtaining first-time sewerage, especially if they are situated at some distance from a higher-order centre.

Similar difficulties to those experienced in the provision of education facilities are presented by the configuration of new housing development and adequate sewerage schemes. There is, however, one basic difference betwen the provision of education and sewerage facilities: and that is the absolute necessity for there to be adequate sewerage services before any new housing is allowed to be built in a specific area. Whereas pupils from settlements with no education facilities can be transported to school, it is not practicable for developers to install their own sewerage systems and so they are dependent on using spare capacity in existing systems. Therefore, while housing in a school-less settlement will be allowed to proceed if other factors are favourable, the very fact that no sewerage facilities are available in a settlement will lead to an embargo on new houses until the situation is alleviated.

This being the case, cooperation between planners and the Water Authority assumes a completely different nature to that between planners and, for example, the Education Committee. The Water Authority are not in a position whereby they are continually trying to catch up with new planning developments. Their power of embargo allows them to assess the various priorities for investment on the basis of what they consider to be the greatest need, rather than being dictated to by planning decisions and settlement categories. In fact, the state of sewerage and sewage disposal can dictate to the planners as to whether or not development should proceed. A situation such as this demands the very closest cooperation between the two policy-making bodies, but again this has unfortunately not been the case in Devon. The discrepancy between demand for facilities and capital available for investment has become increasingly wide as controls on public spending become stricter. This lack of finance has led to a backlog of schemes needing attention, with the result that a settlement has required an ever-increasing number of points before its sewerage needs are met.

The provision (or non-provision) of sewerage facilities is likely to have had a drastic effect on new housing development in rural areas. Although it was the stated intention of the First Review that priority should be given to key settlements, it is inevitable that there will have been some time-lapse in certain of these growth centres before spare sewerage capacity for further development is provided. For example, in 1974, thirty-one key settlements were in need of immediate sewerage improvement and of these, work was only programmed in thirteen cases. The prospect of improvement in the remaining eighteen cases remains remote as the Water Authority themselves do not foresee these modifications being carried out in the near future. Such difficulties have been experienced by the key settlements throughout the Development Plan period, and the non-key settlements generally have even lower priority in sewerage matters. The Devon experience clearly shows that sewerage provision strategies, if divergent from the needs of the key settlement policy, have the ability to undermine the effectiveness of the entire rural settlement policy.

Health Services
By contrast with the provision of education and sewerage facilities discussed above, health service provision in rural Devon would seem to have been more compatible with the needs of the overall key settlements policy. This is perhaps because the task of providing the services of a general practitioner is somewhat less difficult to manage than the provision of, for example, sewerage schemes involving considerable capital expenditure. The Devon Area Health Authority and Family Practitioner Committee would seem

to have the ability to exert a good deal more control over health service provision than was the case in Warwickshire, where it was very much the individual doctor's decision as to where to set up practice. The First Review makes provision for the building of small clinics in the key settlements, and in fact the form of this policy has evolved to the provision of health centres housing three or more doctors, when requested by the Family Practitioner Committee. This autonomous Committee has been able to exert considerable influence on the pattern of rural health services through its financial assistance to help doctors in the setting up or running of surgeries.

The location of doctors' services in rural Devon has been organized strictly according to the needs of the local population, and while the average practice size in Devon is 2500 population, this ranges from 1500 in sparsely populated areas to 3000 in larger centres of population. These parameters have meant that doctors have tended to be located in the key settlements, or even in higher-order settlements, and this trend has gathered momentum now that health service policy has gravitated away from single surgeries to the three or more doctor health centres. Furthermore, the location of new surgeries and health centres is based very much on the concept of viability, and consequently the distribution of patients again favours a key settlement location especially when new practices are provided to serve new housing development. This locational pattern might mean that doctors have to travel long distances to their patients, but such factors of distance are considered secondary to the economic viability of the health service system. Moreover, the Family Practitioner Committee has strict control over the setting up of new practices through the granting or withholding of financial assistance, and although the Committee does not concern itself directly with the Development Plan settlement categorization, the emphasis placed on the viability of surgeries and patient distribution has favoured a key settlement location especially when new practices are provided to serve new housing development.

Naturally, the health centre building programme has been subject to curtailment similar to that affecting other public services, due to the dearth of financial resources for investment. However, the Area Health Authority consider that the present distribution of health centres and doctors is adequate to meet the needs of Devon's rural population, and so there would seem to be no question of a financial backlog in the provision of this service.

It would appear, then, that health service provision does not conflict with the overall key settlement policy. The needs of the non-key settlements are met either by doctors located in the higher-order centres, or by ancillary surgeries which are held perhaps on one day per week in some outlying villages for the benefit of the scattered rural population. Moreover, the larger key settlements would appear to be adequately provided with health service facilities, but it remains to be seen whether some of the smaller key settlements serve large enough rural hinterlands to support the full-time services of a general practitioner.

On the whole, there would seem to be a good deal of friction between, on the one hand, the various strategies for the provision of public utilities and services in rural Devon, and on the other the overall key settlements policy, which aims to promote residential growth and service development in key villages which will then act as centres for the surrounding rural areas. It is also likely that other services provided by public bodies (or which are influenced by directions from the local authority), such as roads, bus transport, social services and so on, will similarly be seeking objectives which do not necessarily correspond to those of the key settlements policy. In so far as the provision of these services is based on a particular need in a particular location, then the rural population would be serviced at an entirely satisfactory level, but it is more often the case that questions of financial viability or expediency are emphasized, or that the limited nature of public investment results in the formulation of a system of priorities, in which case conflicts between overall and specific servicing policies may arise.

5.3   The Policy in Practice

The methods and information inputs employed in the Warwickshire case study are mirrored here. However, one problem particular to the Devon situation stems from the use of the civil parish as a data base. Two of Devon's key settlements are represented by two or more parishes each, while another, Princetown, is notionally included in the parish of Lydford. Therefore, to avoid confusion, any parish containing all or part of a key settlement is referred to in the text as a 'key settlement parish'. In addition, seven key inland towns are represented by parishes, and so the term 'key parish' is used when these are added to key settlement parishes in the analysis.

Several of the hypotheses on which the Devon analysis is based are similar to those considered in Chapter 4 with reference to pressured rural areas. These concern:

(1) The successful polarization of infrastructure and service provision into selected centres.
(2) The nature of the settlement hierarchy on which the promotion of selected key settlements may be founded.
(3) The degree to which key settlements are able to perform growth centre functions.
(4) Attitudes towards growth in non-key settlements.
(5) The performance of planning policies when faced with opposing social, economic and political pressures.

In addition, it has been hypothesized in Chapters 1 and 2 that key settlement policies are able to stem the tide of rural depopulation by creating centres of intervening opportunities in rural areas. These six hypotheses pose the questions which this case study attempts to answer.

5.4 *Population*

Population distribution
Figure 5.3 shows the distribution of population in Devon parishes as recorded by the 1971 Census, and when interpreting this pattern it should be remembered that many of these parishes cover an extensive land area, and often include two or more discrete settlements. A case in point is Lydford parish, which encompasses much of the uninhabited moorland of Dartmoor as well as the major settlement of Princetown (a key settlement) and Lydford. Bearing these factors in mind, the pattern of population in rural Devon falls neatly into three constituent parts. Firstly, those parishes falling within the influence of the major urban centres such as Plymouth, Exeter, Torbay and Barnstaple form belts of relatively highly populated parishes. Around Plymouth, these high levels of population form a collar of sub-urban influence, while a sectoral form of growth, interspersed with smaller settlements, has occurred around the remaining urban nodes (notably Exeter).

The second category of population distribution includes those parishes situated in coastal locations and some specific inland sites which are strongly influenced by the impact of tourism and retire-

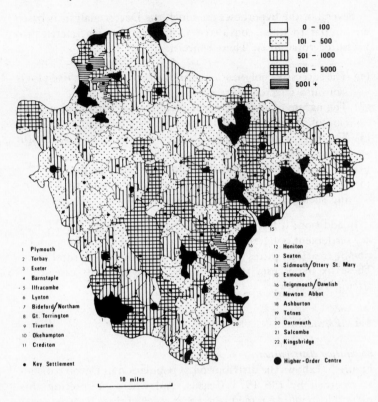

	0 – 100
	101 – 500
	501 – 1000
	1001 – 5000
	5001 +

1 Plymouth
2 Torbay
3 Exeter
4 Barnstaple
5 Ilfracombe
6 Lynton
7 Bideford/Northam
8 Gt. Torrington
9 Tiverton
10 Okehampton
11 Crediton

12 Honiton
13 Seaton
14 Sidmouth/Ottery St. Mary
15 Exmouth
16 Teignmouth/Dawlish
17 Newton Abbot
18 Ashburton
19 Totnes
20 Dartmouth
21 Salcombe
22 Kingsbridge

• Key Settlement

● Higher-Order Centre

10 miles

Fig. 5.3   Population distribution in rural Devon, 1971

ment. These settlements are thus able to sustain greater levels of
population (and also centrality in some cases) than would otherwise
be expected.

   The third component of this pattern broadly covers the remainder of the county, and consists of a large number of very small
settlements occasionally interrupted by more sizeable villages and
market towns. Considerable tracts of west, north and central
Devon fall into this category, and smaller areas bearing similar
characteristics are visible in the South Hams and Axminster areas.
These parts of Devon form an excellent example of an anachronistic
settlement pattern which was originally geared to agricultural

production but which is outmoded under present economic regimes.

One further observation from figure 5.3 is relevant to this analysis. It has been noted that the selection of key settlements in Devon occurred at regular intervals across the county with no weighting in favour of the more problematical remoter areas. What is also evident from the distribution of population is that most of the selected key settlements in these remoter districts are of low population size (some less than 500 population), and so in effect the problem areas are discriminated against, in that investment is spread thinly across a number of small settlements, thereby limiting the success of those larger settlements in the area which have the necessary foundation to create an impetus for growth.

Population change, 1961-71
The Devon key settlement policy has been in operation for a sufficient length of time for a significant assessment to be made of its success in fulfilling its stated aims and objectives. Unfortunately, no population estimates are available for the period between 1971 and the present day, but a review of population change between 1961 and 1971 covers a substantial part of the key settlement policy time-span. Figure 5.4 demonstrates the change in parish populations between these dates.

Considerable population growth has occurred in four areas:

(1) The Barnstaple/Braunton area.
(2) Parishes immediately surrounding Torbay.
(3) Some coastal parishes in the south and east of the county.
(4) The outer ring of parishes surrounding the urban nodes of Plymouth and Exeter.

So far as those inland parishes not mentioned above are concerned, the incidence of population growth of any significant scale is restricted to a few parishes surrounding the key inland towns of Tavistock and Tiverton and to key settlements such as Shebbear and Winkleigh, which were of substantial population size before the key settlement policy was instigated. Elsewhere, patterns of moderate growth are visible, particularly marking the outer influence of Exeter, Plymouth and Barnstaple, but also in areas affected by tourism, especially in the north-western and southern coastal belts. In the really remote areas, most parishes display either a state

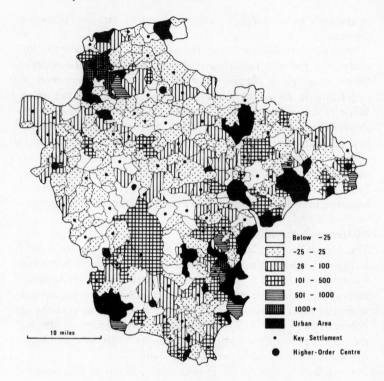

	Below −25
	−25 − 25
	26 − 100
	101 − 500
	501 − 1000
	1000 +
	Urban Area
•	Key Settlement
●	Higher-Order Centre

10 miles

Fig. 5.4   Population change in rural Devon, 1961–71

of stability or have suffered some considerable depopulation. The
performance of key settlements within these areas is mixed but
there would appear to be a significant number showing trends of
zero population growth or depopulation. Having said this, it
should be remembered that due to the considerable size of some
key settlement parishes, an important internal movement of population from the parish peripheries into the central settlement could
be masked by a seemingly stable parish population. There are signs
that this has, in fact, occurred in a number of key parishes.

The relationship between population size and population
change is further explored in tables 5.3 and 5.4. An analysis of all
parishes shows that the great majority of settlements with a

population of less than 500 have either remained stable or have experienced depopulation. Even of those settlements in the 501-1000 category, only half exhibit even moderate growth. Therefore, it is only the settlements of 1000 or more population which show any signs of establishing a regular pattern of growth.

Table 5.4 concentrates on the performance of the selected key settlement parishes. It is evident from these figures that 17 per cent of key settlement parishes have populations under 500, and a further 35 per cent have less than 1000 population. Only five of these small key settlement parishes have shown population increases of over 100 persons. Of those key settlements with more than 1000 population, more than half have been restricted to a growth level of less than 100 persons over this ten-year period.

This distribution of population growth must be viewed in a spatial context. Most of the more highly populated key settlements are situated in the south and east of the county, and so the trend of stagnation and decline is confined largely to the remoter districts. There are, however, some residuals to this pattern in the problem areas of Devon. Shebbear and Winkleigh have already been mentioned in this context, and several other remoter key settlements (for example Lapford, Dolton and Bradworthy) have also demonstrated moderate rates of growth. However, it is also evident that

Table 5.3   Population change in all Devon parishes, 1961-71[1]

Population size	Population change Total	More than -25	-24 to 25	26 to 100	101 to 500	501 to 1000	1000+
0-100	38	4	33	1			
101-500	216	40	142	29	5		
501-1000	79	18	20	26	14	1	
1001-5000	61	11	8	10	25	5	2
5000+	5					1	4
Total	399	73	203	66	44	7	6

Source: 1971 Census

[1] The table demonstrates the number of parishes of a given population size where similar rates of population change have occurred (cf. table 5.4).

Table 5.4   Population change in Devon key settlement parishes, 1961-71[1]

Population size	Population change Total	More than -25	-24 to 25	26 to 100	101 to 500	501 to 1000	1000+
101-500	12	2	7	3			
501-1000	25	3	6	11	4	1	
1001-5000	32	8	5	4	13	2	
5000+	1						1
Total	70	13	18	18	17	3	

Source: 1971 Census

[1] The table details the number of key settlement parishes of a given population size experiencing similar rates of population change.

many key settlements in north and central Devon have failed to reverse depopulation within their own parishes, let alone in those parishes adjacent to them.

If this is the situation in the key settlements, then what of the non-key settlements which have been denied policy aid from planners? Figure 5.4 shows that, apart from parishes within the sphere of influence of urban nodes, there are very few non-key parishes which exhibit population growth. Where growth has been manifested it is often adjacent to the key inland towns or even to some of the larger key settlements. This may be a tentative pointer towards the fact that some of the larger selected settlements have counteracted depopulation on a local scale, but further evidence is required before this suggestion can be substantiated.

Overall, then, the study of population distribution and change has highlighted two opposing trends in Devon. Those rural parishes within the influence of the major urban centres, or bolstered by the influx of tourists or retired people, have shown some population growth. However, cases of increasing population in the northern and west-central remoter areas are isolated within a general pattern of stagnation and depopulation. Therefore, so far as demographic analysis is concerned, the key settlement policy has not fulfilled its objective of reversing the effects of depopulation, except in certain localized areas.

5.5   *Housing*

The distribution of new housing is perhaps the facet of rural life which is most closely linked to the patterns of population change outlined above. One complicating factor concerns the housing occupancy rate in Devon, which has declined from an average of 3.0 persons to 2.7 persons during the period under study and so situations of static population will still produce a demand for new housing. Bearing this in mind, tables 5.5 and 5.6 exhibit the levels of new private and council housing in parishes of varying population size during the key settlement policy period. Between 1965 and 1970, only 10 per cent of parishes received more than 30 new private houses, while a similar level of new council housing was built in only 10 parishes. At the other end of the scale, more than 80 per cent of parishes received less than 10 new private or council houses each.

Two factors in table 5.5 can be seen to be important in the explanation of these statistics. Firstly, the size of settlements has a significant bearing on the expectation that new houses will be built in a particular location. Only 5 per cent of parishes with a population of less than 500 persons received more than 10 new private houses during this period, whereas 87 per cent of parishes over 1000 population provided sites for housing development on this scale. Furthermore, the necessity for a large base population would appear to be even more critical in the establishment of locations for council house building.

The second factor concerns the priority given to building new houses in the key settlements. Table 5.5 shows a limited tendency for the larger selected centres to attract new residential development, but at the same time many key settlements at the lower end of the population range have been confined to little or no new housing. It is also very evident that there has either been a lack of demand or else a lack of planning inclination to establish new housing in the smaller non-key settlements in Devon.

Table 5.6 portrays a similar analysis for the period 1971-5. Over this later time-span, a greater overall level of house building has taken place and it is apparent from these figures that key settlements have been the most prominent recipients of this increase. It is again evident, however, that it is in the larger settlements (that is over 500, and especially over 1000 population) that most of the new housing has been promoted, although there are isolated examples where small amounts of council housing have been

Table 5.5 New housing in rural Devon, 1965–70[1]

Population size	Private						Council				
	Total	0–10	11–30	31–50	51–100	101+	0	1–10	11–30	31–50	51–101
0–100	38	38					37	1			
101–500	216	203(12)	10	3			161(8)	48(4)	6	1	
501–1000	79	59(17)	15(5)	3(1)	1	3(2)	41(6)	29(15)	8(4)	1	
1001–5000	61	18(13)	19(10)	8(3)	9(7)	7(3)	19(11)	21(9)	16(11)	3(3)	2(2)
5000+	5				1	4(3)		1	1(1)	1(1)	2(2)
Total	399	318	42	14	11	14	258	100	31	6	4

[1] The total number of parishes of a given population size experiencing similar rates of new housing are shown in the main body of the table with a concurrent analysis of key parishes alone appearing in brackets.

Table 5.6 New housing in rural Devon, 1971–5[1]

Population size	Total	Private					Council					
		0–10	11–30	31–50	51–100	101+	0	1–10	11–30	31–50	51–100	100+
0–100	38	38					37	1				
101–500	216	200(12)	15		1		186	24(6)	6(6)			
501–1000	79	53(13)	16(6)	4(3)	5(2)	1(1)	49(10)	20(8)	7(5)	3(2)		
1001–5000	61	17(6)	19(12)	8(5)	12(10)	5(3)	29(12)	9(8)	16(11)	5(5)	1	1
5000+	5	1	1	1		3(3)	1(1)	1	1	2(2)		
Total	399	309	50	13	18	9	302	55	30	10	1	1

[1] Again, the body of the table consists of parishes of a given size experiencing similar rates of new housing. Key parishes are shown in brackets.

allowed in low-population non-key settlements.

This evidence suggests that a definite link exists between settlement size and the planned development of new housing under
the key settlement policy. However, for a fuller understanding of
the distribution of new housing in rural Devon these patterns must
be translated to the spatial perspective (figures 5.5 and 5.6). It has
already been remarked that an important dichotomy exists between those parishes influenced by adjacent urban areas or tourism,
and those 'problem' areas which are remote from urban centres and
are thus unlikely to be suffering from the pressures of population
increase. Thus it is to be expected that the lion's share of new
housing development will have taken place in the more urbanized
pole of this rural dichotomy. Figure 5.5 shows this to be the case.
The major private residential developments during the period
1965-70 occurred adjacent to, or within easy commuting distance
from, the urban centres of Plymouth, Torbay, Exeter and Barnstaple. In addition, the south and south-east coastlines show signs of
significant levels of new housing. It is interesting to note that
much of this new development has been successfully steered into
the key settlements of these growth areas.

The performance in this respect of the key settlements serving
the more remote inland areas is less satisfactory. A few of the
isolated centres in these areas stand out as locations for some new
private housing. For example, Winkleigh, North and South Taw-
ton, Chulmleigh, Shebbear and Mary Tavy, all demonstrate significant levels of new housing during this period. These locations may
have flourished in the role of traditional market centres, or as
centres of local employment, or else on account of their proximity
to the key inland towns of Tavistock, Okehampton, Holsworthy
and South Molton. The non-key parish of Cheriton Bishop has also
provided a location which has been attractive to new housing.
However, the remainder of the remoter key settlements and all of
the non-key settlements in the area show little sign of increase in
residential provision. A study of planning permission statistics in
Okehampton R.D. (table 5.7) suggests that non-key settlements
have accounted for about one-third of permitted housing over the
study period. Perhaps of greater importance is the high rate of
planning refusals in non-key settlements, which provides some
evidence of a substantial demand for new housing in the smaller
villages. It would appear likely that the failure to fulfil this
demand resulted from strict planning controls on new development.

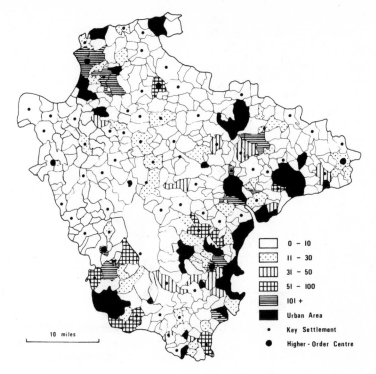

Fig. 5.5   New private housing in rural Devon, 1965–70

One sector in which planners have been able to make a positive contribution to the housing stock in rural areas is through the location of new council house building. Here, planning applications are not merely channelled into appropriate sites but may be instigated by the local authority as part of a comprehensive scheme for the rejuvenation of the remoter rural areas. Figure 5.6 demonstrates the distribution of new council housing between 1965 and 1970. The pattern displayed therein is very similar to that of private housing except that, if anything, the building of council houses has been subject to even greater rationalization than the private sector. Nevertheless, there is further evidence of housing growth in the key settlements named above, which suggests that these centres have gone some way towards meeting this particular objective of the key settlement policy.

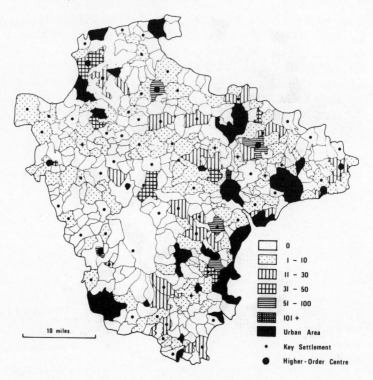

0
1 - 10
11 - 30
31 - 50
51 - 100
101 +
Urban Area
• Key Settlement
● Higher - Order Centre

10 miles

Fig. 5.6   New council housing in rural Devon, 1965–70

A look at the situation concerning new house-building during
the period 1971–5 does suggest a degree of change in the overall
trend. Figure 5.7 shows those parishes where the level of new
housing is higher than that of the previous period. It is evident,
not only from the number of parishes involved but also from their
distribution, that either some relaxation of planning controls took
place during these years or else the demand for new housing in the
county showed a dramatic increase compared with the previous
quinquennium. In practice, both these phenomena were contributory factors to this small but significant upturn in house
building in rural areas. Several non-key parishes are represented in
figure 5.7, which points to the fact that the channelling of all new
housing into key settlements has been less strict, while the greater
demand has led to a more widespread distribution of building.

So far as the remoter areas are concerned, the pre-organization rural districts of Barnstaple, Bideford, Holsworthy, Kingsbridge, Okehampton, South Molton, Tavistock and Torrington account for nearly half of the parishes where building rates had been significantly increased. Within these districts there has been an emphasis on housing provision in the key settlements but it is noticeable that some non-key parishes have also been allowed to expand.

To conclude this review of new housing in rural Devon under the key settlement policy, it is worthwhile placing the housing situation in rural areas in the wider context of the whole of the county. Table 5.8 shows the number of dwellings completed between 1965 and 1975 in different types of settlement in each of the Devon Economic Planning Areas. Clearly, the urban areas have received by far the greatest proportion of new housing, although Barnstaple has received less building than the other sub-regional centres. Of the proportion of dwellings built in the rural areas, the majority occur in those areas influenced by the urban nodes. Thus the levels of building in the North and West Devon areas which correspond to the most remote of the rural areas are very small in comparison. What is more, dwellings completed in non-key settlements in these areas exceed those built in the selected key settlements.

One point in favour of the housing policy in rural Devon is that it has corresponded with the theme of conserving those rural settlements of highest environmental quality. But from this and the preceding analysis of the Devon policy, it is difficult to support the hypothesis that key settlements in remote rural areas are able to concentrate sufficient population and housing into centres of intervening opportunities in order to stabilize situations of depopulation. We may rather construct a secondary hypothesis that the implementation of the key settlement notion in Devon has

Table 5.7   Planning permissions in Okehampton R.D.[1]

	1965–70		1971–5	
	Permissions	*Refusals*	*Permissions*	*Refusals*
Key settlements	62.7	80.2	68.6	51.7
Non-key settlements	37.3	19.8	31.4	48.3

[1] Figures refer to the percentage of the total number of dwellings permitted and refused within Okehampton R.D. between 1965 and 1975

been inappropriate on two counts. Firstly, the policy covers remote and pressured parishes without offering special dispensation for the two different sets of problems covered by the same planning vehicle. Secondly, the number of key settlements in the remote areas is too great for the development of an impetus for growth in any more than a few of them.

5.6 Services

Changes in service provision

One of the areas in which the key settlement policy is most likely to succeed is in the concentration of service provision into key settlements. Indeed, one of the criteria for the original selection of the key centres was the existence of social facilities, public transport and public utilities within the various villages. Bearing in mind that such a policy inherently accepts the 'natural' trends of service rationalization from small centres, then an analysis of service changes should reflect the dominance of key settlements as service centres.

Once again the problem of separating policy ramifications and 'natural' trends is encountered in this instance. It is not certain that the patterns of service change outlined below are a direct consequence of the key settlement policy. However, the service and

Table 5.8   Dwellings completed in various Devon settlement types, 1965-75

	Exeter/ East Devon	South-east Devon/ Torbay	Plymouth	North Devon	West Devon
Sub-regional centres	5200	8400	15820	1380	–
Other urban centres	11120	2680	1800	4290	340
Key settlements	1990	1270	1480	1050	220
Non-key settlements with Outline Plans	390	1040	830	560	–
Other non-key settlements	2220	750	830	940	340

Source: Devon C.C. (1977)

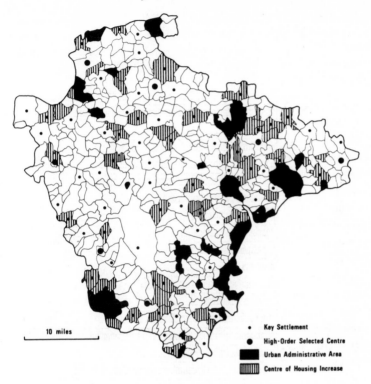

Fig. 5.7   Centres of housing increase in rural Devon 1971–5 compared with 1965–70

infrastructure data resulting from the survey of parish clerks are catalogued in figures 5.8 and 5.9 in order to outline the differences between service development in key and non-key settlements.

Service provision over the period 1965-75 in the key parishes exhibits a trend of stability rather than variation in the number of units representing each phenomenon; it is clear that the key settlement policy has not brought about any widespread increases in the quality of services in the selected centres. Even public transport facilities follow the trend of stability, although the frequency of services has declined in many cases. However, as the key settlements were originally chosen for the adequacy of their services, the policy can at least be seen to have maintained this level of service provision in an environment of decline.

NUMBERS OF PARISHES

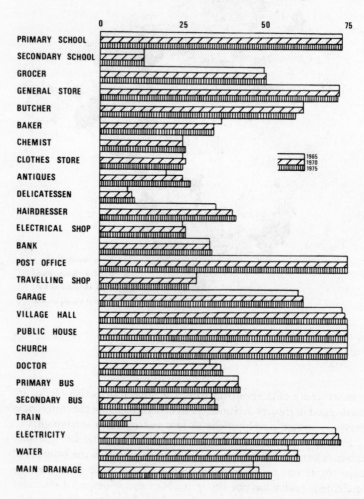

Fig. 5.8 Service provision in Devon key parishes

In addition to this stabilizing effect, the quality of services and facilities has been noticeably improved in the categories of health services and infrastructural facilities. For example, there has been a dramatic rise in the number of key parishes served by a doctor's surgery. This trend was postulated earlier when it was indicated that the unwritten policy for setting up new health service did favour key settlement locations. Moreover, the county policy of establishing purpose-built health centres has further benefited some of the selected centres rather than non-key parishes. It was also suggested above that county policy for the provision of public infrastructure was likely to recognize key settlements as unofficial priority areas. This expected pattern is also manifested in figure 5.8, where the occurrence of electricity, piped water and mains drainage is seen to have significantly increased in the key parishes.

The picture of service provision in non-key settlements is predominantly one of decline. Essential services for everyday living in remoter rural areas have gradually dwindled as a result of public- and private-sector policies of concentration. Food-shops, particularly the ubiquitous general store, have shown a marked decline as has the travelling shop which provides a similar service for more isolated settlements. Professional and health services, notably the village post offices and family doctor concerns, have followed the same trend. Specialist shops, already scarce in rural areas, demonstrate a net pattern of stability but their location often depends on the relative affluence of a particular settlement. In addition to these losses, the village school, which is often the hub of village community life, has also been subject to policies of concentration. Furthermore, all these disbenefits have not been countered by increased in public transport. The recession in provision of primary bus services (defined as more than four buses per day) is hardly compensated by the small increase in secondary service (often one bus per week on market day). This low level of public transport in non-key settlements illustrates the need for a greater planning effort to forge links between growth centres and their hinterlands. Figure 5.9 further emphasizes that only the gradual rise in the levels of community facilities (for example, village halls) and infrastructure counteracts the general trend of decline to any extent.

It should not be forgotten that these figures refer to all rural parishes in Devon, whereas the regional imbalance between the south/east and the north/central areas has already been stressed. Figure 5.10 outlines service changes in the pre-reorganization

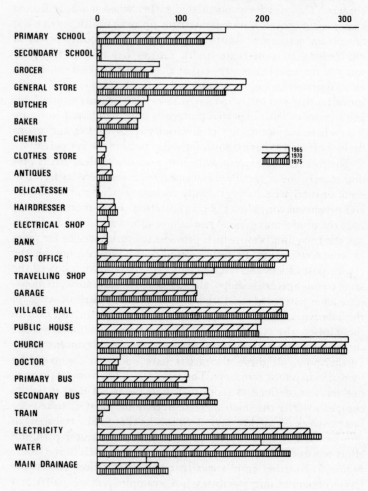

Fig. 5.9 Service provision in Devon non-key parishes

Rural Districts of Barnstaple, Bideford, Holsworthy, Kings-bridge, Okehampton, Tavistock, Torrington and South Molton, which represent the most problematical rural parishes in Devon. At first sight, the level of service introduction into these settlements appears to be high. However, a closer look at the services involved emphasizes that it is often the transient antiques, hairdressers or garage enterprises as well as basic infrastructural facilities (a general increase not shown here) which have been attracted to these areas (table 5.9). Even so, the key settlements are well represented as locations of increased service provision. However, table 5.9 also demonstrates that so far as the primary, general store/post office, food-shop, travelling shop and doctor's surgery categories are concerned, the key settlement policy has done nothing to stem the tide of decline in non-key parishes, and indeed the policy's strictures towards concentration may well have exacerbated the situation.

This evidence is supported by a report by the Standing Conference of Rural Community Councils (1978) on the decline of rural services. Taking Devon as one of its case study areas, the report highlights a 1.5 per cent decline in village post offices, an 11 per cent decline in village shops and a 14 per cent decline in village surgeries during the period 1972 to 1977. A typical recipient of these trends if Stoodleigh, a non-key village with a population of around 300, which since 1970 has lost its primary school, its village shop cum post office, and its twice-weekly bus service, although some positive planning is evident in the setting up of a community minibus service on market days. The report also points out that some smaller key settlements have not escaped this general decline in services. Upottery (population 520) was named a key settlement in 1964 but since that designation has lost its shop/post office, it garage and its daily bus service. What is more, there is a fear among the villagers that this lack of service will prevent young families from moving into the new housing which has been built in the village. This development will use up all the spare sewerage capacity for the settlement, and the resultant embargo on future development will create a considerable negative impact on the village community.

The general conclusion to be drawn from this evidence and from the wider patterns discussed above is that the key settlement policy appears to have fulfilled its stated objective of concentrating public investment into selected centres. At the same time it has exacerbated the ongoing rationalization of services in non-key settlements both directly through public service policies and indirectly through planning restrictions leading to the polarization of new housing (if any) into the growth centres. The key settlements are designed to act as service centres for surrounding rural parishes. Whether or not the level of facilities in key settlements and the quality of linkages between centre and hinterland are sufficient to carry out this function must be seriously questioned in some of the remoter areas.

Settlement size and service thresholds
In a situation where any growth in the services and facilities of a rural area has to be attracted rather than channelled, the relationship between settlement size and service thresholds becomes critical. It has been suggested that the selected key settlements in Devon were too numerous and often too small to achieve the aims of the key settlement policy. One of these aims is to build up a level of facilities in these centres which is sufficient to serve a rural hinterland, and so some measurement of the relationship between size and provision is required in order to suggest which settlements have this capability.

Once again the asymptotic regression curve may be used to quantify the link between these two criteria in the form of a threshold band. In a remote rural area where settlements are often losing population, the minimum point of the band becomes very important. Obviously this lower extreme is not able to close down or establish itself with equal profitability, since the factor of inertia will prolong a service in a depopulating settlement. However, this zone does suggest the approximate mark to which a settlement population should rise to gain the facility in question.

Table 5.10 indicates the threshold bands applicable to Devon parishes and, as in the corresponding Warwickshire analysis, certain services do not allow the construction of a significant regression line. Once again this highlights the fact that some public sector facilities are provided on the basis of an even geographical distribution rather than on the basis of settlement size. The secondary school, secondary bus service and infrastructural facilities fall into this category. Furthermore, transient retail services such as the antiques shop and the delicatessen are likely to follow affluence and fashion rather than a certain threshold of clientele.

The remaining services in table 5.10 did give a good regression

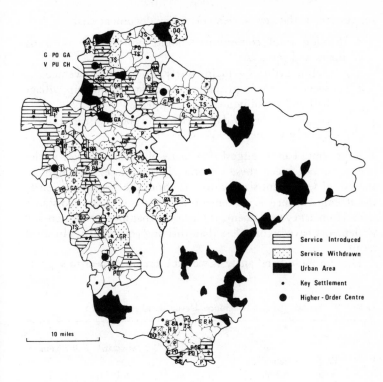

Fig. 5.10   Service changes in remoter Devon parishes, 1965–75. (Letter key as in Table 5.9)

fit. Although the R^2 values in this case are higher than in the Warwickshire analysis, the threshold bands are on the whole wider than were applicable to the pressured rural county. This reflects the essential nature of a certain minimum service level whatever the population structure of the area. However, when it is remembered that many of the key settlements in the most problematical areas of Devon are of relatively low population size (between 450 and 800) it may be realized that services available to settlements of this size are not of the level to support any substantial rural hinterland. Not all of these key settlements can rely on being the exceptional location which, despite low population size, is used to provide the essential minimum service level mentioned above.

Another yardstick with which to measure these bands is the

suggestion in the key settlement policy document that

a thriving rural community should possess the following facilities and services:
(1)   public utilities – mains water, electricity, sewerage;
(2)   social facilities – primary school, place of worship, village hall and possibly a doctor's surgery;
(3)   shops for day-to-day needs, and post office. (Devon County Council, 1964, 45)

The threshold bands suggest that many of the smaller key settlements do not meet these criteria. Furthermore, although no analysis of settlement size by distance from the nearest key centre was attempted since no settlement in Devon is very far (in distance terms) from a key settlement, it is evident that most of the non-key settlements have become less than thriving communities in these terms.

The threshold band analysis would therefore appear to support

Table 5.9   Service changes in remoter Devon parishes, 1965-75

		Introduced	*Withdrawn*
P	Primary school		9
S	Secondary School	1	1
G	General store	3	18
GR	Grocer	1	5
B	Butcher		7
BA	Baker	1	7
C	Chemist	1	
CL	Clothes		2
A	Antiques	8	1
D	Delicatessen	2	1
H	Hairdresser	5	4
E	Electrical and T.V. shop	2	2
PO	Post office	2	10
TS	Travelling shop	2	9
GA	Garage	3	3
V	Village hall	3	1
PU	Public house	1	2
CH	Church		1
DO	Doctor's surgery		2
1	Primary bus service	2	4
2	Secondary bus service	7	2
T	Train		6

Table 5.10   Settlement service thresholds in rural Devon

	R^2	Threshold band
Primary school	0.8417	300-700
Secondary school	–	–
Grocer	0.5972	500-2500
General store	0.7194	250-800
Butcher	0.8151	800-1500
Baker	–	–
Chemist	0.9013	1500-5000
Clothes	0.9120	2000-3500
Antiques shop	–	–
Delicatessen	–	–
Hairdresser	0.6583	900-2500
Electrical and T.V. shop	–	–
Bank	0.5319	1750-3500
Post office	0.7282	150-400
Travelling shop	–	–
Garage	0.7693	500-1000
Village hall	–	–
Public house	0.7439	100-300
Church	–	–
Doctor's surgery	0.5729	1000-2500
Primary bus service	0.8302	500-1200
Secondary bus service	–	–
Train	–	–
Electricity	–	–
Piped water	–	–
Mains drainage	–	–

[1] The threshold band represents a critical level of settlement size below which the service in question is unlikely to occur but above which there will be a high probability of occurrence. The R^2 value indicates the strength of those regressions which were found to be significant.

the hypothesis that key settlements in the remoter parts of Devon are too many and too small to act as viable service centres which will maintain levels of opportunity in the rural hinterland. Evidently, then, many rural dwellers have to look to higher-order settlements, or at least to larger key settlements, for many of the goods and services necessary for rural life. This pattern of service use is inextricably linked with the question of accessibility and transport, to which we continually return in any discussion of rural problems.

5.7   Employment

The final major rural sub-system to be affected by the key settle-ment policy is that of employment. The original Devon policy (Devon County Council, 1964) appears to have been in two minds about the employment role of key settlements. On the one hand, the policy states that 'a thriving rural community should possess . . . employment either in the village or suitably situated nearby' (p. 45) and that 'it will be to those [key] settlements that industries requiring a rural location will be encouraged, if appropriate to go' (p. 46). Indeed, one of the selection requirements for key settle-ments was the location of 'existing sources of employment (exclud-ing agriculture) in or in the vicinity of a village' (p. 46). On the other hand, the same policy document attaches far greater impor-tance to the attraction of new employment into the key inland towns, which are seen as the locations where 'employment oppor-tunities to replace agricultural employment may be best provided' (p. 41).

This basic locational paradox presents two main themes for discussion in any analysis of the relationship between key settle-ments and employment provision. Firstly, it is necessary to dis-cover whether new employment has been attracted to the key settlements in general and the remoter key settlements in particu-lar. Secondly, the relationship between key settlements and the employment provided in their associated key inland towns or higher-order centres should be investigated in order to assess this second employment option afforded by the key settlement policy.

Employment in key settlements
Figure 5.11 outlines the provision of new employment in Devon parishes. It shows that a little over 20 per cent of key settlements attracted new factory jobs between 1965 and 1970, with this figure rising to 25 per cent over the period 1971-5. Other forms of employment appear to be less significant although it is interesting to note that non-key locations have been successful in attracting some office employment as well as some new jobs in the secondary sector. From these figures it would appear that some small success has been achieved in the attraction of new employment into the key settlements.

Other studies have produced results which further expound

these trends. Peter d'Abbs (1975), in a survey of social and economic change in North Devon, outlines the location of new firms which have recently been attracted to the area. In the whole of the study area, which includes the rural districts of Barnstaple, Bideford, Holsworthy, Okehampton, South Molton and Torrington, and therefore covers most of Devon's remoter rural areas, only five out of twenty-six key settlements were found to have provided locations for new firms. Most of the area's new employment was placed in Barnstaple and other higher-order centres (table 5.11). D'Abbs concludes that although there was a substantial influx of new manufacturing industries into North Devon between 1966 and 1974, a noticeable imbalance occurred concerning the size and location of settlements which received this new employment. In particular, he singled out the Okehampton area as one where 'very little industrial growth took place (and) the decline in employment in primary industries resulted in an overall decline of 24 per cent in the number of insured employees' (p. 78).

A survey of key settlements in the Exeter and Plymouth sub-regional areas (Community Council of Devon, 1976) also catalogued the presence of new industry. This survey discovered that three out of seventeen key settlements in the Exeter sub-regional area and one out of thirteen in the Plymouth sub-regional area had attracted new firms in the recent past.

The general conclusion to be drawn from these three different sources of information is that there has been only moderate success in attracting new employment to the key settlements. The signs

Table 5.11 Location of new firms in North Devon

Location	Number of firms
Barnstaple	17
Bideford	4
Holsworthy	3
Ilfracombe	4
Okehampton	3
South Molton	5
Great Torrington	6
Others (including key settlements)	8
Total	50

Source: D'Abbs (1975)

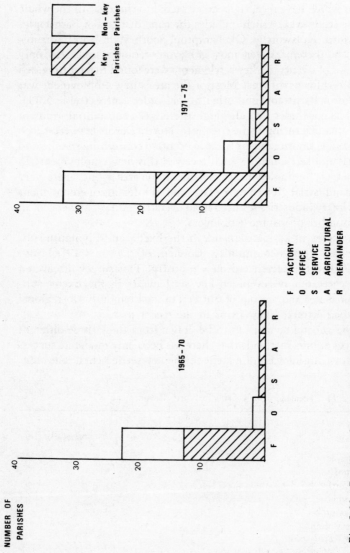

Fig. 5.11 Provision of new employment in Devon parishes

are that the higher-order inland towns in the remoter areas of Devon have received substantially fewer new job opportunities than those in the pressured areas since industrialists have tended to prefer locations near to the major cities of Plymouth and Exeter. Even in those key settlements which have received new employment, the actual rise in the number of jobs has been small. This in itself is not a bad thing. For instance, the work of the Council for Small Industries in Rural Areas has been a major force in the instigation, retention and even expansion of small firms in the rural areas of Devon. These small enterprises are invaluable in the lifting of rural morale as well as in providing further employment opportunities. However, rightly or wrongly, it would appear that the major effort has been directed towards new employment in the higher-order urban centres.

Employment in key inland towns
A comparison between the employment patterns presented in the Development Plan (1964) and the Structure Plan (1977) documentation reveals that the remoter rural areas have remained almost stationary in numbers of employees, the exception being Barnstaple Employment Area which has shown an appreciable increase. These figures mask much of the new employment that has taken place since the out-migration of some workers balances the new jobs provided in the areas. However, it seems likely that only small increases in employment have occurred in areas such as Tavistock and Okehampton. Therefore, the job opportunities in these remoter areas continue to rely heavily on commuting.

It might be imagined that the key settlements with their more extensive public transport services to the key inland towns, would provide good links with these centres of employment. However, a recent study of rural transport in Devon (Department of the Environment, 1974) suggests that public transport is becoming decreasingly important in the journey to work of rural residents. In a case study of the Tiverton area, 77 per cent of workers travelled to work by car, 7 per cent by stage bus, 6 per cent by contract bus and the remainder by motor-cycle, cycle or on foot. The report concludes:

> Public transport does not play a significant part in the journey made to and from work in the outlying areas we examined; even in the one best served by buses. Already more people in these areas travel to work by getting lifts than go by stage bus. There

Table 5.12   Devon key settlement associations with rural sub-systems[1]

	Chi[2]	Significance
Population		
Population 1961	76.5713	.0000
Population change 1961-71	47.0184	.0000
Housing		
Private housing 1965-70	98.8202	.0000
Council housing 1965-70	127.2635	.0000
Private housing 1971-75	133.6174	.0000
Council housing 1971-75	168.2952	.0000
Services		
Primary school	72.1698	.0000
Secondary school	109.1014	.0000
Grocer	60.6197	.0000
General store	46.4089	.0000
Chemist	117.1029	.0000
Bank	114.1946	.0000
Post office	26.4666	.0000
Doctor's surgery	110.8870	.0000
Primary bus service	39.5049	.0000
Employment		
Factory employment 1965-70	124.1626	.0000
Factory employment 1971-75	130.6592	.0000

[1] Associations between key settlement designation and high levels of population, housing, service and employment growth are proved to be highly significant according to the *Chi[2]* statistic.

may be cases, however, where people without access to cars find their choice of employer limited (p. 6).

This last point is important in this context since it is these groups of immobile people who are most helped by the transport facilities provided in the key settlements. Overall, however, the key settlements make only a modest contribution to employment opportunities. Some small industrial estates have been established but in the current economic climate it has not been found easy to attract firms to these sites. It might be concluded that the attraction of new jobs to key settlements would be facilitated if public investment was spread less thinly in fewer centres.

5.8 Conclusions

Clusters of Devon parishes

Having viewed these various patterns of raw data, the need is again apparent to present some statistical corroboration for the trends and relationships discovered above. Table 5.12 demonstrates that significant Chi^2 associations exist between key settlements and the various rural sub-systems, and therefore provides justification for the further analysis of these interrelationships. Once again, cluster analysis may be used to create a spatial juxtaposition of the individual strands of life in rural settlements, and in this case careful scrutiny of the linkage dendrogram and of the cluster fusion levels suggested that five clusters were appropriate to the Devon data.

Cluster 1 (with a high degree of internal correlation) includes thirty-five key settlements along with thirteen other parishes. Settlements represented by this cluster are characterized by the highest levels of centrality. Service provision is high, with primary (and some secondary) schools, food-shops, banks, primary bus services and a full complement of infrastructural facilities being generally available in these locations. It is noticeable that Cluster 1 settlements constitute the centres for health services in rural Devon. Most of the rural doctors' surgeries and all chemists are located in these types of parish. New public and private housing (particularly in the second policy quinquennium) are also concentrated in these settlements along with new employment in many cases.

Cluster 1 settlements can therefore be seen to represent the most successful and viable rural centres in Devon. This status is to be expected from the key settlement contingent but the non-key settlements in this category would appear to be misplaced according to the criteria for key settlement selection. However, figure 5.12 shows that these non-key settlements are either adjacent to urban centres, or adjacent to other Category 1 key settlements and these locational attributes would explain their omission from the key settlement policy. Also visible from figure 5.12 is that large areas of west, central and north Devon lack adequate representation by Cluster 1 settlements and therefore are receiving less than even benefit from growth attracted under the key settlement policy.

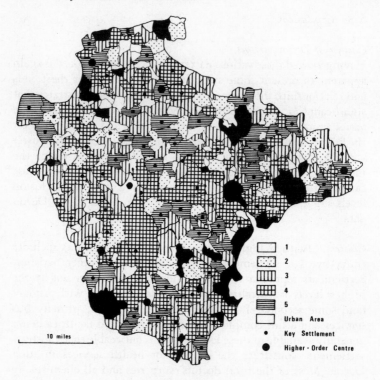

1
2
3
4
5
Urban Area
Key Settlement
Higher - Order Centre

10 miles

Fig. 5.12   Devon clusters

Cluster 2 settlements range in size from 250 to 4000 population.
The association between these widely differing parishes is a functional one depending on a basic level of services (primary school,
general store/post office, bus service and infrastructural facilities)
combined with high rates of housing, particularly in the private
sector, and some new employment. Two spatial groupings emerge
from this cluster. Firstly, groups of suburban parishes of this ilk
can be recognized surrounding the major urban centres of Exeter,
Plymouth, Torbay and Barnstaple. The second constituent grouping consists of smaller inland villages which act as secondary
centres to Cluster 1 settlements. Thirty-one key settlements are
included in this category and these are more evenly distributed
throughout the county than was the case in the previous cluster.
Once again, parishes in this cluster have generally either received

some benefit from the key settlement policy, or else are close enough to urban facilities to be unaffected by rural investment policies.

Cluster 3 includes nearly one-third of all parishes in Devon. Service levels are characterized by the ubiquitous general store/post office, village hall, public house and church combination, while most settlements in this group are also served by public transport and about half possess their own primary school. Little or no new housing has been built in these settlements, and in only seven cases has new employment been attracted during the key settlement policy period. This cluster represents the type of settlement outlined in the previous analysis; namely where the key settlement policy has heightened trends of population and service loss and where continuing standards of rural life are only maintained with the help of public and private transport. Settlements of this cluster are particularly evident in the remoter parts of the county, and even include eight key settlements which would appear to be at a certain disadvantage in the fulfilment of growth centre objectives.

Cluster 4 settlements are of similar service, housing and employment type to those in Cluster 3, with the exception of one vital attribute. Cluster 4 settlements appear to be located away from the major routeways and are therefore subject to pressing problems of accessibility. This relative remoteness is evidenced by a total lack of primary bus services and by a less than even pattern of secondary bus services. Infrastructural patterns (particularly those of mains drainage) are also detrimentally affected by this remoteness. The locational attributes of this cluster have been instrumental in the conditions of relative deprivation which have occurred in the settlements concerned under the key settlement policy. Such settlements are often served by travelling shops, but the lack of bus services has meant that high levels of personal mobility are needed if the facilities provided in the key settlements are to be used. The two key settlements in this group would again appear to have few locational or functional advantages in the fulfilment of the policy's aims and objectives.

Cluster 5 consists of small agricultural hamlets often characterized only by the presence of a church and basic water and electricity provision. These settlements are often of low accessibility and have attracted little or no new housing and no employment. Cluster 5 settlements are mainly found in the west, centre and north of the county and often form remote hinterlands of key settlements in the most disadvantaged rural areas in Devon. The position of the settlements under the key settlement policy differs only because their small size makes them the most difficult part of the rural system to assimilate under a policy of two-way linkages from centralized investment centres.

The results of the cluster analysis, when linked to the findings of the above analyses of housing, services, employment and so on, suggest that only a minority of settlements have as yet received positive benefits from the key settlement policy. Social problems caused by the use of this particular type of planning policy fall into two distinct types. Firstly, there are those problems which the policy attempts to solve but in reality exacerbates in many hinterland settlements. The centralization of resources into key centres represents a move towards the creation of a new purpose for rural settlements. Villages can no longer support large agricultural populations and so a new *raison d'être* is being generated by provision of new employment and increased levels of commuting. However, by creating a new economic and social base in central nodes, the policy inherently withdraws public support and investment from outlying villages and, therefore, contributes directly to situations of no housing or employment growth, and of service losses.

The second set of problems concerns the lack of practical measures to ensure that the benefits accruing from growth in key settlements are spread to the surrounding villages. Key settlement ideology can only be made socially acceptable if equal emphasis is given to concentration of investment and spread of benefits. However, very little evidence has been found of community transport and service schemes designed to counteract the positive discrimination against small villages which has been brought about by resource centralization. As it is, the policy has been effective in the key settlements themselves, but much less so elsewhere.

Key settlement perception

Table 5.13 outlines the responses of parish clerks to questions concerning their knowledge of the key settlement policy. In all, 52.4 per cent of clerks were able correctly to name their nearest key settlement, while a further 19 per cent named a larger urban centre. With no response from 10.3 per cent of parishes, this means that 18.3 per cent of clerks were not aware of their nearest key settlement. Compared with the equivalent response from Warwickshire parishes, this level of knowledge is very high, as would be expected in a situation where the key settlements policy has been operative for fifteen years.

The perception of parish clerks representing key settlements and key inland towns is particularly interesting. All six respondent key inland towns demonstrated an awareness of their status. Furthermore, fifty-seven key settlements also had knowledge of their selected rank in the settlement hierarchy. Thus, allowing for six non-respondent key settlements, only 7 clerks were not aware of their position under the rural settlements policy.

Figure 5.13 demonstrates that the clerks' perception of key settlements occurs in a regular pattern across the county. Parishes that demonstrated no awareness of the policy are also evenly scattered although small groupings of these settlements are visible in the extreme west and east of the county. Certainly, there are few indications to suggest that key settlements in the remoter areas are less well-known than those nearer the major urban centres. On the contrary, many parishes in the more pressured rural areas have closer links with the larger towns and cities and so find the key settlement policy less applicable to their situation.

In the Warwickshire analysis, patterns of perception were used to differentiate between key settlements surrounded by zones of high awareness, and those which were little-known. This formulation of spheres of perceptive influence is not possible in this case. Patterns of awareness are visible around key inland towns such as Tavistock, Okehampton and Crediton, but the key settlements are too numerous for the clarification of spheres of influence.

Table 5.13   Key settlement perception in Devon[1]

	Key parishes	Non-key parishes
1 No response	7	34
2 Correctly named key settlement	57	152
3 Named larger urban centre	6	70
4 Named incorrect village/ don't know	7	66

[1] Parish clerks were asked to name their nearest key settlement, and their replies have been categorized according to the number of correct answers and to the type of incorrect answer proffered by the remainder.

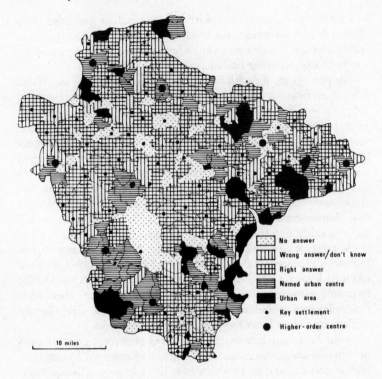

Legend:
- No answer
- Wrong answer/don't know
- Right answer
- Named urban centre
- Urban area
- Key settlement
- Higher-order centre

10 miles

Fig. 5.13   Key settlement perception in Devon

The need for the arrangement of sub-areas around each key
settlement is obvious in this case. At present the pattern of these
centres suggests that their number and location were selected with
little regard for the hinterland areas which they are designed to
service. Once again it is apparent that many parishes are in a
position to be linked to urban centres, whilst others would appear
to require a definite rural centre with which to identify so that
essential rural linkages can be forged. Such a system of hinterlands
linked to centres with an attracted growth impetus would help
overcome some of the small-scale problems encountered in the
non-key settlements.

6
An Assessment of
Key Settlement Performance

6.1 *Fulfilment of Aims and Objectives*

Any assessment of the performance of key settlements should take account of the efficacy with which this particular policy has fulfilled the stated planning aims and objectives in pressured and remote rural areas. Two objectives are common to both situations, namely:

(a) the concentration of residential and employment growth into selected centres in order that the optimum economic pattern of polarized service and infrastructure provision may be effected.

(b) the use of these centralized facilities to improve or stabilize the opportunities for residents of hinterland settlements.

However, the achievement of these objectives is designed to meet fundamentally different requirements in the two types of rural area. In pressured areas, a successful centralizing policy allows the conservation of settlements whose environmental quality is such that further large-scale growth would be inappropriate. Conversely, planners in the remoter areas would hope to stem the tide of rural depopulation by creating centres of intervening opportunities in rural areas.

The foregoing analyses of both types of area suggest that the first common objective has generally met with some success but that the second has received little attention under the key settlement policies as implemented in the two counties under review. Thus, the conservation of rural settlements in pressured areas has been achieved at the cost of stunting the growth of viable non-key settlements. Likewise the stemming of depopulation at the other rural extreme has been partially achieved, but even this has often been due to the internal movement of population from hinterland to key settlement, thus exacerbating the crises in outlying small settlements.

In the case of Warwickshire, it was noticed that the planners have so far found it difficult to restrict increases in population and housing in settlements where an impetus for growth has already been established under previous planning regimes. The impression is gained of a number of settlements in the county where the demand and the suitability for growth has not been seriously questioned and yet whose prospects for such growth are severely limited under the strict key settlement policy. It is also evident that there exists within pressured areas a number of smaller non-key settlements which suffer from the general rural malaise of declining service and transport provision and consequent replacement of traditional rural residents by affluent in-migrants. These settlements also contain pockets of non-mobile and lower-paid population with their inherent problems of accessibility to employment, retail, social and community facilities. The key settlement policy is gradually encouraging these people to migrate towards the centralized services of the key settlements. The plight of these types of pressured rural settlement has often been under-represented by the popular and academic press and yet the social ramifications of the key settlement policy in these areas are an important consideration for the future planning of counties such as Warwickshire.

No such lack of attention has been apparent concerning the remoter rural areas. The public outcry over the planned decline of Durham's 'D' villages set the trend for future thinking on the subject of rural settlement policies. Although it is now recognized that the Durham policy was a special case because of the disused mining elements in the rural environments under consideration, there has nevertheless been a dramatic reversal of academic opinion in both planning and geographical circles about the wisdom of continued use of the key settlement type of policy in remoter rural areas. A series of papers (e.g. Ash, 1976; Hancock, 1976; Martin, 1976; McLaughlin, 1976a; Venner, 1976) has recently resulted in an anti-key settlement policy lobby of substantial proportions. Key settlements are viewed as the villains of the rural peace which have destroyed village life by greedily attracting all rural development into their own already privileged boundaries.

The Devon experience bears out these claims to some extent. For example, the designation of key settlements has coincided with the shrinking of rural transport services, leaving the non-mobile rural population stranded and dependent on local shops and services. Moreover, these local facilities are also tending to concentrate in larger settlements, either because of competitive market forces or as part of a planned policy of centralization. Housing opportunities are also declining. Few, if any, houses are being built in small settlements and those that are constructed are often suitable only for affluent long-distance commuters or as second homes. Young people are forced to move into the key settlements or even further afield if they wish to buy or rent a house. The disappearance of the school, the shop, the bus and the young people all add up to the state of rural deprivation that is the summation of the problems facing some rural communities in remote areas.

These initial reactions to growth centres in pressured and remote rural situations beg various questions about the key settlement policy itself. In what ways has it been successful? Where has it failed to respond to rural planning objectives? Have such failings come about through some intrinsic ineptitude of the policy itself or through the manner in which it has been implemented within the planning system? Only by answering these questions can we make any meaningful assessment of past and present key settlement performance or indeed any recommendations as to more effective ways to plan for the future of our rural settlements. There is no one easy response to these questions. What may be seen as a successful achievement by the planner may represent a removal of opportunities for the rural dweller. Therefore the key settlement question is discussed from three separate viewpoints – the economic, the social and the political – in the knowledge that these three factors are in fact fused together to form that complex equation which we call planning.

6.2   *An Economic Perspective*

Ever since the initiation of key settlement policies, planning practitioners have been preoccupied by the economic and physical aspects of their work. This is partly because the theoretical justification for key settlements stems from the basic economies of scale which they generate, and partly because the tangible results of rural planning are most apparent in rising standards of service provision, or increasing housing levels, or the building of new industrial estates. We would therefore expect considerable achievements from the policy from the economic point of view.

The two case-studies have indicated that, by and large, residential and employment growth has been concentrated in the selected centres where services and infrastructure have been provided. These achievements in themselves should not be understated. Rural areas before the onset of growth centre policies were often lacking in basic infrastructure. The priority given to key settlements in this respect has ensured that at least a majority of rural residents now enjoy the standard of water, electricity and sewage-disposal facilities which they might expect if living in the town. Furthermore, the concentrated effort of house-building and setting up of industrial-estate facilities in key settlements has ensured that rural people have an opportunity to live and work within the rural milieu rather than migrating to higher-order urban centres. The provision of health centres and other public services together with the retention of a certain level of private-sector retail and service outlets have also created some degree of economic viability within the rural settlement pattern. In the light of these advances, it seems fair to accept Woodruffe's (1976, 26) conclusion that 'many village groups have benefited from the improved facilities and amenities that have so far been constructed in the key settlements'. Even McLaughlin, a renowned critic of the key village system, admits that 'for the residents of the key village and its commuting hinterlands, there have probably been definite improvements' (1976b, 55).

When it is borne in mind that the operation of a growth centre policy is a long-term process and that the Warwickshire and Devon case-studies have only investigated fifteen years of this type of planning between them, we may firmly conclude that key settlements have added to the material progress of pressured rural areas and have acted as a stabilizing effect for facilities in remoter rural areas.

Even from the economic viewpoint, however, there have been several failings to be recorded against the key settlement system. The first of these was recognized in the analysis of Devon public service policies but seems to be applicable to all but the latest crop of investment-rationalization policies. The successful implementation of a rural growth centre policy is dependent on strict coordination between the planners and the authorities governing the provision of water, education, health and highway services. A successful key settlement requires both the negative impetus gained from planning permission refusals elsewhere and a positive lead from public service bodies whose priority treatment of the growth centre paves the way for private sector services to follow. Under many development plan regimes, each public service department has allocated priority according to a very specific set of criteria rather than as part of an overall coordinated policy, with the result that the planned development of key settlements has sometimes been delayed or even completely halted due to the lack of sewerage or by-pass facilities. If a comprehensive form of rural planning is to be achieved there is an obvious need for a high degree of collaboration between the various local authority servicing bodies. This situation of close coexistence has now been realized in many counties.

Another apparent failing of the policy involved the several residuals to the expected pattern of growth in housing and employment uncovered by the case-studies. Of particular note was the failure to restrict house-building in some non-key settlements, and this highlights a fundamental difficulty with a policy of planned concentration. It has been found to be almost impossible to refuse some development in villages which have existing infrastructural capacity, especially where an impetus for growth has been established under previous policies. These circumstances are mainly the concern of the planned implementation of key settlements, but there is concern in remoter rural areas that undue development in non-selected centres will prejudice the main tenor of the policy which is to create viable key nodes on which the future of the surrounding rural hinterland may be founded. On the other hand, these residuals may be viewed as a sympathetic reaction to situations of local need, in which case such divergence from the strict policy of concentration is to be welcomed at an appropriate scale.

The focusing of employment into key centres has also fallen short of expectations. Provision of infrastructure, often in the form of small industrial estates, has been adequate but difficulties have been experienced in attracting entrepreneurs to small rural centres. A major deficiency in this respect has been the traditional planning perception of the key settlement policy. There has been a noticeable blind faith that the designation of a key centre will immediately produce a flood of applications from prospective employers. This has patently not been the case. Indeed, special supplementary policies are required for the specific task of luring employment to selected settlements. These problems of attitude and implementation are compounded by an intrinsic quality of key villages, particularly in the remoter rural situation. Here, the selected centres are often too small to act as employment centres, a point reinforced by the Devon example where new ventures have generally opted for the more sizeable urban locations of the key inland towns. Perhaps it would be more appropriate for small rural centres to promote local entrepreneurial talent using schemes similar to those employed by the Highlands and Islands Development Board.

From the overall economic perspective, the key settlement policy has been reasonably successful in the concentration of residential and employment growth so that services and infrastructure may be provided economically. Furthermore, given improvements in policy implementation, there would seem to be little reason why the policy *per se* cannot continue to achieve this objective in the future. But what of the second key settlement task of using these centralized facilities to improve or stabilize the opportunities for residents of hinterland settlements? The standard economic viewpoint is expressed by Ayton (1976b, 67) who argues that

> Although concentration and selection would need to be backed by programmes to maintain reasonable social services in settlements not selected (e.g. mobile libraries, health visitors, meals-on-wheels and public transport) it would not seem sensible to accept development where it would add to the numbers of people in the smaller villages who would have to depend upon such services, imposing extra cost to receive a lower level of service.

Two very important points arise from this type of attitude towards hinterland villages. Firstly, the presumption of providing the absolute minimum of services to small settlements contravenes the original tenor of the key settlement concept. The ideas of Peake and Morris were that centralized facilities should be shared by the surrounding rural population, but in fact little attention has been given to the methods by which such sharing can actually take place. This attitude represents another example of attributing too high a level of expectation to the key settlements. The 'automatic' spread effects of a small growth centre have been shown to be negligible and so there is again a specific need for complementary policies to develop this spread effect artificially.

The second point arises directly from this requirement for specific policies under the key settlement framework. Spread of key centre benefits can be brought about either by mobilizing services for use in the hinterland or by mobilizing the people, enabling them to use the centralized facilities by means of efficient public transport systems. There is little evidence that either of these options have been actively pursued as an integral part of the overall policy. Decreases in mobile services were recorded in the case-study areas, while the principal effort in rural transportation has been through the continued subsidy of stage bus services which tend to link key settlements with higher-order centres rather than with the rural hinterland. If the key settlement policy is to be accepted as an agent for the spread of rural opportunities, then mechanisms for attaining this spread should be provided as an inseparable part of the planning strategy.

One final economic perspective concerns the very theory on which the key settlement policy is based. Traditionally, key settlements have been seen to be cost-effective because the concentrated provision of housing, services and employment is held to be more economic than that on a pattern of dispersal. The work of Gruer (1971) and Norfolk County Council (1976) has put a different complexion on this matter by introducing social costs and investment costs into the question. Gruer demonstrates that when all the costs accruing to both the supplier and beneficiary of a particular service (in this case hospital outpatient care) are taken into consideration, it may be less expensive for a travelling service to visit a scattered population than for the people to travel to a central supply source. If the economics of rural settlement planning are to be calculated in this manner, then a dispersed pattern of village investment becomes a possible alternative to the key settlement system. The stumbling block to this metamorphosis of policy is that this type of equation would take account of personal expenditure by rural dwellers, whereas present financial assessments by local authorities are based upon costs to the exchequer. Should social costs become part of the official planning balance-sheet, the economic justification for key settlements would be much reduced.

6.3 *A Social Perspective*

McLaughlin (1976b, 56) describes the results of key settlement planning as

> a situation where an increasing number of people, particularly the non-mobile, are faced with the choice of either moving to the key village or staying behind to suffer increasing social

deprivation, as transport services, employment opportunities, and social, educational and commercial services withdraw to the relative security of the key village.

This statement is representative of much of the criticism levelled at the social consequences of key settlements. Again, any objective assessment of the planning policy should concentrate on the direct social benefits or disadvantages associated with the key settlement concept rather than bemoaning the lack of social opportunities which are a direct consequence of living in the countryside whatever policy is in operation. This being so, the basic accusation to be answered is that key settlements only bring social benefits to those people living in the selected centres themselves, whilst rural dwellers in the hinterland are disadvantaged because of policies of concentration. Many different social issues are involved here.

Transport

The theme of rural transport is given priority, since the planning options in other sub-systems are often dependent to a large extent on the type and range of available transportation. In the analyses of both the Warwickshire and the Devon key settlement policies it was immediately evident that the provision of transport linkages was hopelessly inadequate to cater for even the basic needs of rural residents. In the pressured rural areas, rural transport levels were available to link the key settlements to higher-order centres, but few regular linkages had been established between key settlements and their hinterlands. Two trends resulted from these patterns. Firstly, the small non-key settlements were deprived of essential accessibility to various services and facilities; and secondly, the transport services that were available facilitated the by-passing of key settlements in favour of larger urban centres on the same route.

Rural transport in Devon was found to be on a predictably lower plane. In this case, not only did similar problems exist in the hinterland villages and hamlets but it was also found that some selected key centres were not regularly linked upwards in the settlement hierarchy, let alone downwards to the outlying villages which they are designed to serve. One conclusion to be drawn from the Devon analysis was that this lack of transport was one of the root causes of the failure of some key settlements to act as viable service centres.

Critics (e.g. MacGregor, 1976) point out, however, that the concentration of services and facilities in key settlements without concern for hinterland transport links has merely exacerbated the plight of the non-mobile population in small villages. High levels of car ownership cannot of themselves solve this problem. Maddocks (1975) points out that even if seventy-five per cent or more households in a settlement own one or more cars, less than half the population will have free access to private transport to fulfil the various linkages required for everyday rural life.

The transport needs for journey-to-work are often fulfilled by high rates of personal mobility, except for the fact that in one-car families the non-mobile wife is prevented from seeking employment by a lack of accessibility. Similarly, a weekly journey-to-shop can be successfully negotiated by the car-owner but is a critical problem for non-mobile groups. Where bus services are available they are generally geared to meet those particular needs, but these services are too often less than satisfactory in terms of frequency and catchment range. Perhaps an even more vital form of deprivation concerns social and recreational trips, the irregular nature and timing of which are unlikely to be catered for by public transport services. Finally, access to welfare services, which again have been subject to concentration both as a direct and indirect result of the key settlement policy, is another need which is difficult to meet through the public transport medium.

As the restriction of development in non-selected centres is integral to the key settlement policy, the need for more wide-ranging transport systems has been directly exacerbated by planning strategy. Some critics might argue that a policy of dispersed investment in the countryside would preclude the need for transport links with higher-order centres, but it is doubtful whether the need for such connections could be disposed of altogether. It would therefore appear that whatever framework is selected for the planning of rural settlements, a solution to the problem of rural accessibility will remain the key issue in the successful implementation of settlement policies.

Employment
Although the data concerning employment provision in Warwickshire and Devon were not as comprehensive as they might have been, it was clear from the above analyses that many employment inadequacies were persisting in both types of rural area. By definition the pressured rural areas, being close to major urban centres, are able to offer a wide range of employment opportunities within comfortable commuting distance. However, with the increasing cost of journeys to work, the distances that people are prepared to

travel for employment may well become shorter in the future. Therefore, two main problems of employment in pressured rural areas have been isolated. In the first instance, the fringe areas within the pressured category are likely to offer an increasingly low level of accessibility to employment and therefore require some increase in employment opportunities, particularly in key settlement locations where concentration of services and housing is already taking place. Secondly, with the decline in primary employment, the residents of small settlements of low accessibility have become dependent on private mobility for the journey to work and there would appear to be a need for increased provision of jobs in key settlements to reduce the reliance on commuting.

In the remoter situation, similar trends are worsened by the fact that not only is there no source of employment within easy commuting distance, but it is also the case that any in-coming entrepreneurs have to be attracted to what has traditionally been viewed as a low-grade area in terms of industrial location. The key settlement policy has attempted to guide any new employment into the key inland towns, and to a lesser extent, the larger of the key settlements. Some success has been achieved in this respect, but it is noticeable that the Exeter and Plymouth areas have attracted the cream of new employment while the concerns guided into rural centres have been the smaller residual types of enterprise.

Criticism of the provision of employment in rural areas has centred mainly around the planners' preference to set up industrial estates in key settlements, and their consequent reluctance to allow small-scale entrepreneurial enterprises in the smaller non-key settlements. McLaughlin (1976a, 159) makes the claim that 'the existence of such an estate is often a perfect justification for the planner when he refuses permission to develop small-scale enterprises in lower-order centres'. It should be said that little evidence of such planning refusals was found in the study of planning permissions in the Southam and Okehampton areas (Cloke, 1977c). Moreover, there are some overall signs to suggest that these local-scale concerns are being set up in the rural areas despite the vogue for industrial estate development.

A strictly interpreted key settlement policy whereby all employment is channelled into the growth centre does constitute an inappropriate form of social planning for employment. As a solution to this problem Ash (1976, 629) has suggested that rural planners should 'replace the concentration of new employment in trading estates on the outskirts of two or three towns by a network of new workshops in towns and villages throughout the area'. However, it seems clear that a scheme such as this will also fail to solve employment problems in rural areas. Neither industrial estates nor workshop enterprises are able to provide sufficient new opportunities in isolation. There would seem to be little reason why the attraction of larger-scale employment to the larger towns and key settlements cannot be accompanied by a flexible attitude towards smaller-scale workshops and businesses in non-key settlements. This flexibility of implementation would not preclude the success of the overall policy.

Housing
A call for flexibility of policy has also been forthcoming with regard to the problems of rural housing under the key settlement policy. In Warwickshire, severe restrictions have been placed on new housing in non-key settlements, regardless of size or need. Similarly, the initial Devon policy took a very strict attitude towards growth in non-key settlements, and even when these restrictions were relaxed after the Second Review of the Development Plan it has been apparent that much of the new housing permitted in non-key settlements has not been geared to the fulfilment of local need. MacGregor (1976, 527) sums up this situation:

> When a local authority puts thirty council houses in one village, and none in surrounding areas, or when planning permission for cheap private housing likely to attract young families is refused and only expensive chalet bungalows are allowed which only the middle-aged and middle class can afford, this nice balance of age and social groups is lost.

Thus, planners using key settlement policies have found it necessary to take away growth from rural hinterlands in order to build up new housing in the key settlements. In doing so, they have placed themselves in the invidious position of having created an exaggerated breed of rural housing problems in small settlements. Not only have young families been forced to leave their villages because of private sector competition from the retired and second-home elements of the market, but this migration is also enforced by the lack of new council dwellings in small settlements. These movements have led to the 'gentrification' of both pressured and remote villages alike.

It can be argued that planning priorities should be directed towards the needs of local rural people. Therefore, a more flexible housing policy is required for the success of any overall policy. After all, attempts to spread the opportunities and benefits from key settlements in order to revitalize small settlements will be nullified if the rural hinterland suffers from a state of planned stagnation or decline.

The housing sector is perhaps the most difficult part of key settlement policy in which to instil flexibility. If no housing development is permitted in small settlements, then an obvious local need is being neglected. If, however, the policy is relaxed and small amounts of housing are allowed in villages which lack public investment, then there is a risk of developing a class-divided countryside. A strict interpretation of key settlement planning encourages the migration of rural dwellers from hinterland to growth centre so that centralized services become more accessible. However, a sympathetic implementation of the policy might permit small amounts of non-key housing to cater for specific local needs without necessarily prejudicing the overall strategy. The difficulty then becomes one of ensuring that housing suitable for local people is built in outlying villages rather than the more expensive luxury housing which developers prefer. There may be a strong case for steering local-authority or housing-association dwellings into smaller settlements when the need arises.

Services
Service provision is interrelated with policies for transport, employment and housing, and forms another factor in the withdrawal of opportunities for many rural dwellers. Key settlement policies in both the pressured and the remote rural situation have allowed the continued decline in levels of service provided in non-key villages. Moreover, with inadequate public transport linkages between key settlement and hinterland, the benefits from centralized service investment are only accessible to the residents of smaller centres through the ownership of private transport.

It has been suggested that public authority policy for the provision of infrastructure was likely to follow the key settlement policy guidelines to the detriment of the non-key villages. This suggestion was substantiated in the main by the analysis of the case-studies, although the impression was gained, particularly in the remoter case, that levels of infrastructure are being gradually improved in the non-key settlements. However, the overall situation in small villages is dominated by the reduction of retail, educational and welfare services, and in many cases the key settlement framework policy has done little or nothing to redress the balance of service provision. Certainly, service levels in the key settlements have generally been improved but no outward linkages have been set up to spread the benefits of these centrally located opportunities.

Service rationalization has been an ongoing feature of the countryside for many decades, with the social benefits of dispersed provision of facilities being discarded in favour of the economies to be gained by centralization. Planners have channelled new services into key settlements and have thus inherently prevented the improvement of local services in non-selected villages. However, the social problems caused by this policy should again be viewed in terms of intrinsicality or implementation. Some form of spread effect whereby benefits of key settlement development are transmitted to hinterland settlements has been an integral part of the key village concept. Unfortunately when it has come to implementing the policy there has been neither the finance, nor the established planning mechanism nor the initiative with which to bring this spread of development and opportunity about. This may appear to be an over-eager defence of the key settlement system. Indeed, should linkages between centre and hinterland prove impossible to establish, then the social requirement for basic services in small settlements will have to be met by planning frameworks more geared towards dispersal investment.

Other social factors
There are also less tangible ways in which key settlement policies have had a direct bearing on the social elements of rural living. One of the consequences of resource-concentration is that it tends to promote the movement of population. The Devon case-study showed that some, but by no means all, parishes were exhibiting a slowing-down or even reversal of depopulation. However, this trend was due in part to the transfer of rural people from hinterland to key settlement, with the result that many rural communities are still experiencing out-migration of young people and in-migration of retired people and mobile, affluent commuters.

Several intangible problems are exacerbated by these demographic movements. The thorny problem of social balance is involved here, with some planners believing that unbalanced rural communities consisting of old and rich people are an inevitable result of key settlement planning. Enforced out-migration also creates difficulties in sustaining a range of village organizations, and these bodies are often important determinants of the opportunities available in small rural settlements. It is clear that a falling population size can be equated with the decline of community groups, although it should be recognized that some aspects of the changing support for such groups are not wholly explicable by demographic changes.

The sense of social cohesion or 'community' is also held to deteriorate when villages lose both local facilities and active population groups. Shaw (1978) notes that such factors as a sense of belonging to a community, involvement in village events and a common view of the quality of life in a village are all influenced by the village stagnation which often results from the key village policy. And yet this is a paradoxical situation. On the one hand, villages feel the need for additional population in the settlement in order to promote the traditional rural community, but on the other hand, too many newcomers will make the village too big with the consequential loss of the feeling of rurality. This balance between in- and out-migration is in theory a fine one to maintain and in practice is almost beyond the scope of land use control planning as we know it in the rural areas.

Problems caused within expanding communities involve the breakdown of social cohesion and the formation of a clique-conscious society. The difficulties of integration experienced by established and newcomer population alike are little different now from Pahl's descriptions in the 1960s. In addition, the social costs of congestion in some key centres, particularly in the pressured rural areas, are a factor which should be considered in any decision to allow rapid growth in rural settlements. A less obvious problem, perhaps, is the suggestion (Cumbria Countryside Conference, 1976) that standards of behaviour deteriorate with increasing population.

The social ramifications of too much or too little growth in the countryside have been the subject of much discussion but little action over the past two or three decades. It is therefore pertinent to assess the extent to which the key settlement policy has helped or hindered the alleviation of rural social ills. A basic criticism of the policy is that it has denied vital growth to small rural settlements. However, this allegation is not as straightforward as it seems, for as Shaw (1978, 100) points out:

> Although population growth in an individual village would
> help it to retain services, and to support group activity, and to

be selected as a location for centralized services, growth would not necessarily solve any social problems, or help the 'traditional' forms of village activity.

What the case-studies have shown is that key settlements policies often lack the flexibility to alleviate particular situations of need in non-selected villages. Obviously, if all rural settlements could achieve the right balance of population and adequate service provision at the village level, then social problems would diminish. However, it is because this ideal situation is unattainable under present financial systems that policies of concentration have been introduced. These strategies have made positive contributions in the retardment of depopulation in some remoter rural areas and in the conservation of some pressured rural settlements where further growth would have been environmentally damaging. Despite these successes, many social problems remain unsolved because of the very nature of key settlement policies. Consequently, an assessment has to be made as to whether other rural settlement strategies are more capable of dealing with these social problems, or whether improved key settlement implementation is to be the preferred planning tactic. These matters are discussed in the final chapter.

6.4   *A Political Planning Perspective*

It is argued above that the ineffectiveness of key settlement policies in both social and economic terms has been due, at least in part, to deficiencies in policy implementation and coordination. Such a conclusion is worthless without specific reference to those parts of the planning system which have served to detract from the overall efficiency and comprehensive nature of the key settlement mechanism.

Firstly, it is worthwhile reiterating at this juncture that during the 1950s and even the 1960s, key settlements were often viewed with an aura of mysticism which led to expectations of rapid results as soon as the policy was introduced. Therefore the early period of key settlement planning was dogged by inexperience and misunderstanding of the various aspects of the planned rural environment. Only with greater experience and expertise have rural planners begun to come to terms with the coordination of various planning tasks into one overall strategy. The early priority of ensuring adequate levels of service provision was emphasized to the detriment of growing problems connected with housing, employment and transport in rural areas, and consequently it was only in the 1960s that a concerted effort was made to achieve multi-role objectives in rural planning. This lack of experience and inevitable learning from mistakes may be viewed as a partial cause of early key settlement ineffectiveness.

Another factor which contributed to sub-optimum key settlement policy performance in many counties was the initial procedure for selecting key centres. More recently, key settlement selection has been on the basis of objective assessments of settlement capability and character, and consequently there has been little room for political pressure of any type in the actual selection process. However, recent choices of key settlements have often mirrored previous nominations, and the early procedures for electing key centres were neither so objective nor so fastidious. There is strong evidence to suggest that some early key settlements were chosen not on the basis of their suitability for this planning role but rather because influential personages happened to live there and were anxious that their village should continue to receive local authority investment. This is not to say that entire key settlement systems were the result of corruption or undue political pressure but it does appear that certain settlements would not have been selected for growth had not these pressures been present. These unwarranted nominations added to the problem of there being too many key settlements in many counties for the successful concentration of economic investment.

Such political pressures need not be the result of a corrupt and forceful manipulation of the planning system. It may have been that certain councillors had a detailed knowledge of conditions in their own village and were therefore able to argue more forcefully in favour of key settlement nomination than would be the case for other settlements. On the other hand, certain financial interests (particularly those associated with commerce and land ownership) are at risk in a potential situation of no-growth and it is possible to visualize the protection of these interests in the selection of key settlements.

Even considering these historical reasons for ineptness, further problems of policy implementation should be identified to explain the continuing failure of the key settlement policy to respond to changing social and economic circumstances. Two major deficiencies are important in this respect. Firstly, planners have been unable to adhere closely to planning strategies in the day-to-day decisions which represent the basic task of land use control in the rural environment. Secondly, the scope of rural planning has not been sufficiently broad to provide effective answers to problems of transport, housing, employment and services in rural areas.

In many ways, the lack of adherence to overall policy directions is understandable given the nature of our present planning system. As Wheeler (1977, 20) points out:

> it is the elected Planning Committee of the Local Authority which agrees to the policies submitted by the professional planning staff, and a change in the political composition of the elected local government may make a substantial difference to the local plans.

Broadly speaking any alternation of free enterprise and socialist ideals within Planning Committees may well have interrupted the long-term application of key settlement policies.

The relationship between District and County levels of planning can also defy the pursuance of a single-minded planning policy. Peel and Sayer (1973, 5) comment on the system whereby a planning policy is passed down from County to District level where it is often received without any analysis:

> Despite protests, the policy usually operates in the form in which it was first presented. In execution, however, the policy is often reversed in details. For example, modest developments in small villages may be recommended for refusal by the planning staff, only for the decision to be reversed in the District Planning Committee and then taken 'to dispute' with the County Planning Committee, which may agree to the development.

These administrative and political cartwheels can be most disruptive even of the most consistent of planning policies. However, when the case can be made for discretionary flexibility within the overall policy, for example with regard to housing development in non-key settlements, the two levels of planning are frequently drawn into disagreement to the disadvantage of the policy as a whole.

Further lack of coordination has been evident between various local government authorities in the provision of basic public services. There have been many instances where growth in particular key settlements has been halted for lack of adequate sewage-disposal or education facilities. In fact, very little is known about the degree of interaction between planners and the various servicing authorities. A simple recognition of the number of authorities involved in decisions being made about roads, public transport, social services, education, health, water, sewerage, housing, employment, emergency services, police, post offices and so on, gives a strong indication of the problems involved in any attempt to coordinate decision-making in the rural environment. Much more research is required in order to understand the circumstances dominating each set of decisions and the way in which these various authorities view their judgements in the light of the overall County Council policy. Peel and Sayer see divergences of policy as tacit rejections of the key settlement system, whereas MacGregor (1976, 525) adopts the opposite viewpoint and sounds a warning against the making of these important decisions by 'unelected committees without public representation'. Whether or not there have been any sinister overtones in this lack of cooperation between different departments, the inability to present a unified planning front to the problems of the rural areas has served to decrease, both conceptually and practically, the efficiency of the key settlement system.

Although the Structure Plans have heralded more effective collaborations between various public authorities, there remains a general recognition that the scope of rural planning is too narrow to provide effective answers to the problems prevalent in the countryside. The opinion that 'few planning departments are able to coordinate, for example, the social, economic and physical aspects of village planning without exceeding their terms of reference' (Moss, 1978, 123), is surely directly relevant to an assessment of key settlement policies which aims at the comprehensive planning of these very factors. How can key settlement planning be compatible with a planning system which does not allow a comprehensive approach? Wheeler (1977, 20-21) outlines this paradox:

> the implementation of development suggested in Structure, or Local Plans is generally mainly dependent on the existence of a demand for development which is not generated by the Local Authority itself, and which most frequently comes from private enterprise. If such a demand is in existence, the Local Planning Authority can influence it very strongly (though it cannot always wholly control it), if it does not exist there is relatively little the Local Planning Authority can do to induce it.

Here, then, we have one of the most important reasons why key settlements have not achieved all of the objectives required of them. The reliance on restrictive rather than positive planning in rural areas has meant that vital stages in the development of key settlements and in the spread of opportunities to their hinterlands are absent from present planning systems. What is more, the continued practice of trend planning, whereby the decisions and methods of previous years are reiterated willy-nilly, has meant that recognition of the need for experimentation in a more positive approach to planning has been a long time in coming. To fulfil its true potential, the key settlement policy should be supplemented by specific positive policies to combat specific problems. Transport and peripatetic service links between key settlement and hinterland require a positive impetus from planning authorities. The establishment of suitable small-scale housing projects and workshop employment also demand policies of attraction rather than mere permission should any application arise. These positive planning actions have begun to appear in isolated cases over the past few years but there remain imposing financial and administrative barriers which prevent any coordinated approach to planning in rural areas.

Given the constraints within which planners have been working over the past two or three decades, some merit may be recognized in their use of key settlement policies. Tangible indicators of growth have been nurtured in remoter key settlements, while considerable steps towards the conservation of certain rural environments have been taken in the more pressured areas. So far, planning priority has been directed to problems of past and present rather than future and this in itself may be meritorious. Wheeler (1977, 21) is of the opinion that 'British planners have been both sensible and correct in dealing with immediate demands as they arise, rather than in attempting to formulate models of a settlement hierarchy for which they could not be sure of implementation in the real world'. However, it would be unwise to continue the pursuance of key settlement planning without regard to its shortcomings, both intrinsic and implementative. The future problems of yesterday are a reality in today's countryside, and experience gained in the formative years of key settlements is invaluable in the decisions which have to be made concerning future policies for rural settlements.

7
Key Settlements
and the Future

7.1 *Alternative Settlement Policies*

A final stage in the process of evaluating key settlements is to
compare the performance of this policy with the planning pos-
sibilities offered by alternative strategies. The recent anti-key
settlement lobby has not been slow to propose replacement policies
on which the future planning of the countryside might be based,
and these alternatives should be closely studied to see if they entail
the potential fulfilment of objectives which the key settlement
policy for one reason or another has been unable to attain. In effect,
the key settlement system must be judged against its competitors
as well as against its own performance. Alternative suggestions
have ranged from complete dispersal of investment into every
settlement to a rigorous concentration of facilities and consequent
abandonment of many villages (figure 7.1). The most feasible of
these proposals are reviewed individually.

The village unit
The village unit concept is concerned with the supposition that
people who live and work in the countryside have a right to the
continuation and proper functioning of their villages. The village
unit is viewed as 'the viable unit on which a more stable future
society could be based' rather than 'a relic of the past, to be
preserved as a museum piece' (Venner, 1976, 39) and as such
represents a movement towards wide dispersal of resources. Peel
and Sayer (1973, 1) note that this approach requires 'the preservation, restoration or introduction as the case may be of the necessary

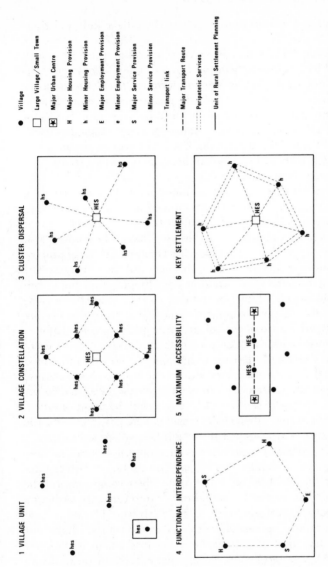

Fig. 7.1 Alternative rural settlement strategies. These diagrams are necessarily schematic as it is extremely difficult to take proper account of different settlement patterns, village sizes, types of services and infrastructure, and so on. However, they do emphasize the level of concentration or dispersal exhibited by different policy options with regard to the basic functions of rural settlement planning.

amenities, and definite steps to assist the village unit and community'.

The desire for future village viability stems from two main sources. Firstly, there remains for many people a folk image of the countryside and its settlements as forming an idyllic back-to-nature existence which must needs be preserved at all costs. Burton (1973, 185) describes the village as 'the type of community that for well over a thousand years was unquestioningly accepted as man's "natural" home'. Rural planning has in the past paid homage to dreams such as these, but rampant idealism is hardly a secure basis for the future of the countryside.

A second more practical generation of support for the retention of village units comes from those commentators who subscribe to Schumacher's philosophy of 'small is beautiful', believing that economics (and planning for that matter) should be studied 'as if people mattered'. From this group has emerged a series of proposals to ensure the survival of rural dwellers and their villages. The list of requirements is an extensive one. Employment both from small-scale modern industries and revived craft industries is to be attracted into villages to supplement the jobs accruing from a more labour-intensive form of agriculture. Adequate accommodation is to be provided with the realization that 'this involves facing up to problems of landlords getting an uneconomic return from rented houses, and of owner-occupiers without the resources to modernise their properties or keep them in good condition' (Peel and Sayer, 1973, 2). A range of services including a church, sub-post office, shop, public house, village hall, school (where possible) and basic infrastructure is also needed to sustain this village unit.

When faced with the prospect of satisfying these needs in every village it is small wonder that village unit protagonists recognize that 'with the pressures that exist today, these components of the unit will not survive or be brought back into existence without a definite policy' (Peel and Sayer, 1973, 2). It would be all too easy to dismiss these proposals as impracticable and yet the village unit approach has given rise to its own pressure group – the New Villages Association (Venner 1976) – and judging by the influence maintained over the years by the Council for the Protection of Rural England in rural planning matters, the environmental lobby for viable villages should not be discounted.

The village constellation

Many schemes have been proposed whereby small rural settlements may be linked together so that services and facilities are shared on a communal basis. Hancock (1976) has argued strongly for the abandonment of the key settlement policy with its very selective provision of opportunities for rural dwellers: 'In its place should be plotted the groups of settlements which are interrelated, first to the city regions, second to small towns and major villages' (p. 522).

The village constellation idea has its appeal. In the case-study of Warwickshire it was found that the arrangement of key settlements and hinterland parishes was not conducive to the establishment of centre-periphery linkages. There appeared to have been little attempt to recognize small-scale functional regions within the countryside and consequently planning area boundaries had little meaning when translated on the ground. The principal strength of a constellation approach is the acknowledgement of existing interrelationships wherever possible and the use of 'natural' rather than superimposed linkages between the various levels of the rural settlement hierarchy. Having established a series of constellations, the provision of housing, employment, services and community transport would be made on the basis of these settlement groups, with greater use being made of voluntary and cooperative efforts.

An integral part of this system would be for each constellation to enjoy vastly increased representation in the local political arena through strengthened parish or neighbourhood councils. In this way the better facets of rural community life may be maintained and harnessed to improve self-help provision of services and facilities.

The primary planning constraint for a series of interrelated settlements of this ilk is the high cost of service provision to every village. Hancock (1976, 523) admits that 'the broad concept of a varied constellation of villages in rural areas would be helped by the rapid development of appropriate technology for sewage disposal and, possibly, energy supply'. Were such breakthroughs to occur, then the village constellation policy might appear attractive to planners in their search for a more socially-orientated strategy for the planning of rural areas.

Cluster-dispersal
The concept of cluster-dispersal was introduced by Parry Lewis in his study of the Cambridge sub-region (Department of the Environment, 1974b). He recognized the social advantages of a dis-

persed pattern of investment whereby the idea of privileged key centres is broken down as far as possible. However, rather than advocating a policy of complete dispersal of resources at the village scale, Parry Lewis realized that clusters of villages would represent a combined population sufficient for the attraction of central service facilities and public and private investment. He therefore suggested that rural development should be based on village clusters centring around established and new rural settlements in which service and employment growth would be attracted so as to serve the entire cluster.

In theory, such a system would provide a collective population threshold equivalent to that of a key settlement while at the same time dispersing growth benefits over a wider area. The cluster-dispersal policy *per se* does not, however, provide any additional incentive for the attraction of employment or housing investment nor does it provide a more efficient settlement pattern to be served by public and community transport. Its advantages stem mainly from the freedom of choice offered by housing and service development in several locations within the cluster rather than the dogmatic centralization of development into one key centre that is integral to the key settlement structure.

Functional interdependence

The premise underlying the concept of functional interdependence is that the key settlement policy represents a complete misunderstanding of the interactions between rural settlements. Planning practitioners such as Martin (1976) suggest that the recognition of a hierarchy of centres and hinterlands within the rural settlement pattern is an erroneous one which disregards the fact that most villages, regardless of size, contribute some service or facility to the surrounding rural area.

> For these 'unique' functions, a village will have a much wider catchment area than its own residents, and people in adjoining villages, instead of going to progressively higher order and, probably, more distant centres for specialist services, may turn to neighbouring villages; to one for electrical goods, to another for furniture, to a third for shoe repairs and so on. (Martin, 1976, 80)

The importance of these interrelationships has led McLaughlin (1976a) to revive the principle of functional interdependence, whereby service, employment and residential opportunities would be spread over a system of perhaps five or six villages or village sub-systems. Once again, such a system would generate a collective population threshold sufficient to support reasonable service levels, only in this case each village would be encouraged to contribute one particular function to the group.

A question mark arises here over the recognition of functionally interdependent settlement systems. In theory, the concept of each part contributing to the whole is one which holds out some hope for the future viability of small settlements. In practice, however, it may be difficult to differentiate between individual interdependent systems of settlements, and yet this would be a necessary task if this concept were to form the basis of planning for all rural areas.

Maximum accessibility
Many policy proposals have incorporated greater degrees of resource concentration than were possible even under the key settlement system. The most reactionary of these suggestions involves the abandonment of large tracts of countryside as being unviable under present economic circumstances. Various levels of settlement relinquishment have been mooted but perhaps the most acceptable of this group is the maximum accessibility approach, based on the German model, which places a major emphasis on accessibility between settlements. Under this system those rural villages which are located on or near the seemingly permanent transport routes between urban centres will receive public investment since they are considered viable settlements. A corollary of this rationalization is the withdrawal of support from those settlements in more peripheral locations.

Rural settlement policies advocating further concentration of resources are unlikely to find favour with the heightened social conscience exhibited by today's rural planning. Even though the maximum accessibility proposal does offer high levels of opportunity for rural people living in supported settlements, the idea of allowing the remoter settlements to become the domain of the affluent minority (which has already occurred in many locations) will not be given official sanction without a great deal of public outcry.

Some preliminary conclusions
These various alternative proposals represent a continuum of policy between the two poles of concentration and dispersal. It would be inappropriate to attempt a critique of each at this juncture, simply

because these approaches warrant individual studies and therefore cannot be adequately described in the short space available here. However, several points of comparison should be made between these concepts and the key settlement policy in order to discover whether the key settlement inadequacies highlighted above are due to the policy itself or to the manner of its implementation.

The first striking conclusion to be drawn from this list of policy alternatives concerns the pressured rural areas. It was concluded from the Warwickshire case-study that stunting the growth of sizeable settlements was an inadequate method of curbing urban growth in the countryside. Consequent to this conclusion is the recommendation that growth could be spread more evenly amongst appropriate rural settlements where an impetus for suitable development had previously been established. The overall object of conserving high-quality environments would remain under this dispersal. However, most suggestions for alternative rural settlement policies advocate the provision of at least some new facilities at village level rather than the establishment of linkages from a growth centre which would be more in keeping with conservation objectives. This is not to say that small pressured settlements should remain sterile. Specific policies are needed to deal with the specific problems created by lack of housing, transport and employment opportunities, but it would appear to make environmental as well as economic sense to concentrate facilities and use these to provide opportunities for small settlements.

Having said this, several further points applicable to both the pressured and remote situations may be made concerning the nature of an appropriate framework for the planning of rural settlements. Firstly, it should be stressed that 'it is doubtful if the village has ever been a self-sufficient unit in social or economic terms' (MacGregor, 1976, 524). However many facilities are located in each village, some linkages with higher-order centres remain a necessity. Therefore the degree of policy alternatives open to the planner refer to the degree of concentration to be adopted rather than whether concentration should take place at all. On the other hand, high degrees of rationalization (for example the maximum accessibility concept) do not give sufficient dispersal to meet the social and political demands of the planning system. Evidently some mid-continuum compromise is required.

The village constellation approach offers one form of compromise between dispersal and concentration. An exploitation of preexisting linkages between rural settlements rather than the superimposition of unworkable and artificial centre-hinterland areas would appear to be a step forward towards sensible rural policies. Indeed, the interrelated nature of settlement systems has been stressed in both case-study analyses. It has been particularly evident that rural settlements dominated by urban centres should be linked into that centre's planning system, rather than be subject to some obscure key settlement in the opposite direction. Many of the difficulties encountered with the establishment of an overall perception of the key settlement policy have been due to the inappropriate designation of the spheres of influence around key centres.

Given this objective of interrelated settlement systems, the basic decision to be made by rural planners concerns the nature of the systems themselves. Should each system revolve around single growth points, clustered growth points, or functionally interdependent and mutually supporting groups of villages? It is obvious that the efficacy of single key centres will depend on the number and spacing of the settlements selected. For example, the Devon policy appeared to have named too many key settlements, leading to a thin spread of investment which in turn discriminated against the small centres in the most needy areas. On the other hand, the policy in Warwickshire is likely to cause hardship to thriving settlements because the designation of key status has been too limited.

With these problems of key settlement policy implementation, the concept of village clusters presents an attractive proposition. On the surface, such a policy offers a share of development to a greater number of constituent settlements along with a greater spatial distribution of any growth that occurs. Indeed, it is evident that such policies have some potential, particularly in the remotest of rural areas where single settlements are often not large enough to create an impetus for growth. But there are disadvantages inherent in a dispersed growth area, however tightly knit, as compared with one single growth settlement. For instance, the economies of scale gained from the building of a large number of dwellings or one discrete sewerage system would be lost if investment were divided between several locations. Also, transportation difficulties, already crucial in rural areas, would be magnified if radial tranport routes had also to link several settlements in the centre of the growth area. Finally, the investment already placed in single growth settlements would be one compelling reason not to abandon those settlements in favour of the promotion of growth in entirely different locations.

In one sense, the choice between one key settlement and a growth area of a few smaller settlements is academic, in that we have seen that the fundamental rural problems occur in the settlements outside the range of rural growth centres. Therefore, policies based on key settlements and on functional interdependence or clustering of smaller settlements share not only the problems of attracting employment and service growth but also the problems of ensuring that the benefits and opportunities derived from this growth are spread to as many parts of the rural settlement hierarchy as is practicable. If these problems are to be given priority in the future, then it seems appropriate to return to the original concept of a key settlement policy as an overview of the settlement pattern as a whole, laying special emphasis on the relationships between the key settlement and other settlements served by it.

7.2   *A Future Rationale for Key Settlements*

There would appear to be two basic reasons why the key settlement framework should not be discarded at this point in time. Firstly, some counties have spent twenty-five years in building up a pattern of rural service centres whose fullest potential will only be realized if these relationships between centre and hinterland are fostered and strengthened. McLaughlin (1976b, 57) argues that key settlement policies 'are in danger of sacrificing long-term improvement for short-term efficiency'. However, the short-term stringencies of the key settlement policy's treatment of small rural settlements may be converted to longer-term benefits if the policy is used as a framework of linkages through which the levels of opportunities in non-key settlements are improved.

The second recommendation for the retention of some kind of key settlement framework stems from the evidence produced from this study. Clearly, some physical, economic and even partial social success has already been achieved through the use of key settlement policies. Therefore, if this framework can be socially strengthened by a package of specific policies for specific rural problems, then economic advantage may be retained alongside social and community advancement in small settlements. There is still a need for a pragmatic approach to rural planning. Moseley (1977, 32) stresses that 'the public expenditure bubble has burst and that the state cannot continue to spend its way out of trouble'.

However, there would seem to be little reason why economic pragmatism should not be linked to a new form of 'initiative planning' in rural areas. Key settlement policies so far have only completed half of their task, that is the establishment of centralized growth. In order to attain the second objective, namely the democratic spread of these benefits, planners should liaise closely with authorities such as the Council for Small Industries in Rural Areas and grasp the initiative by producing flexible but specialized rural sub-system policies.

Specific policies for specific problems
Any future use of key settlement policies will need to recognize that specialized planning remedies are required within the growth centre framework. McLaughlin (1976a, 159) views rural settlements as a human body wherein 'employment opportunities represent the heart that keeps the body alive and the transport system the veins that carry the blood throughout the body'. This analogy could be extended to include rural housing and population, which form the various limbs of the body (with differing degrees of mobility), and rural services, which provide nourishment for both the body and the mind of rural settlements. This use of the systems analogue model serves to emphasize the interrelated nature of these sub-systems and, although individualistic remedial measures are suggested here, it should be remembered that the various facets of rural life have to be interlinked in any planned rural system.

The problems associated with *rural transport* are not new. Moseley (1977, 32) admits that 'for twenty years official committees and academic researchers have described the decline of public transport and the demise of rural jobs and services which combine to pose real difficulties of accessibility for rural residents who lack a car'. However, the 1970s have seen a number of major research projects designed to produce some answers to these problems (e.g. the studies by Moseley, 1977; Clout *et al.*, 1973; Department of the Environment, 1971b, 1971c), and two major points have been established. Firstly, it has been suggested that the functional and locational scope of conventional stage bus services should be determined. For example, these services could sensibly be restricted to small town and key settlement interconnections. Then a concurrent effort could be made to establish a 'low-cost package of policies' (Moseley, 1977, 34) which would be better suited to the needs of small rural settlements. These would include:

(1) The relaxation of route licensing systems so that fare-paying passengers may be carried by private vehicles.
(2) The encouragement and organization of community minibus schemes.
(3) The wider usage of school bus facilities.
(4) The revision of post-bus routing and timing so as to make the carrying of passengers a practical proposition.
(5) The broader-scale establishment of welfare and hospital car schemes.

Experimentation with these themes has produced some success in solving the problems of rural accessibility. However, a comprehensive scheme of community transport is required for each and every hinterland rural area. This in turn dictates some recognized organizational structure, whether this be part of the County or District authority's duties or else the duty of a specially employed community transport officer in each area. If such a comprehensive system of community transport could be brought about, then many of the rural social problems highlighted by policies of concentration would be appeased.

A second sector where unique difficulties are encountered is *employment*. There would appear to be two strands to the problem of much-needed new employment in the rural areas. The first concerns the attraction of sizeable firms into centralized locations. Spooner (1972) outlines the advantages and disadvantages of the peripheral rural location as a possible destination for migrating enterprises. He argues that the problems associated with the sparse population distribution, the lack of services and the distance from market contacts can be overcome because of the environmental attractions and lack of economic social and institutional rigidities displayed by the rural areas. However, he adds the proviso that centres of population, such as they are, provide the best employment locations. Gilg (1976, 166) agrees with this assessment in his verdict that 'within the rural regions as a whole, however, employment could be made to grow quite markedly by vigorously pursuing the type of approach employed by the Highlands and Islands Development Board, and by concentrating investment in key centres'. Thus, it seems clear that this broad-scale approach to employment attraction should continue, with additional efforts being made to attract new jobs, and perhaps the widening of emphasis to include tertiary and quaternary types of employment. This expansion of the scope of rural employment would appear to be a salient feature of any new planning approach. So far, undue reliance has been placed on directing manufacturing industry into rural locations, whereas such enterprises as professional services, research and development and all-year-round formalized recreation and tourism facilities are ideally placed within the rural environment, and could make a significant contribution to rural employment.

The second strand of the rural employment problem concerns the promotion of small-scale workshops at the village level in order to provide small amounts of new employment in rural settlements. It should be stressed at this point that not all villagers are in favour of any form of growth. 'Our village is quiet and peaceful and we want it to stay that way' is a comment typical of many replies received from parish clerks. Furthermore, where social needs do indicate a desire for small-scale workshops, the physical planning standards in villages must be maintained. MacGregor (1976, 526) stresses that 'if we are to have workplaces in villages they must be very carefully sited, with strict controls on their expansion'.

While the need for localized rural employment in many settlements is clearcut, the mechanism through which such enterprises are to be encouraged is less well-established. Peel and Sayer (1973, 19) suggest the establishment of government assistance in the form of 'tax reliefs, allowing businesses with a small turnover, whether companies or not, a small amount of untaxed profit and perhaps a subsidised credit system to assist in capital works and the provision of starting capital'. The Development Commission, and particularly the Council for Small Industries in Rural Areas (CoSIRA), are able to provide the organizational and financial facilities to aid these small-scale workshops and businesses. CoSIRA have already been instrumental in promoting a range of rural activities, from the building of advance factories to the granting of financial and advisory aid to small-scale entrepreneurs. However, with a recent increase in spending power, this organization is now able to play a major part in the encouragement of small-scale businesses in rural areas. It is to be hoped that the pressured rural areas will also form part of CoSIRA's new horizons and that planners in all rural areas will be instrumental in establishing the organizational environment in which CoSIRA can work to its fullest effect.

The problems of providing adequate *housing* for the local needs of small rural settlements again require a positive planning response. No single policy can provide universal appeasement of housing difficulties, since the social and political decisions to be enforced as part of housing strategies will differ in the pressured and remote rural contexts. In pressured rural areas it is not only the smaller settlements where growth is being prohibited. The Warwickshire case-study showed clear examples of the problems associated with stunting growth in settlements of, for example, over 1000 population. It may well be that even with rigid growth targets to keep to, political pressures will be brought to bear for additional housing to aid the continued growth of these settlements, if at a moderate scale. Such a decision would be part and parcel of an overall policy because flexibility providing for housing development in non-selected settlements would have a dramatic effect on rural population growth projections.

At a lower level, several individual schemes have been proposed to counteract the lack of housing for local people in both pressured and remote rural settlements. Much rural housing research is currently being undertaken and so the forthcoming results should provide invaluable input into local-scale policy formation. However, an impressive appraisal of housing in rural areas has recently been produced by the Community Council of Devon (Scott-Miller, 1976). This outlines several less conventional means with which local councils can promote or encourage an increased housing stock in rural areas to cope with local need. These suggestions are summarized below as they contain the essence of any future flexible housing policy in rural areas.

(1) The council can require builders to construct a range of dwelling types through its powers as a planning authority.

(2) Compulsory purchase and Community Land legislation allow controls to minimize the land-element cost in house prices.

(3) The council can plan for there to be a controlled supply of land at current-use value available for residential development.

(4) Councils may build dwellings to be sold to local needy families at cost price. Concomitant easy mortgage terms could be arranged.

(5) The council can enter into more short-term letting agreements to ensure that houses do not stand empty unnecessarily.

(6) Councils should regard rehabilitation of existing property as an integral part of an authority's housing programme.

(7) Starter-home, shell-home, equity-sharing and self-build schemes may be appropriate in rural settlements.

(8) Even within a reduced private sector, councils can encourage local housing associations and societies to provide an alternative source of rented accommodation.

Many of these suggestions entail increased public expenditure and, therefore, particular schemes should be suited to particular needs. It is again the case that not all rural communities wish to see further housing growth within their village. However, it is apparent that the implementation of schemes such as these where the need prevails would counteract some out-migration of young local families without necessarily prejudicing the overall objectives of a framework of investment concentration.

The final rural sub-system where specific policies could reduce social discrimination in non-key settlements is in the field of *service provision*. Key settlement policies have generally failed to establish outward linkages so as to spread the benefits of centrally located opportunities. Two basic methods of linkage are available to the planner. The first has been dealt with under the heading of transport. Should a comprehensive system of community transport be a practical proposition in rural areas, then the centralized services in key settlements would be more accessible to the smaller hinterland settlements.

However, linkages may also be achieved centrifugally through the mobilization of various services. The travelling shop has been a regular component of life in many of the smaller rural settlements, and has met with varying viability in different areas. As a means of providing 'last-minute' or 'additional' food items, the itinerant trader continues to have a regular role to play in the countryside. However, as the only source of regular food items the travelling shop has obvious limitations concerning the range, quality and price of goods stocked.

Greater promise is offered by the mobilization of public services. Moseley (1977) includes a system such as this in his suggested low-cost package of policies for low-access areas. He proposes 'an emphasis on various public sector peripatetic services clustering together in time and in space (e.g. mobile chiropodist, family planning clinic, library, post office and "play-school bus" meeting every Tuesday afternoon on a certain village green)' (p. 34). To this list could be added the mobile doctor's surgery and even the mobile bank, which has been the subject of successful experimentation in the North Yorkshire Moors and the Scottish Highlands and Islands. Once again, the establishment of this mobile service market is dependent on a preconceived organizational system, and this is a form of 'initiative planning' which will be a new venture for most rural areas.

MacGregor (1976) reports on an educational experiment in

Oxfordshire whereby five village schools were served by one head-master and one set of specialist staff moving around from school to school. Similar experiments have also been taking place with team ministries in the churches. This type of alternative should be explored as a further method by which various services can be brought to outlying settlements. If the mobile public service market can be allied with other itinerant services, then some of the benefits accruing to the key settlements can be spread to the rural hinterland.

Key settlements: a practical approach

Ideally, a broad-scale key settlement policy, when allied to these specific policies for specific problems, would form a logical and workable planning response to the difficulties associated with living in the countryside. Economies of scale would be generated for the bulk of investment in housing and infrastructure, while discretionary flexibility would allow situations of local need to be alleviated. However, critics of the key settlement policy are likely to argue that if the financial and manpower resources are available to support these specific policies, then a more dispersed pattern of investment should be considered. Reasoning such as this can lead to rural planning securing a permanent location between the devil and the deep blue sea. When an increase in experience, administrative capacity or financial allocation allows an improvement to existing policies, this very increase will always be seen by some as the chance to raise planning aims and objectives and initiate a different policy to meet these more demanding requirements. In this way, no policy is given the sustained opportunity and resource back-up needed to achieve its goals. This is not to say that an established policy *per se* is the appropriate one for use in any situation, but merely that the switching from one framework to another should be supported by strong if not undeniable evidence that the in-coming strategy is more appropriate than its predecessor.

In the light of these comments it is difficult to be totally objective in the assessment of various future rural planning strategies. However, it is obvious that at the local level there are opportunities for progressive changes in the planning system which would not detract from any likely future planning framework for the countryside. The collective efforts in the fields of transport, employment, housing and services (described above) can bring about positive improvements to village life, and the attainment of these objectives is not beyond the reach of present planning resources.

Two areas of responsibility should be officially reviewed as soon as possible. Firstly, the administration of local-scale rural planning schemes could be coordinated by a community or neighbourhood officer who would mould local authority and community efforts into a comprehensive scheme of facilities for his parish or group of parishes. This officer would need to be specially appointed to serve as a link between the parish councils and higher-order administrative bodies. His or her full-time task would be to continue at the local level the type of work begun by countryside officers at the county level. Thus far, the lack of a coordinating factor in local-scale rural planning has been one of the principal factors in the continuation of 'experiments' in rural transport, housing and employment rather than comprehensive working schemes to aid these basic elements of rural living.

The second factor for review concerns finance. In some ways, the more successful these special policies for rural areas are, the greater the financial cost to be incurred. It is not enough to merely state that money should be found from one source or another, particularly when it is realized that there is unlikely to be a central or local government spending spree in rural areas. However, positive planning measures will incur additional costs, and even if these measures are restricted to the employment of community officers, some reallocation or improvement of rural resources must take place. Financial resources are most likely to be gleaned either from a slightly increased central government contribution through organizations such as the Development Commission, or from a gradual reallocation process within the local government system. For example, there is little evidence to show that salaries cannot be transferred from overmanned local authority departments in order to establish community officer posts. Similar redistributions in other sectors are possible if the case for rural area investment is made sufficiently strongly.

The time has come when academics and planning practitioners alike must advocate a practical approach to problem-solving in rural areas. Lobbying for increased financial focus on the countryside must continue, but meanwhile we must look to relatively low-cost packages to secure the best possible advantage from planning activities. Thus far, no real evidence has been advanced to demonstrate that alternative planning frameworks would provide a more practical or successful approach to rural planning than would the key settlement system. Therefore, until such evidence is brought forward, and until financial stringencies are lifted, the establishment of two-way links between growth in the key settlements and natural increase in the rural hinterland appears to be the most likely method by which the long-term stability of rural areas in general, and village life in particular, can be assured. Any thought of abandoning the key settlement framework at this point in time could be akin to throwing out the baby with the bathwater.

7.3   *Epilogue: A Reappraisal of Policy Evaluation Methods*

This study has merely paved the way for discussion and action on the question of future planning strategies in rural areas. The intention of the study was to make some assessment of the advantages and disadvantages of the key settlement policy as seen from its actual implementation in two differing types of rural areas. Such an evaluation has been attempted with the conclusion that the key settlement policy framework, when accompanied by specific policies to deal with individual rural problems, would appear to be a reasonable future approach for the planning of rural settlements. However, this conclusion was reached by a process of broad-scale comparisons between policy alternatives, and was constrained by a situation where the only detailed evidence of policy performance available for assessment was that relating to key settlements. Consequently, the objectivity and accuracy of the overall conclusions is low-powered. What this study has shown is that there is a glaring need for some kind of methodology whereby various rural planning policy alternatives may be evaluated in terms of both economic and social factors. It is obvious that present policies are weighed up in terms of exchequer costs rather than personal, social or opportunity costs. Therefore, policies of concentration are favoured without regard to the fact that the savings made by the public purse are simply passed on to rural residents in the form of increased travel and living costs.

Some attempts at the comprehensive costing of alternative patterns of development have already been made. The classic forerunner in this respect was the South Atcham Study (Warford, 1969), which dealt with the provision of water services. More recently, the North Walsham Area Study (Norfolk County Council, 1976) measured the relative costs of concentrated and dispersed housing development in Norfolk. The general conclusion reached by this study was that policies of concentration are less costly in both capital and revenue terms than policies of dispersal. However, the study suggested that a number of non-monetary costs and benefits were not amenable to quantification but that there were strong social arguments in favour of accepting the higher cost of dispersal. The difficulties involved in this type of evaluation exercise are highlighted by the study's final conclusion which states that

> for those who would prefer the closer and more personal atmosphere of village life the Dispersal strategy would be the most desirable, while for those others who value greater independence and a wider variety of organizations and people, the Concentration strategy would be best. (para. 87)

How, then, should social factors be included in the policy evaluation process? At present, rural planners appear to be restricted to the type of mutual compatability matrix shown in figure 7.2. Here various settlement policy options are seen in terms of their ramifications on rural sectors such as employment and housing and on the planning system itself, particularly as regards finance. Policy decisions are made in the light of this matrix, which therefore acts as an aid but not a positive guide to the most appropriate selection. In the Rutland example, little attention is paid to social issues, although it should be realized that this matrix represents a simplification of planning processes for the benefit of public understanding.

Another example of a matrix approach is the attempt by Bather et al. (1976) to carry out a development potential analysis on alternative growth scenarios contained within the West Berkshire Structure Plan (figure 7.3). Their policy impact matrix was again able to isolate social arguments but failed to include social factors into the analysis.

Several other urban- and regional-scale techniques are available to the rural planner in his quest for a balanced assessment of policy alternatives. Basic cost-benefit methods have been refined to provide a more reasonable orientation towards the goals and objectives of planning. Hill's (1972) 'goals achievement matrix', Lichfield's (1975) 'planning balance sheet', and Schimpeler and Grecco's (1972) 'systems evaluation by community goals and objectives' represent the methodological progressions which have been available to planners for a number of years. Considerable potential may be foreseen from extensions of the threshold analysis technique (Kozlowski and Hughes, 1972), and other more quantitative tools

	Settlement Policy	Population	Employment
1	Concentration (Concentrating further growth in no more than 4/5 centre)	✓	✓
2	Concentration/new village. (As above but with much of the growth going to a new village.)	Difficult if growth restricted because of limited amount of development to distribute.	✓
3	Sub-Centres (Development in a number of medium-sized villages rather than the larger settlements.)	Difficult to implement if population growth restricted as amounts of growth allowed in each sub-centre small.	Inconsistent with increased commuting i.e. limit job growth to existing firms not in sub-centres. Current pattern difficult for same reasons.
4	Quality areas (Careful development in conservation villages to create an attractive environment for new homes.)	Difficult if growth encouraged as scale of development makes sensitive approach difficult, as does no population control as growth levels uncertain.	Inconsistent with job balance and reducing commuting i.e. employees scattered and job growth unacceptable in many villages. Difficult to attract sufficient jobs.
5	Dispersal (Would seek to disperse development among a large number of villages.)	Incompatible with restricting population growth and probably difficult to achieve unless population growth encouraged.	Incompatible with job balance and reduced commuting; inconsistent with population/job match because labour and facilities scattered.
6	Social policy (Concentrate most growth in the larger settlements but allow some small developments in declining villages for social reasons.)	Incompatible with encouraging population growth which would make the social element hard to implement.	As with Quality Areas policy.

Fig. 7.2 Mutual compatability of rural settlement policies. After Leicestershire County Council (1975)

Housing	Movement	Recreation	Finance
✓	Inconsistent with concentration on roads as would encourage congestion i.e. car's advantage is freedom of movement.	Inconsistent with policy of major development which would encourage more broadly distributed growth.	Trend possible but some new investment required and change in service priorities may be necessary.
✓	✓	As above.	Trend unacceptable – considerable new investment, especially private, required, or larger proportion of County budget.
✓	Inconsistent with private transport extreme as some public transport would be needed to serve these areas.	✓	Trend probably unacceptable – limited new investment required; change in service priorities and more private investment likely.
More Council housing could help the effective control of development standards.	As above.	Inconsistent with restricted or limited development around Reservoir i.e. quality area. Difficult to implement if major recreation development is encouraged.	Trend probably unacceptable – limited new investment required – change in service priorities necessary and some more private investment.
Inconsistent with increasing Council housing as this group has lower mobility i.e. negates advantage of dispersal.	Unacceptable with either public transport choice.	Incompatible with restricted development or limited development as dispersal would encourage development in a large number of villages.	Trend unacceptable – considerable new investment likely to be needed, particularly from private sector.
Reduction incompatible and trend unlikely as more council housing might be needed to implement the social policies.	Probably incompatible with either private transport choice as reasonable bus services would be essential.	Inconsistent with major development as this would make social element difficult to fulfil due to general growth pressures.	Trend may be acceptable but change in service priorities probably required.

POLICY
IMPACT
MATRIX

POLICY AREAS	POLICY OPTIONS	PROBLEMS	Manufacturing industry in urban areas has shortage of skilled workers
Policies towards manufacturing industry	Restrictive	1	□ 4 9 14
	Less restrictive	2	△ 4 9 14
	Promotional	3	● 6
Location of new manufacturing industry	Main Centre	4	□ 1 9 14
	Expanded village	5	△ 3
	Key villages	6	⬤ 3 12
	Satellite settlements	7	● 3 12
	Secondary centre	8	△ 3
Public transport	Improve	9	□ 4
	Maintain	10	●
	Decrease	11	⬤ 4
Scale of growth in rural settlements	Large scale	12	⬤ 3 6
	Environmental capacity	13	● 3 6
	Natural growth	14	□ 4 9

High detrimental impact (worse)   ⬤
Low detrimental impact (bad)   ●
Low beneficial impact (good)   △
High beneficial impact (better)   □
No discernable impact   blank

Fig. 7.3 Policy impact matrix. After Bather *et al*. (1976)

Workers in rural areas experience difficulty in getting employment	Environmental damage caused by growth in rural settlements	No spare capacity at rural dewage works
△ 6 9 12	□ 4	△ 4
△ 6 9 12	• 6 12	• 6 12
□ 6 9 12	● 6	● 6
• 9	□ 14	△ 14
△ 9	● 3	● 3
□ 3 9 12	● 3 12	● 3 12
△ 9 12	• 3 12	● 3 12
• 9 12	△ 1	△ 1
□ 6	□ 4	
•	△	
● 4	•	
□ 3 6	● 3 6	● 3 6
△ 1 6 9	△ 1	• 3 6
•	□ 1	△ 1 4

The impact of the policy option is increased
if taken in conjunction with policy option 9 etc.

such as potential surface analysis may well provide the foundation on which an objective policy assessment method may be built.

Wilson (1974, 351) isolates the three crucial problems which have so far prevented the acceptance of a universal method for policy selection: 'first, to ensure that the indicators are adequate measures of impact; second, to measure impact on different groups of people and organizations who are affected; and third, to weight different indicators so that they can be combined into a single measure'. Thus far, the complex nature of these problems has dictated that the techniques mentioned above cannot individually provide a comprehensive evaluation of alternative policies for rural areas. It may well be that some combination of these and other methods could provide the basis for a research project designed to effect this evaluation. Clearly, such a project is a vital prerequisite for any further progress in the discussion of future planning policies in rural areas.

Bibliography

Allen, K. and Hermansen, T. (1968) 'Economic growth – regional problems and growth centres'. In EFTA, 1968, *Regional Policy in EFTA: An Examination of the Growth Centre Idea*, Oliver & Boyd, Edinburgh.

An Foras Forbartha (1971) *The Application of Geographical Techniques to Physical Planning*, An Foras Forbartha, Dublin.

Ash, M. (1976) 'Time for change in rural settlement policy'. *Town and Country Planning*, 44, 528-31.

Ashby, Q.W. (1939) 'The effects of urban growth in the countryside'. *Sociological Review*, 31, 345-69.

Ashton, J. and Long, W.H. (1972) (eds) *The Remoter Rural Areas of Britain*, Oliver & Boyd, Edinburgh.

Ayton, J.B. (1976) 'Structure planning for rural area'. Paper presented to the Conference of the Institute of British Geographers.

Ayton, J.B. (1976b) 'Rural settlement policy: problems and conflicts'. In P.J. Drudy (ed.), 1976, *Regional and Rural Development*, Alpha Academic, Chalfont St Giles.

Bailey, J. (1975) *Social Theory for Planning*, Routledge, London.

Barr, J. (1969) 'Durham's murdered villages'. *New Society*, 340, 523-5.

Bather, N.J., Williams, C.M. and Sutton, A. (1976) *Strategic Choice in Practice: The West Berkshire Structure Plan Experience*, Dept Geog., Univ. Reading, Geog. Papers no. 50.

Berry, B.J.L. (1967) *Market Centres and Retail Distribution*, McGraw-Hill, New York.

242   *Key Settlements in Rural Areas*

Berry, B.J.L. (1970) 'Labour market participation and regional potential'. *Growth and Change*, 1, 3-10.
Berry, B.J.L. and Garrison, W.L. (1958) 'The functional bases of the central place hierarchy'. *Economic Geography*, 34, 145-54.
Berry, B.J.L. and Neils, E. (1969) 'Location, size and shape of cities as influenced by environmental factors: the urban environment unit at large'. In H.S. Perloff (ed.), 1969, *The Quality of the Urban Environment*, Johns Hopkins Press, Baltimore.
Bertrand, Y. (1970) 'Aspects de la diffusion du développement dans un cadre regional à partir d'implantations industrielles récentes'. *Bulletin de conjoncture regionale*, 15, 1-2.
Best, R.H. (1965) 'Recent changes and future prospects of land use in England and Wales'. *Geographical J.*, 131, 1-12.
Best, R.H. and Champion, A.G. (1970) 'Regional conversions of agricultural land to urban use in England and Wales, 1945-67'. *Trans. I.B.G.*, 49, 15-32.
Best, R.H. and Rogers, A.W. (1973) *The Urban Countryside*, Faber, London.
Bielckus, C.L., Rogers, A.W. and Wibberley, G.P. (1972) *Second Homes in England and Wales*. Wye College Land Use Studies no. 11.
Blowers, A. (1972) 'The declining villages of County Durham'. In Open University, 1972. *Social Geography*, Open University Press, Bletchley.
Bonham-Carter, V. (1951) *The English Village*, Penguin, Harmondsworth.
Bracey, H.E. (1952) *Social Provision in Rural Wiltshire*, Methuen, London.
Bracey, H.E. (1953) 'Towns as rural service centres: an index of centrality with special reference to Somerset'. *Trans. I.B.G.*, 19, 95-105.
Bracey, H.E. (1956) 'A rural component of centrality applied to six southern counties in the United Kingdom'. *Economic Geography*, 32, 38-50.
Bracey, H.E. (1958) 'Some aspects of rural depopulation in the United Kingdom'. *Rural Sociology*, 23, 385-91.
Bracey, H.E. (1962) 'English central villages'. In K. Norborg (ed.), 1962, *I.G.U. Symposium, Urban Geography*, I.G.U., Lund.
Bracey, H.E. (1970) *People and the Countryside*, Routledge, London.

Brush, J.E. and Bracey, H.E. (1955) 'Rural service centres in South-western Wisconsin and Southern England'. *Geographical Review*, 45, 559–69.

Burton, S.H. (1973) *Devon Villages*, Hale, London.

Bylund, E. (1972) 'Growth centre and administrative area problems within the framework of Swedish location policy'. In A.R. Kulinski (ed.), 1972, *Growth Poles and Growth Centres in Regional Planning*, Mouton, Paris.

Cambridgeshire C.C. (1954) *County Development Plan*.

Cambridgeshire C.C. (1966) 'Cambridgeshire: a rural planning policy and its implementation'. *Official Architecture and Planning*, 29, 1126-41.

Cambridgeshire C.C. (1968) *Development Plan Review*.

Cambridgeshire Joint Town Planning Committee (1934) *Cambridgeshire Regional Planning Report*.

Carol, H. (1966) *Geographic Identification of Regional Growth Centres and Development Regions in Southern Ontario*, Dept. of Economics and Development, Univ. Province of Ontario, Toronto.

Carruthers, I. (1957) 'A classification of service centres in England and Wales'. *Geographical J.*, 123, 371–86.

Carter, H. (1972) *The Study of Urban Geography*, Edward Arnold, London.

Carter, H. and Davies, W.K.D. (eds.) (1970) *Urban Essays: Studies in the Geography of Wales*, Edward Arnold, London.

Centre for Urban Studies (1964) *Symposium of the Centre for Urban Studies*, Macgibbon & Kee, London.

Champion, A.G. (1974) 'An estimate of the changing extent and distribution of urban land in England and Wales, 1950-70'. Centre for Environmental Studies Research Paper 10.

Cherry, G.E. (ed.) (1976) *Rural Planning Problems*, Hill, London.

Cheshire C.C. (1959) *County Development Plan*.

Christakis, A.N. (1975) 'Towards a symbiotic appreciation of the morphology of human settlements'. *Ekistics*, 40, 449-63.

Christaller, W. (trans. C.W. Baskin) (1966) *Central Places in Southern Germany*, Prentice/Hall, Englewood Cliffs, N.J.

Clawson, M. (1966) 'Factors and forces affecting the optimum future rural settlement pattern in the United States'. *Economic Geography*, 42, 283-93,

Clawson, M. (1968) *Policy Directions For U.S. Agriculture*, Resources for the Future Inc., Baltimore.

Cloke, P.J. (1977a) 'An index of rurality for England and Wales'. *Regional Studies*, 11(1), 31-46.

Cloke, P.J. (1977b) 'In defence of key settlement policies'. *The Village*, 32, 7-11.

Cloke, P.J. (1977c) 'The use of key settlement policies in the planning of rural areas'. Unpub. PhD thesis, Univ. London.

Cloke, P.J. (1978) 'Changing patterns of urbanization in the rural areas of England and Wales, 1961-71'. *Regional Studies*, 12. 603–17.

Clout, H.D. (1972) *Rural Geography – an Introductory Survey*, Pergamon, Oxford.

Clout, H.D., Hollis, G.E. and Munton, R.J.C. (1973) *A Study of Public Transport in Norfolk*, Dept Geog., Univ. Coll. London, Occ. Paper no. 18.

Community Council of Devon (1976) *Key Settlements in the Exeter and Plymouth Sub-Regional Areas*, internal report.

Cornwall C.C. (1969) *First Review of County Development Plan.*

Courtney, D.S. (1972) *The Newfoundland Resettlement Program: a Case Study in Spatial Reorganisation and Growth Centre Strategy*, Dept Geog., Univ. Newfoundland.

Coventry City Council, Solihull County Borough Council and Warwickshire County Council (1971) *Coventry-Solihull-Warwickshire: a Strategy for the Sub-Region*.

Cumberland C.C. (1955) *County Development Plan*.

Cumberland C.C. (1964) *First Review of County Development Plan*.

Cumbria Countryside Conference (1976) Press release.

D'Abbs, P. (1975) *North Devon 1966-1974 – Aspects of Social and Economic Change*, Community Council of Devon, Exeter.

Darwent, D.F. (1969) 'Growth poles and growth centres in regional planning – a review'. *Environment and Planning*, 1, 5-32.

Davidson, J. and Wibberley, G.P. (1977) *Planning and the Rural Environment*. Pergamon, Oxford.

Davies, W.K.D. and Lewis, C.R. (1970) 'Regional Structures in Wales: two studies of connectivity'. In H. Carter and W.K.D. Davies (eds.), 1970, *Urban Essays: Studies in the Geography of Wales*, Edward Arnold, London.

Department of the Environment (1971a) 'The nature of rural areas of England and Wales'. D.o.E. internal working paper.

Department of the Environment (1971b) *Study of Rural Transport in Devon*, H.M.S.O., London.

Department of the Environment (1971c) *Study of Rural Transport in West Suffolk*, H.M.S.O., London.

Department of the Environment (1972) 'The nature of small towns of England and Wales'. D.o.E. internal working paper.

Department of the Environment (1974a) *Rural Transport in Devon*.

Report by the Steering Group.

Department of the Environment (1974b) *Study of the Cambridge Sub-Region*, H.M.S.O., London.

Devon C.C. (1953) *County Development Plan*.

Devon C.C. (1964) *County Development Plan — First Review*.

Devon C.C. (1967-74) *Annual Survey of Settlement Pattern*.

Devon C.C. (1970) *County Development Plan — Second Review*.

Devon C.C. (1977) *County Structure Plan — Report of the Survey*.

Devon C.C. (1978) *County Structure Plan — Draft Written Statement*.

Dickinson, R.E. (1932) 'The distribution and functions of the smaller urban settlements of East Anglia'. *Geography*, 17, 19-31.

Dickinson, R.E. (1942) 'The social basis of physical planning, I and II'. *Sociological Review*, 34, 51-67 and 165-82.

Dorset C.C. (1965) *West Hants/Bournemouth/East Dorset Land Use Transportation Study*.

Dorset C.C. (1972) *Lythchett Matravers — Village Policy Report and Plan*.

Drake, M.M., McLoughlin, B., Thompson, R. and Thornley, J. (1975) *Aspects of Structure Planning in Britain*, Centre for Environmental Studies Research Paper 20.

Drudy, P.J. (1976) (ed.) *Regional and Rural Development*, Alpha Academic, Chalfont St Giles.

Durham C.C. (1932) *North-East Durham Joint Town Planning Scheme*.

Durham C.C. (1954) *County Development Plan*.

Durham C.C. (1964) *County Development Plan Amendment*.

East Anglia Consultative Committee (1972) *Small Towns Study*, East Anglia Consultative Committee and East Anglia Planning Council, Cambridge.

East Sussex C.C. (1953) *County Development Plan*.

Economic Associates Ltd (1966) *A New Town for Mid-Wales*, H.M.S.O., London.

Economic Committee of the Community Council of Devon (1969) *An Economic and Social Survey of North Devon*, Devon County Council, Exeter.

EFTA (1968) *Regional Policy in EFTA: an Examination of the Growth Centre Idea*, Oliver & Boyd, Edinburgh.

Emerson, A.E. and Compton, R. (1968) *Some Social Trends*, Report to the Suffolk Rural Community Council.

Everson, J.A. and Fitzgerald, B.P. (1969) *Settlement Patterns*, Longman, London.

Fairbrother, N. (1970) *New Lives, New Landscapes*, Penguin, Harmondsworth.

Fox, C. (1966) *The Role of Growth Centres in Regional Economic Development*, Dept Economics, Univ. Iowa.

Frankenberg, R. (1966) *Communities in Britain*, Penguin, Harmondsworth.

Garbett-Edwards, D.P. (1972) 'The establishment of new industries'. In J. Ashton and W.H. Long, 1972, *The Remoter Rural Areas of Britain*, Oliver & Boyd, Edinburgh.

Gilg, A.W. (1976) Rural Employment. In G.E. Cherry (ed.), 1976, *Rural Planning Problems*, Hill, London.

Gilg, A.W. (1978) *Countryside Planning*, David & Charles, Newton Abbot.

Gillette, J.M. (1923) *Rural Sociology*, Macmillan, New York.

Green, F.H.W. (1950) 'Urban hinterlands in England and Wales: an analaysis of bus services'. *Geographical J.*, 116, 64-88.

Green, R.J. (1966) 'The remote countryside – a plan for contraction'. *Planning Outlook*, 1, 17–37.

Green, R.J. (1971) *Country Planning – the Future of the Rural Regions*, Manchester University Press.

Green, R.J. and Ayton, J.B. (1967) 'Changes in the pattern of rural settlement'. Paper given to the Town Planning Institute Research Conference.

Gruer, R. (1971) 'Economics of outpatient care'. *The Lancet*, 20 Feb. 390-4.

Hall, P. (ed.), (1973) *The Containment of Urban England*, Allen & Unwin, London.

Hampshire C.C. (1955) *County Development Plan*.

Hampshire C.C. and Mass Observation Ltd (1966) *Village Life in Hampshire*, Hampshire C.C., Winchester.

Hampshire C.C. (1969) *Village Planning in Hampshire*.

Hancock, T. (1976) 'Planning in rural settlements', *Town and Country Planning*, 44, 520-3.

Hannan, D.F. (1969) 'Migration motives and migration differentials among Irish rural youth'. *Sociologia Ruralis*, 9, 195-220.

Hereford and Worcester C.C. (1973) *Worcestershire Structure Plan*.

Hereford and Worcester C.C. (1976) *Herefordshire Structure Plan*.

Hermansen, T. (1972) 'Development poles and development centres in national and regional development, elements of a theoretical framework'. In A.R. Kulinski (ed.), 1972, *Growth Poles and Growth Centres in Regional Planning*, Mouton, Paris.

Higgs, J. (ed.) (1966) *People in the Countryside*, National Council of Social Service, London.

Hill, M. (1972) 'A goals achievement matrix for evaluating alternative plans'. In I.M. Robinson (ed.), 1972, *Decision-making in Urban Planning*, Sage, London.

Hirschmann, A.O. (1958) *The Strategy of Economic Development*, Yale University Press, New Haven.

H.M. Treasury (1976) 'Rural depopulation'. Report of the inter-departmental working group.

Hodge, G. (1966) 'Do villages grow – some perspectives and predictions'. *Rural Sociology*, 31, 183-96.

House, J.W. (1965) *Rural North-East England 1951-61*, Papers on Migration and Mobility in N.E. England no. 1, Dept Geog., Univ. Newcastle-upon-Tyne.

Hudson, J.C. (1969) 'A location theory for rural settlement'. *Annals of the Assn of American Geographers*, 59, 365-81.

Humphreys, R. (1974) 'Population changes in two rural districts of South Devon'. Unpub. B.Sc. dissertation, Dept Geog., Univ. Southampton.

Huntingdonshire C.C. (1954) *County Development Plan*.

Huntingdonshire C.C. (1959) *First Review of County Development Plan*.

International Geographical Union (1975) *Report of the Working Group for Rural Planning and Development*, I.G.U., Budapest.

Jackson, M. and Nolan, M. (1971) 'Threshold analysis: concept, criticisms and current usage'. *Chartered Surveyor*, 104, 288-93.

Jackson, M. and Nolan, M. (1973) 'Threshold analysis II: urban growth and programming'. *Chartered Surveyor*, 105, 308-15.

Johnston, R.J. (1965) 'Components of rural population change'. *Town Planning Review*, 36, 279-93.

Johnston, R.J. (1966) 'An index of accessibility and its use in the study of bus services and settlement patterns'. *Tijdschrift voor Economische en Sociale Geografie*, 57, 33-7.

Jones, A.R. (1974) 'The use of development indices in rural settlement planning'. Unpub. discussion paper. Univ. East Anglia.

Jones, A.R. (1975) Personal communication concerning rural settlement planning research study, Univ. East Anglia.

Kendall, D. (1963) 'Portrait of a disappearing English village'. *Sociologia Ruralis*, 3, 157-65.

Kent C.C. (1958) *County Development Plan*.

Kozlowski, J. and Hughes, J.T. (1972) *Threshold Analysis*, Architectural Press, London.

Kulinski, A.R. (ed.) (1972) *Growth Poles and Growth Centres in Regional Planning*, Mouton, Paris.

Lancashire C.C. (1962) *First Review of County Development Plan*.

Leicestershire C.C. (1966) *Interim Settlement Policy*.

Leicestershire C.C. (1971) *Leicestershire: A Strategy for the Countryside*.

Leicestershire C.C. (1973) *Leicestershire County Structure Plan*.

Leicestershire C.C. (1975) *Rutland Structure Plan: the Main Choices*.

Lemon, A. (1973) *Planning and the Future of Small Towns in East Anglia*, Regional Studies Association, Discussion Paper no. 3.

Lewis, J.C. and Prescott, J.R. (1972) 'Urban regional development and growth centres: an econometric study'. *Journal of Regional Science*, 12, 57-70.

Lichfield, N., Kettle, P. and Whitbread, M. (1975) *Evaluation in the Planning Process*, Pergamon, Oxford.

Lindsey, Lincolnshire C.C. (1955) *County Development Plan*.

Losch, A. (1938-9) 'The nature of economic regions'. *Southern Economic Journal*, 5, 71-8.

Lowenthal, D. and Comitas, L. (1962) 'Emigration and depopulation – some neglected aspects of population geography'. *Geographical Review*, 52, 195-210.

Lucey, D.I.F. and Kaldor, D.R. (1969) *Rural Industrialization: the Impact of Industrialization on Two Rural Communities in Western Ireland*, Chapman, London.

MacGregor, M. (1976) 'Village life: facts and myths'. *Towns and Country Planning*, 44, 524-7.

McLaughlin, B.P. (1976a) 'Rural settlement planning; a new approach'. *Town and Country Planning*, 44, 156-60.

McLaughlin, B.P. (1976b) 'The future of the village: a planner's view'. *The Village*, 31, 54-7.

Maddocks, T. (1975) 'Mobility and accessibility problems in a small rural village'. *Reading Geographer*, 4, 70-5.

Malisz, B. (1969) 'Implications of threshold theory for urban and regional planning'. *Journal of the Town Planning Institute*, 55, 108-10.

Martin, I. (1976) 'Rural communities'. In G.E. Cherry (ed.), 1976, *Rural Planning Problems*, Hill, London.

Masser, F.I. and Stroud, D.C. (1965) 'The metropolitan village'. *Town Planning Review*, 36, 111-24.

Ministry of Education (1960) *Manual of Guidance for Schools* (No. 1), H.M.S.O., London.

Ministry of Housing and Local Government (1967) *Settlement in the Countryside*, Planning Bulletin no. 8, H.M.S.O., London.

Ministry of Town and Country Planning (1950) *Notes on the Siting of New Houses in Country Districts*, H.M.S.O., London.

Misra, R.P. (1972) 'Growth poles and growth centres in the context of India's urban and regional development patterns'. In A.R. Kulinski (ed.), 1972, *Growth Poles and Growth Centres in Regional Planning*, Mouton, Paris.

Mitchell, G.D. (1950) 'Depopulation and rural social structure'. *Sociological Review*, 42, 69-85.

Mitchell, G.D. (1951) 'The relevance of group dynamics to rural planning problems'. *Sociological Review*, 43, 1-16.

Mitchell, G.F.C. (1973) 'Rural-urban preferences with respect to agricultural policy objectives'. Dept Economics, Univ. Bristol, occasional paper.

Morrill, R.L. (1973) 'On the size and spacing of growth centres'. *Growth and Change*, 4, 21-4.

Morris, H. (1925) *The Village College − being a memorandum on the provision of educational and social facilities for the countryside, with special reference to Cambridgeshire*, Cambridge University Press.

Morris, H. (1942) 'Education and the Community'. In D. Needham, 1942, *The Teacher of Nations*, Cambridge University Press.

Moseley, M.J. (1973a) 'The impact of growth centres in rural regions: I − an analysis of spatial patterns in Brittany'. *Regional Studies*, 7, 57-75.

Moseley, M.J. (1973b) 'The impact of growth centres in rural regions: II − an analysis of spatial flows in East Anglia'. *Regional Studies*, 7, 77-94.

Moseley, M.J. (1974) *Growth Centres in Spatial Planning*, Pergamon, Oxford.

Moseley, M.J. (1977) 'A look at rural transport and accessibility'. *The Village*, 32, 33-5.

Moseley, M.J. (ed.) (1978) *Social Issues in Rural Norfolk*, C.E.A.S., Univ. East Anglia.

Moss, G. (1978) 'Rural settlements', *Architects Journal*, 18 January, 100-39.

Myrdal, G. (1957) *Economic Theory and Underdeveloped Regions*, Duckworth, London.

Needham, D. (ed.) (1942) *The Teacher of Nations*, Cambridge University Press.

Newman, J. (1967) *New Dimensions in Regional Planning, a Case Study of Ireland*, An Foras Forbartha, Dublin.

Nichols, V. (1969) 'Growth poles: an evaluation of their propulsive effect'. *Environment and Planning*, 1, 193-208.

Norborg, K. (ed.) (1962) *I.G.U. Symposium, Urban Geography*, I.G.U., Lund.

Norfolk C.C. (1974) *Interim Settlement Policy*.

Norfolk C.C. (1976) *The North Walsham Area*.

Norfolk C.C. (1977) *County Structure Plan*.

Northamptonshire C.C. (1977) *County Structure Plan*.

Northumberland C.C. (1956) *County Development Plan*.

Northumberland C.C. (1966) *County Development Plan – First Review*.

Nottinghamshire C.C. (1959) *County Development Plan*.

Nottinghamshire C.C. (1966) *Rural Nottinghamshire 1. East Retford R.D.*

Nottinghamshire C.C. (1966) *Rural Nottinghamshire 2. Worksop R.D.*

Nottinghamshire C.C. (1967) *Rural Nottinghamshire 3. Eastern Area*.

Nottinghamshire C.C. (1968) *Rural Nottinghamshire 4. South Notts*.

Nottinghamshire C.C. (1969) *Rural Nottinghamshire 5. Central Notts*.

O'Farrell, P.N. (1968) 'A proposed methodological basis for the determination of the centrality and rank of central places'. *Administration*, 16, 17-32.

Open University (1972) *Social Geography*, Open University Press, Bletchley.

O'Riagain, P. (1971) 'The selection of village growth points'. In An Foras Forbartha, 1971, *The Application of Geographical Techniques to Physical Planning*, An Foras Forbartha, Dublin.

Osborne, R.H. (1964) Population. In J.W. Watson, and J.B. Sissons, (eds.), 1964, *The British Isle: A Systematic Geography*, Nelson, London.

Pahl, R.E. (1965a) *Urbs in Rure*, London School of Economics Geographical Papers no. 2.

Pahl, R.E. (1965b) 'Class and community in English commuter villages'. *Sociologia Ruralis*, 5, 5-23.

Pahl, R.E. (1966a) 'The rural-urban continuum'. *Sociologia Ruralis*, 6, 299-329.

Pahl, R.E. (1966b) 'Commuting and social change in rural areas'. *Official Architecture and Planning*, July, 996-9.

Parsons, D. (1976) 'Village planning in England'. Unpub. Ph.D. thesis, Dept Geog., Univ. Nottingham.

Peake, H. (1916-18) 'The regrouping of rural population'. *Town*

Planning Review, 7, 243-50.

Peake, H. (1922) *The English Village*, Benn, London.

Peel, J. and Sayer, M. (1973) *Towards a Rural Policy and its Application to Norfolk*.

Perloff, H.S. (ed.) (1969) *The Quality of the Urban Environment*, John Hopkins Press, Baltimore.

Perroux, F. (1950) 'Economic space, theory and applications'. *Quarterly J. of Economics*, 64, 90–7.

Polish Academy of Sciences (1961) *Problems of Applied Geography*, Polish Academy of Sciences, Geographical Studies no. 25, Warsaw.

Poster, C. (1969) 'Village colleges today'. *New Society*, 9 October, 548-50.

Queen, S.A. and Carpenter, D.B. (1953) *The American City*, McGraw-Hill, New York.

Ratcliffe, J. (1974) *An Introduction to Town and Country Planning*, Hutchinson, London.

Rawson, M.J. and Rogers, A.W. (1976) 'Rural housing and structure plans'. Countryside Planning Unit, Wye College, Working Paper no. 1.

Redfield, R. (1941) *The Folk Culture of Yucatan*, University of Chicago Press.

Ree, H. (1969) 'Henry Morris'. *New Society*, 9 October, 547-8.

Ree, H. (1973) *Educator Extraordinary*, Longman, London.

Richardson, H.W. (1969) *Regional Economics*, Weidenfeld, London.

Richardson, H.W. (1973) *The Economics of Urban Size*, Saxon House, London.

Robinson, I.M. (ed.) (1972) *Decision-making in Urban Planning*, Sage, London.

Rowley, G. (1967) 'The middle order towns of Wales'. Unpub. Ph.D. thesis, Dept Geog., Univ. Aberystwyth.

Ryan, G. (1970) 'The criteria for selecting growth centres in Appalachia'. *Proceedings of the Assn. of American Geographers*, 2, 118-23.

Sarre, P. (ed.) (1972) *The Future City*, Open University, Bletchley.

Saville, J. (1957) *Depopulation in England and Wales, 1851-1951*, Routledge, London.

Saville, J. (1966) Urbanization and the Countryside. In J. Higgs (ed.), 1966, *People in the Countryside*, National Council of Social Service, London.

Schimpeler, C.G. and Grecco, W.L. (1972) 'Systems evaluation:

an approach based on community structure and value'. In I.M. Robinson (ed.), 1972, *Decision-making in Urban Planning*, Sage, London.

Schnore, L.F. (1966) 'The rural-urban variable: an urbanite's perspective'. *Rural Sociology*, 31, 131-43.

Scott-Miller, R. (1976) 'Housing in rural areas'. Internal dicsussion paper, Community Council for Devon.

Shackleford, J. (1970) 'On thresholds, take-offs and spurts: a place for S.M.S.A.'s in growth centre strategy'. Discussion Paper no. 27, Univ. Kentucky.

Shaw, M. (1970) 'An examination of key village policy in the Peak District'. Unpub. M.A. thesis, Univ. Sheffield.

Shaw, M. (1976) 'Can we afford villages?' *Built Environment*, 2, 135-7.

Shaw, M. (1978) 'Social implications of village development'. In M.J. Moseley (ed.), 1978, *Social Issues in Rural Norfolk*, C.E.A.S., Univ. East Anglia.

Shropshire C.C. (1960) *County Development Plan*.

Smailes, A.E. (1944) 'The urban hierarchy in England and Wales'. *Geography*, 29, 41-51.

Smailes, A.E. (1961) The urbanization of Britain. In Polish Academy of Sciences, 1961. *Problems of Applied Geography*, Polish Academy of Sciences, Geographical Studies no. 25, Warsaw.

Smith, R.D.P. (1968) 'The changing urban hierarchy'. *Regional Studies*, 2, 1-19.

Smith, R.D.P. (1970) 'The changing urban hierarchy in Wales'. *Regional Studies*, 4, 85-96.

Somerset C.C. (1958) *County Development Plan*.

Somerset C.C. (1964) *First Review of County Development Plan*.

Sorokin, P.A. and Zimmerman, C.C. (1929) *Principles of Rural-Urban Sociology*, Henry Holt, New York.

Speare, A. (1971) 'A cost-benefit model of rural to urban migration in Taiwan'. *Population Studies*, 25, 117-30.

Spooner, D.J. (1972) 'Industrial movement and the rural periphery: the case of Devon and Cornwall'. *Regional Studies*, 6, 197-215.

Staffordshire C.C. (1960) *County Development Plan*.

Staffordshire C.C. (1973) *Staffordshire County Structure Plan*.

Standing Conference of Rural Community Councils (1978) *The Decline of Rural Services*, National Council of Social Service, London.

Stewart, C.T. (1958) 'The urban-rural dichotomy: concepts and uses'. *Amer. J. Sociol.* 64, 152-8.

Thijsse, J.P. (1968) 'Second thoughts about a rural pattern for the future in the Netherlands'. *Papers and Proceedings of the Regional Science Association*, 20, 69-75.

Thomas, M.D. (1972) 'The regional problem, structural change and growth pole theory'. In A.R. Kulinski (ed.), 1972, *Growth Poles and Growth Centres in Regional Planning*, Mouton, Paris.

Thorburn, A. (1966) Discussion at Town and Country Planning School. In R.J. Green, 1971, *Country Planning – The Future of the Rural Regions*, Manchester University Press.

Thorburn, A. (1971) *Planning Villages*, Estates Gazette, London.

Thorns, D.C. (1968) 'The changing system of social stratification'. *Sociologia Ruralis*, 8, 161-78.

U.S. Bureau of the Census (1966) In L.F. Schnore, 1966, 'The rural-urban variable: an urbanite's perspective'. *Rural Sociology*, 31, 131-43.

Venner, D.G. (1976) 'The village has a future'. *The Village*, 31, 39-41.

Wallace, D.B. and Drudy, P.J. (1975) 'Social problems of rural communities'. Conference paper.

Warford, J.J. (1969) *The South Atcham Scheme*, H.M.S.O., London.

Warwickshire C.C. (1956) *County Development Plan*.

Warwickshire C.C. (1966) *County Development Plan: An Interim Policy Statement*.

Warwickshire C.C. (1973a) *County Structure Plan – Report of Survey*.

Warwickshire C.C. (1973b) *County Structure Plan – Supplementary Report No. 5 Rural Settlements*.

Warwickshire C.C. (1975) *County Structure Plan – Approved Written Statement*.

Warwickshire C.C. (1976) *Parish Population Estimates*.

Warwickshire Joint Planning Committee (1935) *Town and Country Planning in Warwickshire*.

Watson, J.W. and Sissons, J.B. (eds) (1964) *The British Isles: a Systematic Geography*, Nelson, London.

West Suffolk C.C. (1963) *First Review of County Development Plan*.

West Suffolk C.C. (1968) *Rural Planning in West Suffolk*.

Wheeler, P. (1977) 'The concept of the growth village'. Paper presented to the Anglo-Hungarian Conference.

Whitby, M.C., Robins, D.L.J., Tansey, A.W. and Willis, K.G. (1974) *Rural Resource Development*, Methuen, London.

Wibberley, G.P. (1972) 'Rural activities and rural settlements'. Paper presented to the Town and Country Planning Assn. Conference, 17 February, 1972.

Wilson, A.G. (1974) *Urban and Regional Models in Geography and Planning*, Wiley, London.

Wiltshire County Council (1953) *County Development Plan*.

Winter, G. (1971) 'Plenty of space – too few people; the anomaly of rural depopulation'. *Country Life*, 4 February, 236-8.

Woodruffe, B.J. (1973) 'Rural settlement planning in Britain'. Paper presented to 'erstes Deutsch-Englisches Symposium zur angewandten Geographie Giessen-Würzburg-München 1973'.

Woodruffe, B.J. (1976) *Rural Settlement Policies and Plans*, Oxford University Press.

Index